Y0-BCL-018

Marisa —

I really enjoyed listening to you tell about Holy Week; your descriptions and excitement radiated throughout your stories! Thank you for being part of "Coming Home."

# Coming

*"I remember the summer vacations spent at my aunt's*

*house in the country, the smell of eucalyptus, the*

*beautiful waterfalls and how I quenched my thirst on hot*

*summer days.  This is the Portugal that I miss most."*

Maria Pingree
Portugal

# Coming

Joanne Alfonso Pizarro

Igloo Publishing

Published by Igloo Publishing
P.O. Box 41986
Fredericksburg, Virginia 22404

Copyright © 1997 by Joanne Alfonso Pizarro
Edited by Della Fay Reese
Cover painting by Claudia Olivos

10 9 8 7 6 5 4 3 2 1

All rights reserved, including the right of
reproduction in whole or in part in any form.

Library of Congress Cataloging-in-Publication Number: 96-095150

ISBN: 0-9655184-1-8


Printed in the United States of America

# contents

## f o r e w o r d

An archeological expedition is one way of digging into the past to find out about peoples' lives. Another way is to hear the stories directly from the people themselves. It is in this spirit that *Coming Home* is written.

*Coming Home* is, at first glance, a cookbook. The common thread throughout is the sharing of good food among friends and loved ones. However, it is more than a cookbook in that you, the reader, will embark upon a journey through the hearts and hearths of over 100 residents of the Fredericksburg, Virginia, area. The journey will take you through forty-four countries and many years of the histories, traditions, and cultures of the individuals who shared their experiences in *Coming Home.*

I am reminded of the family gatherings of my youth. It was not uncommon for someone to say, "Food's ready now; y'all dig in!" I invite you to do the same here. This collection of stories and recipes is replete with repast for the palate and soul.

Della Fay Reese
*Editor*

*Spice vendors in India*

## introduction

The genesis of *Coming Home* came from my love for travelling. I had travelled great distances because I sought to learn and experience other cultures in our world. When I returned home after each trip, it seemed that the Fredericksburg area was changing into an "international" community, an atmosphere much different from when my family moved here in 1972. As Filipinos moving into the countryside, we were quite a curiosity! I realized I had overlooked my own backyard, and I did not always need intercontinental travel to learn about other peoples.

The community has been remarkably generous in providing me the recollections contained in this book. I learned a great deal more from the people than I possibly could have had I been a foreigner, or an outsider, visiting their country. We openly discussed subjects ranging from beliefs and customs to struggles and triumphs, including "sensitive" issues, such as arranged marriages, polygamy, and even death, which I would not have entertained asking for fear of offending. But they were not reluctant to answer, and I discovered that the cultural chasm that I thought sometimes existed was only in my imagination. They were as eager to

relate their likes and differences as much as I was
eager to learn about them.

In my travels, I found that food transcended all
language barriers, whether I was ordering a meal
by imitating the animals or dividing a five-stick
pack of chewing gum with fourteen children.  Many
times I was invited for a drink or a lavish meal,
even with families who had the least to offer.
Somehow the sharing of food always brought me
closer to the people and to the soul of the country.

Come and experience the hospitality and warmth
as I have by sharing the memories that spurred
the appetite or visa versa.

Joanne Alfonso Pizarro

## dedication

To my mother.

*"Do what you want. You'll do it anyway."*

I was travelling to Europe—alone—at eighteen.
I was moving to England with $500 in
my pocket.
I was going to Greece—a fourth time.
I was travelling around the world into many
unknowns: languages, disease, political
instability, terrorism, unfamiliarity.

You protested for safety's sake, but you
always knew I *had* to go.

I found your words liberating.

□  □  □

To Clint.

Thank you for exploring the world with me.

**nostalgia** (nos-TALja) *noun*
a longing for persons, places, or things
which are past or distant.
[Greek *nostos* a return home + *algos* pain]

**My grandfather** had a title: "Aga." In my country, Bosnia, Aga was a very rich, well-respected man of great influence. He was not always rich with material wealth; he was rich with his brain.

On Wednesdays people from all over the country came—sometimes in cars, but usually on horses, carriages, or carts—to his town, Nevesinje, to sell different foods and goods that represent their city or town. One part of Aga's huge house was like a hotel where people would spend the night. Rich people paid to sleep in the house, but poor people did not have to pay. Aga had an obligation to make food for all these people, and his wife and daughters prepared the meals.

Before dinner all the men staying at his house would go to Aga's room. His room had a bed and many pillows. Aga never liked sitting in chairs so they sat Turkish-style. The men read and talked. They usually drank Turkish coffee or tea served in tiny glasses and ate Bosnian-Turkish sweets called *lokum*. When the Turkish empire was there, many traditions mixed with our culture and we call them Bosnian.

Aga travelled to different parts of the country and the world. He told the men stories about other peoples and their customs. He also taught them the Koran, which he read daily. He would go to his room on top of the house and read about Islam every day from three o'clock to five o'clock in the afternoon. No one disturbed him during this time. Then just before dinner they would all read the Koran together and thank God for the food they were about to eat.

*My husband was the first love of my life. He never died, he always lives in my heart. I drink coffee with him; I made my yard in memory of him. People have asked me if I will marry again. I say to them that I am still married. We just have different living arrangements: I am here in the home, and he is in the cemetery.*

When they were ready for dinner, Aga would bang on the floor three times with his cane to let the women know to bring the food. Sitting on pillows, the men ate at a huge round table about a foot high. The table was always round to show that everyone is equal. They ate very slowly; there was no talking at all.

After dinner he would bang on the floor again, and a woman would come in with a towel and a huge brass urn filled with water. Each man washed his hands while she poured the water; then she would leave again.

When women came into Aga's room—for dinner, tea, or any reason—they never left the room with their backs to him. Men had no obligation to this custom, only the women, even my grandmother. She respected her husband, and everyone respected Aga. It was not because of terror; it was because of respect. No one forced anyone to act that way.

It is not like this any longer. My grandfather was the last Aga for the town. His son was the only man-child, but he was weak and not good for the role of Aga. Every generation brought more of the modern world, so people forgot.

I have a nice feeling in my heart because Aga taught me so much and gave me a nice life. I am poor now because I am a war refugee, but my blood is very rich. My background is one that I can be very proud of, and no one can deny it—not one army in the world. I have lost everything, but I will always carry the blood and memories of my background no matter where I am going.

□ For many years my father and his friends would get together and play cards on Thursdays. Whoever lost had to prepare dinner and invite everyone to his house. My father never cooked unless he lost. *Brodet* was the first meal he ever made.

—Essa Miletic

## BRODET
### Fish with Tomato Sauce

| | |
|---|---|
| 1 | lb. any white fish fillet |
| | flour for coating |
| | oil for frying |
| 3 | medium red onions, sliced |
| 3 | Tbsp. olive oil |
| | salt to taste |
| 1 | tsp. black peppercorns |
| 4 | bay leaves |
| 2 | tsp. flour |
| ¹/₂ | cup water |
| 1 | Tbsp. tomato paste |

Dredge fish in flour. Cook fish in vegetable oil over medium heat until golden; set aside.

In another pan, cook onions in olive oil until golden. Place fish on onions; cover with water, adding salt, peppercorns, and bay leaves. Cook over low-medium heat until fish is done. Mix flour, water, and tomato paste; stir in to thicken sauce. Serve with wine.
*4 to 5 servings*

□ After my husband and I married, we made a promise to each other that every Saturday I would make a special lunch, and he would bring flowers as a present. He never forgot. For twenty-one years we always held the same tradition.

When the war started, we didn't have money; we lost everything. Humanitarian organizations gave us money, and even then he wanted to keep his promise and the tradition, so he would buy at least one flower. There was a forest beside our house where my husband walked because he had heart problems. Many of the flowers in the forest burned or dried out; sometimes he even brought these flowers home.

The war and our promise were so connected. Before the war, the bouquet on the table was huge and the plates were full. During the war, there was only one flower in the vase and a little piece of meat and something else on the plate. Our house was taken in the end; my grandparents' fortune was destroyed—everything was gone. My husband told me to be strong. He said that much was destroyed because there was nothing he could do, but he would never let our love be destroyed. The flowers were part of our love.

*Begova chorba* was one of his favorite recipes.

## BEGOVA CHORBA
### King Soup

| | |
|---|---|
| 1 | large red onion, chopped |
| 2 | Tbsp. oil |
| | salt and pepper to taste |
| 1 | lb. boneless chicken breast or veal, cubed |
| 1 | Tbsp. Vegeta* or soup base |
| 1 | tsp. paprika |
| 2 | carrots, chopped |
| 1 | bunch parsley, chopped |
| 5 | cups water |
| 1 | egg |
| 1 | cup sour cream |

Cook onion in oil over medium heat until golden; add salt and pepper. Add chicken or veal; cook for 10 minutes. Stir in Vegeta and paprika. Add carrots, parsley and 1 cup water; cook until carrots are done. Add remaining 4 cups water; bring to a boil over medium heat. Remove from heat.

Beat egg and sour cream together. Return pan to heat; add egg and sour cream mixture. Bring to a boil over medium heat. Garnish with parsley and a squeeze of lemon.
*8 to 10 servings*

**I may be the only person** in the world who loves the smell of seafood markets. I loved to visit the *mercado fresco* in Chile, where sometimes we would see men pushing wheelbarrows full of conch or crates filled with crabs, which Chile is well-known for. When I think of Chile and its food, I think of seafood and *empanadas,* meat pastries made fresh every Sunday at the local bakeries, and, of course, Chilean wine.

Chile has the Pacific Ocean bordering its side from the most northern tip below Peru to the most southern tip at Cape Horn, making the beach an intricate part of life in Chile. Many Argentines join the throngs of Chileans at the beach each summer, where tanning and eating seafood are among the top main attractions. Lining the waterfront at the most popular beach resort, *Viña del Mar,* are restaurants serving fish, clams, oysters, crabs, *locos,* or conch, sea urchin and more—all freshly caught in the icy waters of the Pacific. The water is so cold, in fact, that few venture in for more than a few seconds, and it is not unusual to see penguins and sea-lions nearby.

*The summer I remember most vividly was the summer I was seven years old. It was the summer I read my first poem by Pablo Neruda. I remember thinking there could be no better place on earth but right there, with the smell of eucalyptus trees and salty ocean waters mixing in the air.*

I have many memories of summers spent at the beach, building castles in the sand or digging the hole that would finally bring bring me to China. I remember men trudging through the sand with a cooler full of ice cream bars that we begged my mother to buy. At sunset, there would appear another man, this time carrying a wicker basket full of *pan de huevo,* a sweet bread that satisfied our appetite until dinner time. Evenings were spent taking long walks on the beach or sliding down nearby sand dunes that could reach up to forty feet high.

The summer I remember most vividly was the summer I was seven years old. I discovered moras in the woods that we picked and ate with sugar, making believe they were as delicious as they had been fun to pick. It was the summer my mother graduated from college, and we feasted on crabs and *locos.*

I have a memory of runaway crabs in the kitchen. I desperately tried to catch them although I was afraid of their claws. I recall the sound of my dad and his friends outside banging an inner tube full of *locos,* with their shells removed, against the cement terrace to get them soft and ready for cooking. It was the summer I read my first poem by Pablo Neruda. I remember thinking there could be no better place on earth but right there, with the smell of eucalyptus trees and salty ocean waters mixing in the air.

I have always loved seafood, which brings back memories of my childhood in Chile.

People in Chile enjoy eating outside. Cafés, with chairs and a bunch of little tables with parasols, are everywhere. Although there are not many tourists, the menus are posted outside. You can sit at a café for hours, and no one will pressure you to leave.

*Pebre*, a typical Chilean condiment, is served in a bowl on the table. It can be spread on steak and seafood, eaten with bread, or added to soups. When tomato is added to *pebre*, it becomes *chancho en piedra*, literally translated as "pig on the rocks."

### PEBRE
### Cilantro Condiment

| | |
|---|---|
| 1 | bunch cilantro, finely chopped |
| 2 | vidalia onions, finely chopped |
| 1 | green chili pepper, chopped |
| | juice of 2 or 3 lemons |
| 5 | Tbsp. olive oil |
| 1/2 | tsp. cumin |
| | salt to taste |
| 2 | tomatoes, chopped (optional) |

Combine all ingredients; mix well.

Memories of my grandmother often revolve around eating. When my sister and I were little, we spent many Saturdays with her. She would have *machas a la Parmesana*, clams with a bit of bacon and fresh Parmesan cheese, or *bistec a lo pobre*, steak, french fries, sautéed onions, and a fried egg, ready for us when we arrived. *Bistec a lo pobre* means "beef steak of the poor," and is obviously a play on words. She sometimes gave us sweet wine with strawberries in it!

My grandmother and I loved having tea time together. For tea we would have fresh bread, paté, marmalade, fresh cheese, and mashed avocado with salt, lemon, and pepper.

She truly enjoyed preparing foods for us. After we moved to the U.S., she would prepare for our visits to Chile months ahead. She made *humitas*, mashed corn with basil wrapped in corn husks, which she would freeze, *pimentones,* and fresh

preserves including my favorite, *naranjas confitadas*. As soon as we arrived at her house from the airport, she would begin pulling out the delicacies that she had prepared for our stay.

*Pimentones* is one of my grandmother's specialties. The red peppers are delicious in this recipe. They can be used on pasta or as a garnish, but are most delicious when mixed with a dab of mayonnaise and boneless chicken. The chicken and pimiento mixture is great for canapés.

### PIMENTONES
### Pimentos

| | |
|---|---|
| 12 | red peppers |
| 4-5 | garlic cloves |
| 1/2 | cup olive oil |
| 2 | bay leaves |
| | dash of pepper |
| | salt (optional) |

Wash red peppers; broil in oven until skin blisters. Remove skin, seeds, and stem; cut into wide slices. Cook garlic in oil over medium-hot heat until golden.

Combine red peppers, garlic and oil mixture, bay leaves, pepper, and salt (optional). Place in canning jars, covering tightly. Place jars in a pot with water; boil over high heat for 40 minutes. Cool in jars.

**Every September** 18 is National Day in Chile. On *Fiesta Patrias,* we Chileans celebrate our independence from Spain. The holiday is like America's Fourth of July. It is a time for Chileans to enjoy their traditions through food and dance.

The festivities begin on September 17 all over Chile, and one of the most popular places to celebrate is in Parque O'Higgings in Santiago, the capital. *Fondas*, buildings with leaves on top set up for the dancing and food, are built just for National Day. The insides of the *fondas* have many colored lights and look like a mixture of a disco and restaurant. They also are adorned with typical Chilean decorations such as garlic strands and many different copper ornaments. Copper is symbolic in Chile because the country mines the mineral as well as gold and silver.

Some *fondas* have professional bands with folk music and dance. One typical dance is called *la cueca*, which is about a rooster trying to conquer a hen. The rooster tries to seduce her—but in a very kind way. A man puts his handkerchief over a woman's head, positioning her for a kiss, but she is trying to be very shy. It's all just a game.

People who know the traditional dances may join the professionals. Mostly older people know these particular folk dances, but as years passed, the younger people dance to rock n' roll and other music. When we go to the *fondas*, we dance salsa, merengue, cumbia, and to different Latin American music. There are a few *cuecas* especially because it is National Day. However, most of the music is modern.

The *fondas* also have restaurants underneath. People serve Chilean food like *cazuela*, chicken soup cooked in clay pots. Another traditional food is *empanadas*, or meat pastries. This day is a special time to make more Chilean food than the rest of the year. After getting their food and wine, people can sit down and eat, drink, or dance. There are many *fondas* in the park; each may specialize in a particular food. Throughout the night people will go walking around to the different *fondas*.

Claudia with her children.

*When I was growing up in Chile, I was more interested in music sung in English. It wasn't until I moved to America that I discovered my love for Latin American music. Now I am a Latin American singer.*

The highlight of the holiday is the *la parada militar* on the next day. National Day also celebrates the day of the glories of the army. Besides the military being the main attraction, the parade includes other professional dancers like the ones who dance *la cueca*. Traditionally, the president of Chile opens the parade by drinking *chicha*, a sort of cider, from a cow horn.

I remember when I was little—maybe six years old—I was on my way to the festivities and saw the parade. I wondered when it was going to be my turn to march. I was even practicing! I wanted to march and be a part of the parade because everyone looked like they were really enjoying themselves.

▫ Empanadas are very typical of Chile. They can be seen everywhere, like hamburgers in the United States.

### EMPANADAS
#### Meat-Filled Pastries

| | |
|---|---|
| 4 | onions, chopped |
| 1¹/₂ | lbs. ground beef |
| ¹/₂ | tsp. cumin |
| | salt and pepper to taste |
| 1 | tsp. paprika |
| 4 | Tbsp. raisins |
| | chili powder (optional) |
| 1 | tsp. cornstarch (optional) |
| 3-4 | hard-boiled eggs, quartered |
| | pitted black olives |
| 1 | egg, beaten |

**dough:**

| | |
|---|---|
| 2¹/₂ | lbs. flour |
| 2 | Tbsp. shortening, melted |
| 1 | tsp. salt |
| 4 | cups water |

Cook onions over medium-high heat until tender. Add ground beef; sprinkle with cumin, salt and pepper. When meat is done, stir in paprika and raisins. Add chili and cornstarch, if desired.

Prepare dough. Make a well in flour. Add shortening. While mixing with both hands, add 1 cup of water at a time until dough does not stick to hands. Knead until smooth. Cover with cloth; leave dough in a warm place.

Cut off 1¹/₂-inch pieces; roll into rectangular shapes. Do not roll too thin. Place 2 tablespoons meat, 1 quarter of egg, and 1 olive on half of dough. Fold and press edges to stick together. Fold edge again and seal. Brush with egg. Bake at 400° for 15 minutes or until lightly brown.

*8 to 10 servings*

▫ My mother made *cazuela* for me when I was leaving Chile for America. She said that I would not be able to have *cazuela* here because food was so different. She was right—a little—because it took me a long time to find ingredients or good substitutes. For example, I use sweet potatoes for *cazuela* instead of the pumpkins we used in Chile.

Mom was a working woman; she was not the kind who stayed home and cooked for us. When she made two pots of *cazuela* for me, it was like "Wow!"

*Cazuela* can be made with any meat, but it must have bones for the flavor. *Cazuela de pollo* is the soup with chicken; *cazuela de chancho* is with pork; and *cazuela de vacuno* is with beef.

### CAZUELA DE POLLO
#### Chicken Soup

| | |
|---|---|
| 1 | large onion, chopped |
| ¹/₄ | cup oil |
| 3 | garlic cloves, chopped |
| 1 | tsp. of <u>each</u>: cumin, coarse black pepper, paprika, parsley, and cilantro |
| 1 | chicken, cut into pieces |
| 3 | large potatoes, halved |
| 3 | large sweet potatoes, halved |
| 1 | lb. frozen mixed vegetables |
| 2 | tsp. salt |
| 6-8 | ears of corn |

In a large pot, cook onion in oil over medium-high heat. Add garlic and spices; cook for 2 minutes. Add chicken; cook for 10 to 15 minutes. Add potatoes, sweet potatoes, mixed vegetables, and salt. Fill pot with hot water; reduce heat to medium. Cook until chicken and potatoes are done. When almost done, add corn.

*6 to 8 servings*

**Once there was** a very beautiful woman. She was so beautiful that the emperor of China wanted to keep her for his own. But the woman was married. She wanted to refuse the emperor, but no one ever denied the emperor anything. The only way for her to refuse was to kill herself. Afterwards, her soul flew up to the moon. So that is why every year on August 15 on the Chinese calendar, the Chinese celebrate Moon Cake Day, or *Zong Cho Jea*.

The celebration is no longer like it used to be. Generally, the Chinese just give moon cakes to others. Moon cakes are flat, round pastries with sweet bean paste inside. The giving of the moon cakes is to remember the woman who kept her pride and didn't want to ruin her name by sharing herself with the emperor. It's sad really; she had to kill herself just to refuse him.

We wrap a few moon cakes nicely in colored paper to give to families. It's not very nice to just give one moon cake especially if the family has children. The Chinese always wrap gifts very nicely for any occasion. It shows respect for the person receiving the gift. But we don't wrap for the kids, just for family and friends. The kids just want to eat the moon cakes because they're sweet!

Many cities also have dragon boat races down the river or in the lakes. In China, the dragon represents the emperor. The story behind the dragon boat race is that the emperor would not believe that the beautiful woman was gone, so the dragon boats tried to search for her by following the moon on the river. Today the boat race is a competition. The boats are all different sizes; some hold up to twenty people, ten on each side. The dragon head is the only decoration and must be on the front of the boat.

*My family and I took a month vacation touring China. We are in Tiananmen Square in Beijing.*

Moon Cake Day began thousands of years ago. This is the story that was passed to me. But stories change—especially one that has been passed down for that long! Now the new generation doesn't even know the story. Still Chinese all over the world celebrate Moon Cake Day: China, Hong Kong, Taiwan, Singapore. My family celebrates it here by giving out moon cakes also. We pass them to family, friends, and employees. And, yes, we still wrap them beautifully.

# Hsiang-Ling (Peter) Yin

□ Soy sauce, white wine, vinegar, sugar, msg (monosodium glutamate), green onions, garlic, and black beans—Chinese cooking will always have a combination of a few of these ingredients. People don't like msg here; they're scared of it, but we grew up on it for many, many years and have no problems. Chinese food can be difficult to prepare but all these recipes are very easy.

## LIANG BAN WONG GWA
### Chilled Cucumber Salad

| | |
|---|---|
| 4 | cucumbers, peeled and halved |
| | salt |
| 4-5 | drops sesame oil |
| 4 | tsp. white vinegar |
| 2-3 | tsp. sugar |
| | dash of white pepper |
| | dash of msg |

Remove seeds from cucumbers. Slice $^1/_2$-inch pieces diagonally. Sprinkle with salt. Set aside for 15 minutes; drain. Add oil, vinegar, sugar, white pepper, and msg; mix well. Chill before serving.
*4 servings*

## HI SHIN TUNG
### Seafood Soup

| | |
|---|---|
| 8 | shrimp, shells removed |
| 8 | scallops |
| $^1/_4$ | lb. crab meat |
| $^1/_4$ | lb. squid |
| 7 | cups water |
| $^1/_2$ | Chinese cabbage, cut into pieces |
| $^1/_4$ | lb. mushrooms, halved |
| $^1/_4$ | lb. snow peas |
| $^1/_4$ | tsp. salt |
| 4 | Tbsp. white wine |
| $^1/_4$ | tsp. white pepper |
| $^1/_4$ | tsp. msg |
| $^1/_2$ | bunch spinach, cut into pieces |

Clean seafood. Cook in boiling water over high heat for 4 minutes; remove seafood. Add cabbage, mushrooms, snow peas, salt, wine, white pepper, and msg; boil for 15 minutes. Add spinach and seafood. Bring to a boil, covered; remove from heat.
*4 servings*

□ *Tong chu shau pi gu* is served as a main dish. Have the butcher cut the ribs in half for smaller pieces. Cornstarch makes the sauce stick to the meat, but do not overcook the cornstarch. After adding cornstarch, remove the pot from the stove while the sauce thickens.

## TONG CHU SHAU PI GU
### Sweet and Sour Spare Ribs

| | |
|---|---|
| 2 | lbs. pork ribs, cut into half |
| $^1/_2$ | Tbsp. salt |
| 1 | Tbsp. soybean oil |
| 6 | Tbsp. white wine |
| 4-5 | Tbsp. sugar |
| 4 | Tbsp. soy sauce |
| 4 | Tbsp. vinegar |
| 2 | Tbsp. cornstarch |
| | oil for frying |

Combine ribs and salt. Set aside for 3 to 4 hours; drain. Deep-fry until golden brown.

In a wok, cook soybean oil, wine, sugar, soy sauce, and vinegar over medium-high heat, stirring constantly. Reduce heat to low; cook for 5 minutes. Add ribs; cook for 10 minutes. Stir in cornstarch and remove pan from heat.
*4 servings*

**In China** we do not prepare food the same way we do in the Chinese restaurants here in America. We make the food here for the Americans; this is American-Chinese food. We follow the examples of the people who have opened restaurants before us. For example, in China we eat monosodium glutamate (msg), from childhood to old age. Here, people say it makes them sick. We used to cook with msg; now we don't. We still use it at home.

American-Chinese food is easy to cook. People here like stir-fried or deep-fried foods—that's all. Like for chicken broccoli, we take the skin off a whole chicken and thinly slice the meat. The chicken is stir-fried with the vegetables, then a sauce is added. Here, there are only brown, white, lemon, or sweet and sour sauces which are made, and the sauce is added to the food. All the sauces still take at least half an hour to prepare.

The Chinese don't have a "brown sauce." If we cook chicken in a Chinese way, we may use *hoisin* sauce, msg, salt, and soy sauce. In China every dish has a different sauce. If we steam shrimp, we would use only salt and pepper, then we'd have a sauce like *shuan tou jang*, a sauce with soy sauce, garlic, and sesame oil, for dipping.

I don't eat much meat; I eat mostly vegetables and seafood. I grew up close to the ocean in Fuzhou, so there was a lot of fresh seafood. My family would steam whole fish, some which cannot be found here, and season it with soy sauce, green onion, and ginger. Sometimes we cut the fish, leaving the bone in, and deep-fry it to a brown color. If it is New Year's Day, we'll make the fish red with food coloring.

Many Chinese also never drink iced tea—always hot tea. Even our plain water must always be hot. My father and I used to boil water often. One time we found a big hot water pot and kept it in the corner so we could have hot water for drinking any time.

Sometimes people will see us eating our food in the restaurant. They'll ask, "What is that?" or "What kind of vegetable is that?" Many people have never seen some of the vegetables that we eat because we buy them from the Asian stores, or maybe they have seen the vegetables but just don't know how to fix them.

I have been in the States for a while, and I have learned a lot about the Chinese food prepared here. It's totally different from the food we prepare, from the soups to the fortune cookie which is given at the end of meals. No one in China even knows what a fortune cookie is!

*China is so big that I will never see all of it. My country is beautiful, with huge mountains covered with green, sharp cliffs, and winding rivers. I took a cruise to see the Lesser Three Gorges before the gorges are flooded soon to make a hydroelectric plant.*

# Mei Wen (Christine) Dan

□ The Chinese like their food very fresh. They go to the market every day to purchase the freshest food. The market sells everything; all the material for *zhen zhao* can be bought at one time.

### ZHEN ZHAO
### Steamed or Fried Dumplings

| | |
|---|---|
| 5 | Tbsp. oil |
| 1 | lb. pork, finely chopped |
| 5 | dried mushrooms, soaked and chopped |
| $^1/_2$ | cup shrimp, chopped |
| $^1/_2$ | cup chopped bamboo shoots |
| $^1/_2$ | cup chopped bokchoy (optional) |
| 1 | Tbsp. chopped ginger |
| 1 | Tbsp. chopped green onion |
| $2^1/_2$ | cups flour |
| $2^1/_2$ | cups boiling water |
| $1^1/_2$ | cups cold water |

Heat oil over medium-high heat; cook pork and mushroom until pork is done. Add shrimp, bamboo shoots, bokchoy (optional), ginger, and green onion; cook for 2 to 4 minutes and remove from pan.

In a large bowl, gradually add boiling water to flour. Mix well, pressing flour until evenly mixed. Add cold water; knead until smooth. Cover and set aside for 20 minutes.

Knead dough again until smooth. Flatten small portions, forming circles 4 to 5 inches in diameter. Hold wrapper in one hand and place a small amount of mixture onto the wrapper. Fold, pressing dough to form dumplings.

Steamed: Arrange dumplings on a clean wet cloth in a steaming basket. Steam for 10 to 15 minutes.

Fried: Grease pan with 2 tablespoons oil; arrange dumplings in pan. Cook over medium heat until golden brown.

*4 to 6 servings*

□ The Chinese never eat soup before their meal as an appetizer. The main course and the soup are served next to each other.

### LO MEIN TONG
### Noodle Soup with Meat

| | |
|---|---|
| 1 | lb. pork, sliced |
| 6 | Tbsp. salted soybean paste* |
| 1 | green onion, chopped |
| 1 | tsp. wine |
| 5 | Tbsp. vegetable oil |
| 1 | tsp. sugar |
| 6 | cups chicken stock |
| | salt to taste |
| 1 | slice of ginger |
| 1 | tsp. sesame oil |
| 2 | eggs |
| $^1/_2$ | lb. bean sprouts |
| $^1/_2$ | package lo mein noodles* |

Prepare meat sauce. Cook pork, bean paste, green onion, and wine in vegetable oil over medium-high heat until pork is done and paste turns yellow. Add sugar, stock, salt, and ginger; set aside. Add sesame oil just before mixing with noodles.

Cook eggs, scrambled; set aside. Cook sprouts until half done; set aside. Boil noodles until done; drain. In a large bowl, mix noodles with egg and sprouts. Add noodles to stock mixture.

Optional: add chili sauce or vinegar.

*6 to 8 servings*

**We Colombians begin** celebrating the Christmas season on December 7, the Day of the Lights, or *día de los alumbrados.* It is like a contest of whoever has the most lights. People have candles around the front yard and in the windows. There is also a parade for two days in each community. Everyone walks with a candle, singing and praying. For these two days, there is a lot of dancing and drinking. For the Colombians, this is when Christmas begins.

Every day there is something to do. December 16 is *día de los aguinaldos,* when neighbors, friends, boyfriends, and girlfriends give and receive gifts. After December 16, we still celebrate with the family and cook food until January 6. People start going over to eat at friends' and families' houses; they bring different dishes with them to share. We cook for other people and actually eat just a little of our own food because everyone is bringing us a dish.

December 16 also begins *la novena del nino Jesus.* Some people fix a nativity for Jesus. These people with the nativities invite all the kids in the neighborhood to come after dinner to pray every day until Jesus "is born." The kids get together around the nativity and pray, but they also play games, make stories, laugh, and sing. I remember we used to smash beer bottle caps and wire the flattened pieces together for a musical instrument to play while we sang.

Margarita (left) with her friend visiting Columbia.

*I remember walking about five miles to school each day. I had to carry a big book bag, and I didn't even have good shoes. My mom bought whatever she could afford. I had to take care of those shoes because they were to last for at least two years!*

These get-togethers are like contests and are a lot of fun for the kids. The grown-up of the house gives a prize each day to whoever is the best singer or has the best joke. There is also a big box with a toy or prize under the Christmas tree for the child who doesn't miss one day until the 25th. After prayers, the lady of the house gives candy to every kid. Since every single kid likes candy, his intention may not even be to go and pray!

On December 25 Jesus "is born" and put into the nativity scenes. Until this day, the manger is empty. Everyone comes to see Jesus and welcome him. They wonder how big he is or what he looks like. Is he going to be wrapped in white? It's only a piece of ceramic, but people still have in their minds what he looks like. The kids welcome and thank him for their gifts because in Colombia we believe that Jesus brings the gifts; we don't believe in Santa Claus. The kids also make promises to Jesus that they will be good.

The nativity is kept until January 6 because this is the day that the three kings come. The three kings are added to the nativity scene, and all the kids will come again to see the kings. January 6 is the last day, and families get together and have picnics to end the one-month celebration.

Christmas in the U.S. is nothing like the way we celebrate in Colombia. Everyone in Colombia is so excited once December 7 comes. The grown-ups also have so much fun. They drink and dance from morning until the sun comes up again; it is non-stop. People receive invitations almost every day from the different homes in the neighborhood to come and eat and dance. They have to be ready to go and have fun.

❑ Because I am Spanish, rice was the first food that my mom taught me to cook. We ate rice every day. We'd have *arroz con pollo* on special occasions like Mother's Day, First Communion, or weddings. This rice and chicken dish can be served with salad or plantains. It's better the day after it's made.

## ARROZ CON POLLO
### Chicken with Rice

| | |
|---|---|
| 4 | chicken breasts, 2 without skin |
| 6 | cups water |
| 1 | Tbsp. salt |
| 1 | tsp. garlic powder |
| 4 | cups rice |
| 2 | cups frozen carrots and peas |

**Creole sauce:**

| | |
|---|---|
| 2 | medium onions, chopped |
| 2 | medium tomatoes, chopped |
| 1/2 | green, yellow, or red pepper, chopped |
| 5 | Tbsp. olive oil |
| | salt and pepper to taste |
| | garlic powder to taste |
| 1 | envelope sazon y achiote (optional) * |
| 1 | cup tomato sauce |

Boil chicken in water with salt and garlic powder until tender. Remove from pot and reserve water. Shred and set aside. Cook rice in reserved water. When rice is almost done, add carrots and peas.

Prepare Creole sauce while rice is cooking. Cook onions, tomatoes, and chopped pepper in oil over low-medium heat until tender. Sprinkle salt, pepper, and garlic to taste or envelope of sazon y achiote. Add tomato sauce; cook over medium heat for 5 minutes. Add chicken; cook for 2 minutes. Mix with rice; cook over low heat for 15 minutes.
*6 to 8 servings*

❑ There were twelve kids in my family. We had to cook, iron, clean, and wash clothes for the whole family. We washed clothes by hand with a big stone. Forget it, it was no luxury. But we were happy, and we enjoyed our childhood so much.

We kids made money by delivering milk, newspapers, and groceries to the neighbors. They would give us money the day before, and we had to deliver by a certain time. We woke up early and got in line for milk; they paid us just to stand in line and deliver. With that money we could buy what we wanted, like junk food. Junk food was a luxury for us.

Unlike junk food, *papas guisadas* is pretty healthy. Potatoes Parmesan is really easy and quick to prepare.

## PAPAS GUISADAS
### Potatoes Parmesan

| | |
|---|---|
| 6 | red potatoes, |
| 1/8 | tsp. salt |
| 1/8 | tsp. garlic powder |
| 1/3 | cup milk |
| 2 | medium tomatoes, chopped |
| 2 | medium onions, chopped |
| 5 | Tbsp. olive oil |
| | salt and pepper to taste |
| | garlic powder |
| 1/2 | cup Parmesan cheese |

Boil potatoes in water with salt, $1/4$ teaspoon garlic powder, and milk until cooked but firm.

In a separate pan, cook tomatoes and onions in oil over medium heat. Sprinkle salt, pepper, and garlic powder (or substitute these seasonings with Cajun seasoning). Add drained potatoes to mixture; mix well. Stir in Parmesan.
*4 to 6 servings*

My family has always been close. Back in Cuba, where I was born and lived for almost twelve years, family time was important to us. My parents, my brother, Carlos, my sister, Helena, and I sat down together for dinner every single day to enjoy my mother's most delicious plates. Yes, I know those were other times. But for my family and I, being together at the table, sharing the food, and talking about what happened during the school day or any other topic was a very significant time.

Sundays were even more important. After going to church, we all went for lunch at my maternal grandparents' house. And when I say "all," I really mean everybody: my three cousins, aunts and uncles, godfather and godmother, and sometimes even the neighbors. Sundays were definitely special! I will never forget all of us sitting at the big table, laughing and telling stories while sharing the delicious food. I will always miss having all the love of the family on those Sundays in Cuba.

Mom's cooking, rich in flavor (calories, too!) reflected the family's Spanish and Cuban heritage. Being a housewife, Mom had time to prepare the most impressive special plates and desserts. I have always been a sweets lover. Dinner for me was not finished until I had eaten something sweet for dessert. Custards, fruits, gelatin, chocolate pudding, and, of course, my favorite, bread pudding, were present—days and nights—to satisfy my appetite. Sometimes at night, after my parents had retired to their bedroom, Carlos and I used to sneak out of our beds and attack the refrigerator, looking for that last piece of pudding or any leftover to cure our "sweets need."

How good were those moments! They were good because my brother and I indulged in all that delicious food that Mom prepared for us. But they were especially good because those moments highlighted aspects of yesterday's life which are disappearing in society today: the appreciation for our parents' sacrifices to give us all that we needed and the spirit of family love, togetherness, and sharing. With all my love, thanks, Mom and Dad, for lots of good memories.

Tony with his family and mother, Rosa Gibert.

*Life is so fast now. Sometimes even my own family cannot be all together for meals. The times we do spend together remind me of my childhood in Cuba, a long time ago, when life seemed less complicated and moved at a slower pace.*

□ Being of Spanish heritage, our Cuban menu is full of tasty and abundant plates. However, Mom's croquettes are my favorite. I was always the first in line to help in the kitchen when croquettes were on the menu. I thought that by helping Mom, I would get extras as a reward. But sometimes being the youngest is not necessarily a good thing; most of the time my older brother and sister got more *croquetas*.

I hope that while preparing this recipe, you will think about my mother. I also hope that you love Mom's Cuban croquettes as much as I.

### CROQUETAS CUBANAS
#### Cuban Croquettes

| | |
|---|---|
| 1 | lb. skirt or flank steak |
| 1 | beef or chicken bouillon cube |
| 1 | medium onion |
| 3 | Tbsp. oil |
| | salt and pepper to taste |
| 2 | Tbsp. flour |
| 1½ | oz. milk or broth |
| 2 | eggs, beaten |
| 1 | box cracker crumbs |
| | oil for frying |

Boil meat with bouillon cube until tender; drain. Grind meat with onion. Cook in oil over medium-high heat, stirring constantly. Add salt and pepper. Combine flour and milk; add to meat. Mix well and cool.

Place eggs and cracker crumbs in separate wide containers. Dip 1 tablespoon of mixture in egg, then in cracker crumbs until well-covered. Roll into cylindrical shape. Cook a small amount at a time in oil over medium-high heat until golden.
*4 servings*

□ After a long, hard day at school, Carlos and I were in desperate need of some filling snacks. The waiting period between lunch and dinner seemed too long to survive. Our family, like many in our culture, had late dinners around seven o'clock in the evening. A piece of bread pudding with a glass of milk, juice, or water was the most beautiful experience for a couple of hungry, young boys.

### PUDIN DE PAN
#### Bread Pudding

| | |
|---|---|
| 1½ | lbs. French bread, crust removed |
| 8½ | cups milk |
| 2½ | cups sugar |
| 1½ | tsp. salt |
| 1 | Tbsp. vanilla extract |
| ½ | cup butter, melted |
| 4 | eggs |

Soak bread in milk until soft. Break into small pieces with fork.

Melt butter over low heat. Grease a 9 x 13 glass pan with butter. Add sugar, salt, vanilla, and remaining butter to bread and milk mixture; mix well. Add eggs; mix well. Bake in a 375° preheated oven for about 1½ hours.
*8 to 10 servings*

My memories of our Cuban kitchen don't revolve around one special dish or even a holiday celebration. They float back to the everyday, to the wonderful aromas and fabulous tastes that other kids in our middle-class, suburban Washington, D.C., neighborhood never got to appreciate: the succulent taste of pork and chicken marinated for hours in *mojo criollo,* the heavenly harmony of black beans and white rice, and the savory mix of guava and cream cheese to cap a meal. Of course, a strong expresso was a must at the end of a meal. It had to be doused with plenty of sugar, a sweet reminder of the fertile fields of my parents' Caribbean island.

I can bring those sights and sounds to mind as if they took place yesterday, though it was many yesterdays ago. I guess that's a tribute to a great cook—as my mother is—and a lesson about how ordinary meals can leave lasting impressions.

Maria Carrillo with her mother, Josefina Carrillo, in the late 1960's.

One of my favorite meals was, and still is, *arroz con pollo.* Simply translated, it's chicken with rice. But that really is too simple a description.

The meal would be colorfully dressed up with asparagus spears, hard-boiled egg slices, and red pimentos. It looked almost too perfect to serve, as if you didn't want a single bit of rice to fall out of place. The chicken was always tender and the yellow rice perfectly cooked. They were a terrific blend and a hearty meal.

My mother always made plenty so that the rice nearly overflowed from a large earthenware dish. She would usually heat some rolls to complement the dish, but it was hardly necessary to have more food. There was definitely enough to feed a hungry family.

I hope you all enjoy.

□ This recipe for *arroz con pollo* calls for *Bijol*, a Spanish spice that turns the rice yellow. It can be purchased at specialty food stores and some larger food chains.

## ARROZ CON POLLO
### Chicken with Rice

| | |
|---|---|
| 2 | whole chickens, cut into pieces |
| 3 | garlic cloves |
| | juice of 1 lemon |
| | olive oil |
| 1 | onion, quartered |
| 1 | green pepper, quartered |
| 1 | cup chicken broth |
| 3 | cups water |
| 1/2 | cup wine |
| 2 | tsp. Bijol or paprika |
| 1 | large can tomato sauce |
| 2 | 2 oz. jars red pimentos |
| 1 | 15.25 oz. can peas |
| 1 | bay leaf |
| 1 | Tbsp. salt |
| 1/2 | tsp. black pepper |
| 3 | cups Uncle Ben's® rice |
| 1 | 15 oz. asparagus |
| | hard-boiled eggs, sliced |

Marinate chicken in garlic and lemon juice. Cook in oil over medium heat until brown. Combine onion and green pepper in blender; add to chicken. Cook for about 1 hour. Let chicken cool. Remove bones and skin, breaking meat into pieces.

In a separate pot, add chicken, broth, water, wine, Bijol, tomato sauce, pimentos, peas, bay leaf, salt and pepper. Bring to a boil; reduce heat to low. Stir in rice. Cover with aluminum foil first, then a lid. Cook ¹/₂ hour, stirring occasionally. Do not add more liquid. Cook until rice is tender. Sometimes Mom sticks it in the oven at 350° for the last 15 to 20 minutes. Decorate dish with peas, asparagus, pimentos, and hard-boiled eggs.
*8 servings*

□ Another favorite meal around our house was a Spanish stew—literally *caldo gallego*—that Mom would start making once the weather turned cold. There was nothing better on a day when we'd been out playing in the snow and needed to warm up fast.

## CALDO GALLEGO
### Spanish Stew with Sausage

| | |
|---|---|
| 8 | cups water |
| 2 | lbs. navy beans or 2 packages frozen collard greens |
| 8 | Spanish sausages |
| 2 | lbs. Virginia ham, bone-in |
| 1 | garlic clove, chopped |
| 1 | green pepper, chopped |
| 1 | onion, chopped |
| 2 | lbs. potatoes, quartered |
| 8 | turnips, peeled and cubed |

Boil water. Add beans or collard greens, sausages, ham, garlic, green pepper, and onion; cook over medium heat for 1 hour or until beans are soft. Add potatoes and turnips; cook until potatoes and turnips are done.
*8 servings*

I remember happy times of long ago when most of the members of my family still lived in Cuba, the place of my birth, and when we were still celebrating important occasions together. Memories of those years always centered around my maternal grandparents and their home on the northern coast of the island, a dreamy place we called Barrederas.

My grandparents, Enrique and Maria Dolores, had a large family—seven children in all, the oldest daughter being my mother, Ana Maria. By the time my sister, Isabel, and I were in our early teens, my grandparents were welcoming their first great-grandchild, and celebrations around the baby's christening were taking place. My memories of these events are nostalgic, for sure, but what has stayed with me the most, even after all of these years, is the distinct feeling that this was a celebration unique to our family, in which European traditions went hand in hand with Cuban ways.

*Memories of those years [in Cuba] always centered around my maternal grandparents and their home on the northern coast of the island, a dreamy place we called Barrederas.*

For the christening, my grandmother prepared a special drink made with egg yolks, sugar, and rum. The very young children could enjoy only a small sip. It was called *crème de vie,* or *crema de vida* in Spanish. Eggnog reminds me a bit of it, but our *crema de vida* was much thicker. The recipe had very likely—though no one is certain—descended from my great-grandmother, Ursula, whose family had immigrated to Cuba from French Louisiana, which explains the French name of the drink.

Made only for christenings, I got to have a good taste of it only when my nephew, Leonardo, was born. I was about fourteen then. For the adults in the family, an additional beverage called *aliñado* was also made and served late in the afternoon with supper. It was a much stronger fermented liquor with an orange flavor.

Since we lived near the coast, supper was frequently fish or seafood. My father loved octopus, but the sight of it in the refrigerator, waiting to be prepared for supper, made my sister and me howl in disgust! During the "winter" months, roasted pork or lamb was served instead. Rice, black or red beans, plantains, and yucca or cassava, steamed and served with garlic sauce completed the meal.

After supper, we watched our old great-aunts, Luisa and Caridad, play solitaire. But on steamy nights, we sat on the wicker chairs on the front porch and talked until the evening got cool enough to allow everyone to finally go to bed.

❏ For a hearty lunch or dinner, I often prepare *Picadillo Cubano*. When I make it for my family, I use golden raisins or small currants instead of the traditional raisins. In addition to the raisins, my children object to Spanish olives, but I use them generously anyway because they are an essential part of the dish. My husband and I find many "extra olives" on our plates.

Usually at the end of the semester, I prepare this dish for my Mary Washington College students enrolled in a class I teach on Latin American culture. For them, I triple this recipe.

This is a very popular food and almost all Latin American countries, including Brazil, have a variation of it. Leftovers may be used as filling for *empanadas* [see page 19], small meat pastries popular all over Latin America as well. *¡Que les aproveche!*

### PICADILLO CUBANO
#### Cuban Picadillo

| 1 | large onion, chopped |
| 2-3 | garlic cloves, crushed |
| 1-2 | Tbsp. olive oil |
| 1½ | lbs. ground beef or turkey |
| 2 | 14.5 oz. cans Del Monte® Mexican recipe stewed tomatoes |
| 15 | Spanish stuffed olives |
| ½ | cup raisins |
| ¼ | cup capers |
| 1-2 | tsp. oregano |
| | salt and pepper to taste |
| 1 | Tbsp. cumin |

Lightly cook onion and garlic in oil over medium heat. Brown meat; remove excess fat. Add remaining ingredients except cumin. Cook over low heat for about 1 hour. Add cumin; simmer for 15 to 20 minutes. Serve over white rice cooked with olive oil and a bay leaf.
*6 to 8 servings*

❏ Plantains, *plátanos* in Spanish, are a staple food in all of the Caribbean region and many areas of Central America. They look like oversized bananas, but unlike bananas, they cannot be eaten raw. I frequently find them in the produce section of most of the local supermarkets.

They can be steamed, baked, or fried. Don't throw them away when the skin turns almost black! This only means they are ripe and at their sweetest. This recipe, however, is for green plantains and is very popular in Cuba. Children love these crispy and salty treats!

### TOSTONES
#### Fried Green Plantains

| 2 | large green plantains |
| | oil for frying |
| | salt |

Slice plantains into 1-inch rounds. Peel and cook in oil over medium heat until golden on each side. Use vegetable oil; do not use olive oil. Line kitchen counter with grocery paper bags or any thick paper. Remove plantains; press between two thick pieces of paper until partially flattened.

Return plantains to pan; cook each side for a few seconds until golden. Sprinkle with salt. Serve tostones warm.
*4 servings*

My fondest childhood food memories revolve around holidays spent at our farm just outside Havana when the family gathered and a suckling pig was barbecued over a pit of glowing coals.

The party started the day before the feast when a sixty- to seventy-pound pig would be chosen and prepared. The son of the tenant farmer dispatched the animal with one stab of his foot-long blade inserted into the animal's heart, causing a prompt and painless death. The pig was gutted and cleaned. This included a straight razor shave and a warm water bath. The animal hung outside overnight, and before dawn on the following morning, a bed of coals was prepared in a *barbacoa,* a pit dug specifically for this occasion. The pig was trussed spread-eagle on a grill and basted with a wine and spice mixture.

*My father-in-law and I (front) used to goose hunt almost every day during the season.*

The smells, as the fat and basting drippings fell on the fire, could be sensed for miles. During the first few minutes, the hot fires seared the flesh. Then the fires were banked. Leaves from a nearby guava tree were added to the coals for the sweetness of their smoke. The pig was covered with banana leaves to trap the heat and smoke, then it was cooked slowly until the family gathered around two o'clock.

Tables and chairs were set up, and the rest of the meal was brought out under a palm thatch shelter near the pit. Along with the suckling pig, we enjoyed black beans and white rice; *yuca con mojo,* yucca with garlic and lime sauce; *tostones,* fried green plantains; salad, avocado slices, tons of Cuban bread, fresh fruit, and dessert. Cold beer washed down the meal. At the end of the feast, strong Cuban coffee and hand-rolled cigars appeared while the children went off to play or resume an interrupted baseball game.

□ Traditionally, the excess fat from the pork being cooked was rendered to make crackling and lard. The old-fashioned way of cooking black beans was to use this lard instead of olive oil when making the *sofrito*, which is a blend of onion, peppers, garlic, and spices. The crackling was then incorporated into the beans during the last step of cooking. If you do this, add 2 tablespoons of olive oil to the beans prior to serving. Serve over white rice or by itself as a soup.

### FRIJOLES NEGROS
### Black Beans

| | |
|---|---|
| 1 | lb. black beans, cleaned |
| 10 | cups water |
| 2 | bay leaves |
| 1 | large onion, finely chopped |
| 1/2 | cup olive oil |
| 1 | medium green pepper, chopped |
| 1 | medium red pepper, chopped |
| 2 | Tbsp. minced garlic |
| 2 | tsp. sugar |
| 1/2 | tsp. *each*: black pepper, oregano, and cumin |
| 3 | Tbsp. vinegar |
| 2 | Tbsp. wine |
| 1 | cup green olives |
| 1/2 | cup pimentos |

Soak beans overnight. Combine beans, water, and bay leaves; boil until beans are tender. If beans are not soaked, boil as usual, adding hot water as needed.

Prepare sofrito while beans are cooking. Cook onion in oil over medium-high heat for 3 minutes. Add green and red peppers; cook for 3 minutes. Add garlic; cook for 3 to 5 minutes. Pour into beans. Stir in sugar, pepper, oregano, and cumin; cook over medium heat for 30 minutes to 1 hour.

Add vinegar, wine, olives, and pimentos; cook for 1 hour. If too thin, mash some beans and mix into broth to thicken.

### YUCA CON MOJO
### Yucca with Garlic and Lime Sauce

| | |
|---|---|
| 3 | lbs. yucca, peeled and cut into 2-inch slices |
| 1 | tsp. salt |

**mojo:**

| | |
|---|---|
| 1 | large onion, sliced |
| 1/2 | cup olive oil |
| 10 | garlic cloves, chopped |
| 1/2 | cup sour orange or lime juice |
| 1 | tsp. salt |

Add yucca to a large pot of water; bring to a boil. When boiling, add 2 cups cold water. Return to a boil; cook for 15 minutes or until tender. Remove pot from heat. Add 1 teaspoon salt. Let yucca soak for 3 to 5 minutes; drain.

Prepare mojo. Cook onion in oil over medium-high heat until tender. Add garlic; cook for 2 minutes. Add sour orange or lime juice and salt; cook until juice is warm. Pour over yucca.
*8 to 10 servings*

□ Depending upon the size, *lechon asado* takes about four hours to bake after being marinated.

### LECHON ASADO
### Roast Pork

| | |
|---|---|
| 1 | 6 to 8 lb. pork roast |
| 1 | whole head of garlic, chopped |
| 2 | tsp. cumin |
| 2 | tsp. oregano |
| 2 | Tbsp. salt |
| 1 | tsp. black pepper |
| 1 | cup sour orange juice |
| 2 | bay leaves |
| 1 | lb. onions, thinly sliced into ringlets |
| 1 | cup white wine |

Score roast diagonally. Prepare marinade by combining garlic, cumin, oregano, salt, pepper, and orange juice. Cover roast with marinade. Add bay leaves and onion; marinate for 12 hours.

Add wine to roast; bake in a 350° preheated oven. Baste with pan juices every hour until meat thermometer reads at least 150° to 185°. Remove from oven. Drain pan juices with garlic and onion; after removing fat, mix in blender. Strain the resulting gravy. Serve with pork.

Set aside pork for 10 minutes before cutting.
*14 to 16 servings*

**When I left Peristerona**, my village in Cyprus, twenty years ago, there were only about 350 people. On Easter's Great Sunday, every person in the village was supposed to be in the church just before midnight to celebrate the resurrection of Christ. We all knew each other in my village. When someone was missing, a person was sent to the home to call him to church. Perhaps he was asleep; we didn't have electricity so everyone went to bed when it became dark. We didn't have alarm clocks either and the rooster wasn't crowing at that time. We knew straight away if someone was missing, and we couldn't begin the joyous celebration without everyone being in the church.

Before midnight, all the candles were blown out except for the Holy Light, the one on the altar. The Holy Light is on, day and night, and is never turned off. Imagine how dark the church was with only the Holy Light on at the altar. At midnight brand-new candles were lit, beginning with the priest lighting his own candle from the Holy Light. He went to the congregation and said, "Receive the Holy Light of Christ." Then the altar boys lit the new candles and passed the light to the people in the church until everyone's candle was lit.

Carrying our candles, we went outside for a service. We walked around the church, stopping at each corner, while the priest read a gospel. At every corner, after the priest said "Cristos Anesti," some people exploded homemade firecrackers!

Here in the States people bring eggs, hard-boiled and dyed red to symbolize the blood of Christ, to church. At the end of the service, there is a contest of cracking the eggs by tapping the tips together. The object is to keep the eggs intact. Before tapping, one says, "Christ has risen"; the other says, "Truly He has risen."

In Cyprus, we did not break the eggs in church, just at home. But some people brought their eggs to church because, after fasting and being at church until two or three o'clock in the morning, they were hungry. When church finished, they would eat the egg right from their pockets. By the time we came home at three o'clock in the morning, we were also very hungry. We hadn't eaten all day. Imagine! Before sleeping, we'd have some *avgolemono,* an egg and lemon soup with rice, and chicken *flaounes*, pastries with cheese.

The next day was the most celebrated day of all. There was so much rejoicing and happiness and many families and friends got together for parties. About two years ago, I had a big party for about fifty people at my house. I roasted a full lamb and had many dishes such as *pastitsio*, a macaroni and meat pie; *moussaka*, an eggplant casserole; spinach pies, and many different salads. People were drinking and dancing. The kids were hunting for eggs. Hunting for eggs is not typical for Cypriots, but we did it for the kids. Everyone was having a wonderful time. Easter Sunday was just a great day of joy for families and friends.

Chryse and her son, Danny.

*My village in Cyprus was so small that if anyone was missing at church, we would know straight away.*

▢ When my mom cooks, food tastes extraordinary. It's so much different from other Greek-Cypriot cooking. There can be 1,000 ways of making one dish—for instance, *pastitsio*—and depending on the person, it may have more cheese or more meat. But the way my mom makes it...it's special.

—George Kartoudi

### PASTITSIO
**Macaroni and Meat Pie**

| | |
|---|---|
| 2 | lbs. ground beef |
| | salt and pepper to taste |
| 1/2 | bunch parsley, chopped |
| 4 | cups milk |
| 2 | cups butter |
| 4-5 | eggs, beaten |
| 1 | Tbsp. cornstarch |
| 2 | Tbsp. flour |
| 1 | lb. macaroni, cooked |
| | Parmesan cheese |
| | Cheddar cheese |
| | cinnamon |

Cook meat in 1 tablespoon butter over medium-high heat. Sprinkle with salt, pepper, and parsley.

In a separate pan, boil 3 cups milk and butter.

In a separate bowl, add cornstarch and flour to eggs; mix well. Add remaining milk; mix well. Pour this mixture into hot milk, stirring constantly. When sauce thickens, remove from heat.

Spread half of macaroni in a greased 9 x 13 pan. Sprinkle with Parmesan and Cheddar cheese. Layer meat and remaining macaroni. Spread sauce on top; lightly sprinkle with cinnamon. Bake at 350° for 1 hour or until brown on top.
*12 servings*

▢ In Cyprus, we never counted anything when we cooked; we never measured. I learned a lot of cooking from cookbooks. I make these *koulourakia*, or butter cookies, for any occasion: Easter, Christmas, Greek festivals, or just any day.

### KOULOURAKIA
**Butter Cookies**

| | |
|---|---|
| 4 | cups margarine, room temperature |
| 2 | cups unsalted butter, room temperature |
| 2 | cups sugar |
| 6 | eggs |
| 4 | lbs. flour |
| 1 | tsp. vanilla extract |
| 8 | Tbsp. baking powder |

Cream margarine, butter, and sugar with mixer. Add eggs individually while mixing. Add flour by spoonfuls until dough does not stick to hands. Test by pinching dough occasionally. Add vanilla and baking powder.

Roll small amounts into thick strings, fold in half, and twist. Lightly brush with beaten egg for a gloss. Bake at 350° for 15 minutes or until bottoms are lightly brown.
*6 to 8 dozen*

Hardly a day passes by that the sky in Cyprus is not blue. The winters are usually quite mild, but they do have their share of harsh rains. On these rainy days during the winter, *kouneli stifado,* or rabbit stew, is a popular food.

*Kouneli stifado,* a type of stew that contains lots of onions, is a favorite among Cypriots, and like lamb, it is sometimes served at special gatherings. *Stifado* is also commonly made with beef or lamb because rabbit is an expensive ingredient in Cyprus. My family enjoys *kouneli stifado* along with a large slice of crusty Greek bread which we dip in the savory juices of the stew.

The Cypriots call a wild rabbit "*lagos*." *Lagos* has a stronger flavor than the farm-grown *kouneli,* or rabbit, and it is best when stewed. Other parts of the rabbits, such as the fur, are also used. We comb the fur of the largest rabbits and spin the fur into yarn to make sweaters.

Most families in Cyprus own a small piece of land where they can raise their own rabbits for food. Some do, but with the industrial and modern growth of the island, there is less land now. So during the winter months when it is hunting time, most of the men head for the mountains where the rabbits are plentiful. When the uncles, brothers, and fathers come back, they share the rabbits with family and friends.

The land we owned in Cyprus is no longer our family's because of the Turkish occupation of the northern part of Cyprus in 1974, but when we lived there, my father and grandfather raised rabbits as well as goats and other animals on their farm. We also had a citrus grove where we grew oranges, lemons, tangerines, and grapefruits. After working the land all day, it was a great blessing to come home to a plate of *kouneli stifado* to satisfy a hungry appetite.

*I (right) am making loukoumades, donut-like pastries, with my nephew, John, at the Greek Festival in Fredericksburg. The festival is not only a fund raiser for the the Greek Orthodox Church; it also adds ethnic flavor to the community.*

# Anastasia Papadopoulou

□ Red wine, olive oil, bay leaves, garlic, and cinnamon are largely used in Greek-Cypriot cooking. These ingredients, when combined, add great flavor to foods and are commonly used to marinate meat.

### KOUNELI STIFADO
### Baked Rabbit Stew

| | |
|---|---|
| 3/4 | cup olive oil |
| 1 | medium rabbit, cut into pieces |
| 2 | large garlic cloves, crushed |
| 2 | Tbsp. wine vinegar |
| 8 | Tbsp. red wine |
| 1 | cinnamon stick |
| 1 | bay leaf |
| 3 | medium tomatoes, crushed |
| 2 | cups hot water |
| | salt to taste |
| | freshly ground pepper |
| 2 | large onions, chopped |

In a large pan, heat 3 tablespoons oil over medium-high heat. Add rabbit; cook all sides well. Add garlic and cook quickly. Add vinegar, wine, cinnamon, bay leaf, tomatoes, water, salt and pepper, stirring well. Place rabbit in baking pan; bake in a 350° preheated oven for 45 to 50 minutes.

Heat remaining oil over low-medium heat. Add onions; cook for 15 minutes or until golden. Drain oil, if desired; add onions to rabbit. Bake an additional 20 minutes. Stifado should have a rich, thick sauce. If too thin, reduce liquid over medium heat.

*4 to 6 servings*

□ *Kaloprama* means "good thing" in Greek. This wonderfully easy dessert is exactly that. The moist cake-like pudding is also called *shamali, revani,* or *basbosa,* depending on where you eat it in the Middle East.

In Cyprus, another common name is *halva.* *Halva* is usually associated with the sweet sesame paste dessert, but *halva* simply means "sweet." *Kaloprama* is a popular dessert found in most Greek confectionery bakeries in Cyprus; it is also made in most homes.

### KALOPRAMA
### Almond and Semolina Pudding

| | |
|---|---|
| 1/2 | cup butter |
| 1/2 | cup sugar |
| | peel of 1 lemon, grated |
| 3 | eggs |
| 1 | cup semolina or cream of wheat |
| 1/2 | cup flour |
| 3 | tsp. baking powder |
| 1/4 | cup milk |
| 1/4 | cup toasted almonds, finely chopped |
| | blanched split almonds for decorating |

**syrup:**

| | |
|---|---|
| 1 1/4 | cups sugar |
| 1 1/2 | cups water |
| 2 | Tbsp. lemon juice |

Prepare syrup. Dissolve sugar in water over medium heat. Add lemon juice; bring to a boil. Cook for 10 minutes; remove from heat. Set aside to cool.

Cream butter, sugar, and lemon peel until fluffy. Add eggs individually, beating well after each. Fold in semolina, flour, and baking powder, alternating with milk. Stir in chopped almonds. Spread mixture into buttered 7 x 11 baking pan. Bake at 325° to 350° for 50 minutes or until golden and pudding pulls away slightly from sides.

When done, poke holes with thin skewer. Pour cooled syrup over hot pudding. Cool in pan; decorate with blanched almonds. Cut into squares and serve.

*10 to 12 servings*

**Electricity came** in the sixties when I was about eleven or twelve years old. Running water came around the same time, within a year. Now tractors, cars, and motorcycles are everywhere. All the life I knew faded out when machinery came.

I had grown up in my village Philia very differently. We had a fifteen-acre farm in Cyprus; two acres were just for the vegetables. My mother worked on the farm, and my father worked in the city. There were eight children, and by the age of three, we had to help my mother on the farm. Imagine raising all of us! We always had something to do and we never wasted time. If we weren't picking beans or getting water from the river, we were crocheting or sewing.

On our farm, we had chickens, goats, and pigs. There wasn't a store. If we wanted to eat chicken, we'd just go out to the yard and pick one. The butcher sold sheep and lamb, but that was only on the weekends. We only ate meat on the weekends anyway; the rest of the week we ate vegetables from the garden. When my mother killed a rooster, we'd have half of it on Saturday and half on Sunday, or half for lunch and half for dinner. It depended on how many chickens we had. If there were too many roosters—we didn't need them—we'd wait for them to grow and eat them. Or we ate the old chickens and kept the young ones. With all the animals, nothing was wasted. We never threw anything in the garbage. Potato peels, beans, watermelons, leftovers—all were thrown out in the yard for the animals.

We made our own bread and cheese. We made cheese in the summer because the goats didn't make milk year round, only after they had babies in the early spring. We collected the milk from the mothers and made *haloumi* and ricotta cheese. The cheese, covered

Maria (left) with her two daughters (far right), niece, and a family friend.

*One thing nice about Cyprus is that all the neighbors help each other.*

in juice and stored in a jar, lasted until the next year.

The farm was about four miles from the city, and we rode our donkey to get there. My mother would put huge saddlebags on both sides of the donkey. She had stuff in one side and stuff in the other; or stuff in one side and a kid in the other! Sometimes she'd hold one kid in front of her. Not all eight of us could go at one time; we only had one donkey. Our donkey was more than transportation. He carried wood and vegetables for us, like when we had artichokes. After my mother cut a lot of artichokes, we'd load the donkey, walk home and unload, walk the donkey back to the farm, and load again.

I was so happy when the electricity came because I didn't have to wash lamps anymore. We were using kerosene for the lamps and stove. Every night the glass on the lamps turned black, and it was my job to wash those lamps after school. If my mom came home and the glasses weren't clean, I was in trouble because we wouldn't be able to see.

I remember wishing we had running water, then one day we had it. My mother now has a washing machine which she never had before. But she still has her oven outside. Every Sunday, she lights it up to cook a chicken over the wood. There is nothing like it.

□ There was nothing like Sunday in Cyprus. We never worked, and we never missed church. After church we had chicken soup for breakfast, then we would begin preparing Sunday dinner which was always very special because we would have meat.

Meat was a big treat. My sister and I helped my mother prepare the meal. Usually we had roasted chicken and potatoes, but a really special treat would be when we had *keftedes*, Greek meatballs.

Today when I have friends coming over, I make *keftedes*. My friends don't want anything else. They eat the meatballs like candies!

### KEFTEDES
#### Greek Meatballs

| | |
|---|---|
| 2 | large onions |
| 3 | garlic cloves |
| 2 | lbs. potatoes, peeled and finely grated |
| 3 | lbs. ground beef |
| 3-4 | bread slices |
| 4 | eggs |
| 1 | sprig of parsley, chopped |
| | salt and pepper to taste |
| 1-2 | lemons |

Finely chop onions and garlic by hand or in a blender; set aside.

Strain grated potatoes for 15 minutes. Add onions, garlic, and remaining ingredients except lemons; mix well. Set aside for $1/2$ hour.

Shape into balls; deep-fry until meat is done. Squeeze lemons over meatballs before serving. Serve with fried potatoes or rice pilaf.
*10 to 12 servings*

□ *Boulgoure,* or cracked wheat, can also be served with *keftedes* instead of fried potatoes or rice pilaf.

### BOULGOURE
#### Cracked Wheat

| | |
|---|---|
| 1 | large onion, finely chopped |
| $1/3$ | cup oil |
| 1 | cup chopped tomatoes |
| 4 | cups chicken broth |
| 2 | cups bulgur wheat* |
| | salt and pepper to taste |

Cook onions in oil over medium heat. Add tomatoes; cook for 5 minutes. Add broth and bring to a boil. Add wheat; cook over low heat until broth is absorbed. Add salt and pepper.
*6 to 8 servings*

**Growing up** in Pennsylvania, where so many rich ethnic heritages are preserved, I learned to know and love the music, customs, and especially many of the foods that my Czech and Slovak grandparents brought with them to America. When my husband and I moved to Germany for a missionary assignment, I eagerly looked forward to "building bridges" with my long-lost relatives and their culture in what was then called Czechoslovakia.

We got our chance just after the so-called "Velvet Revolution" of 1989-1990, when we were called on to help establish the first international English-language Protestant congregation in Prague after the fall of the Communist government. In Prague we met Michal, a Czech scientist, and his wife, Jitka, who offered to help find my family in the hilly province of Moravia.

In their home in the mining city of Turnov, Bohemia, we were treated to *kolace*, a wonderful plum pastry. Writing down the recipe, which I hoped to take home with me, was most interesting. Jitka, who spoke no English, gave the recipe from memory to Michal, who translated it into English for us, but only until the phone rang and he was called away. Then Michal's mother translated it into German and my husband turned the German into English. After all that, I still had to convert the metric measurements and temperature readings into American! Yet somehow, Jitka's wonderful treat still comes through.

*Michal and two of my long-lost relatives, Ana and Frantiska.*

Then we went for our adventure. With my parents from Pennsylvania along, we drove through Moravian farming and mining country to a lovely town called Hroznova Lhota, which consisted of a one-mile-long street packed tightly with houses and barns. The Catholic church was at one end and the Lutheran church at the other.

After we arrived, the "clan" began to gather to meet these strange American relatives. It seemed that we were related to about half the town. One cousin was a businessman in the city; others were still working on the farms and in the mines. One young woman was taking advantage of the recent political and economic upheaval by taking a job at a new casino!

Our one day spent with them was mostly filled with food. Everyone brought something and the tables were overflowing. A cousin made rich, homemade noodles, spooned high into soup bowls, with chicken broth poured over to make a delicious soup. Appetizers included *kolace* shaped into little buns and filled with either chopped nuts or dry cottage cheese, along with fresh vegetables, and homemade breads. The main dish was *rouladen,* a speciality made of thinly sliced beef, seasoned and wrapped around a hard-boiled egg, then topped with gravy. For dessert, the crowning glory was a chocolate cake and whipped cream torte with an extra touch of liqueur served with coffee.

Late into the night, everyone told his story, which was a special challenge because none of us spoke Czech, and none of our relatives spoke English. Michal had to translate everything! Finally, out came two guitars and the homemade plum wine, and

*Going to what was then called Czechoslovakia was a once-in-a-lifetime opportunity to visit the land of my heritage.*

the singing began. Much to our surprise, two of the favorites were "My Darling Clementine" and "Comin' Round the Mountain"—both sung in Czech before we took our turn in good ol' American English! It was a day, an evening, and a meal to be remembered for a lifetime.

◻ *Kolace* is a Czech-Slovak sweet dough filled with a fruit, poppy seed, cinnamon, and/or chopped nut filling. There are many kinds of *kolace* made by Central European bakers. My family's style is to roll out the dough, spread the filling, then roll up the pastry like a jelly roll. We discovered this authentic Bohemian recipe when we returned home to the Czech Republic to meet relatives and friends there.

### PLUM KOLACE
**Bohemian Plum Pastry**

| | |
|---|---|
| 3 | cups flour |
| 2 | envelopes dry yeast |
| 1/4 | cup sugar |
| | dash of salt |
| 1/2 | cup milk |
| 1/2 | cup butter or margarine |
| 1 | tsp. vanilla extract |
| 2 | large cans plums |

**streusel:**

| | |
|---|---|
| 1/2 | cup butter or margarine, softened |
| 1 | cup sugar |
| 1 | cup flour |
| 1 | tsp. vanilla extract |

In a large bowl, mix flour, yeast, sugar, and salt. Set aside.

Cook milk and butter over medium heat until butter melts; add vanilla. Mix liquid into dry ingredients, using hands to form a stiff dough. Cover; let rise for 1/2 hour in a warm place.

Drain plums, remove pits, and cut each in half. Pat dough into greased cookie sheet evenly. Spread fruit within 1/2 inch from edge.

Combine streusel ingredients and sprinkle over fruit. Bake at 325° for 15 minutes. Reduce heat to 300°; bake for 35 to 40 minutes or until light brown on edges.

*12 to 15 servings*

◻ *Halushki* are little potato dumplings similar to Italian gnocchi. I always thought of *halushki* as the name for the dumpling and cabbage dish. When we visited Prague, I ordered *halushki* to see how the authentic dish compared to our family recipe. To my surprise, the *halushki* was not served with cabbage, but with meat.

### HALUSHKI
**Potato Dumplings (with Fried Cabbage)**

| | |
|---|---|
| 3 | large potatoes, finely grated |
| 1 | tsp. salt |
| 1 | egg, beaten |
| 2 1/2 | cups flour |

**fried cabbage:**

| | |
|---|---|
| 1 | large cabbage, cut into 1/2-inch pieces |
| 1 | lb. bacon, sliced into 1/2-inch strips |
| | salt and pepper to taste |

Combine potatoes, salt, and egg; mix well. Add flour until dough is soft, adding more if needed until dough is not sticky. Place dough on a board; scrape off 1 teaspoon at a time. Boil in salted water until dumplings float, about 10 to 15 minutes. Stir often to prevent sticking. Drain and rinse in cool water. Return dumplings to pan.

Cook bacon until almost crisp. Remove bacon, reserving 1/4 to 1/3 cup drippings. Add bacon to dumplings.

Cook cabbage in drippings until tender; sprinkle with salt and pepper. Add to bacon and dumplings. Heat mixture over low heat, stirring often. Serve warm.

*6 to 8 servings*

**I have many** cherished memories of my mother, who is of Slovak descent from what was formerly known as Czechoslovakia, and her cooking. My mother spent a lot of time in the kitchen making the dishes that we all liked.

As a child, when I came home from school, she would have everything ready. I remember watching her prepare meals, all from scratch, for six kids. My mother cooked anything and everything. Besides the Slavic food, she also cooked chili, different soups, Swedish pancakes, lemon pie, apple crisp. She even made her own bread, rolls, and raised donuts. I think, boy, all the time she took to make the food for us, and she did it all by herself!

My mother passed away at a very early age, so I never really learned how to cook from her, but my older sisters knew how to make many of the Slavic dishes. With the help and know-how of my older sisters, it didn't take me long to learn. When I lived in Pennsylvania, one of my sisters lived about two miles away. She would come and show me how to fix different Slavic dishes or we'd do them together. We always had fun, although the cooking was a lot of work.

Mary (standing, second from left) and her brothers and sisters.

*I would like my children to know how to make the recipes that were passed to me, but they've got to start learning.*

Sometimes I call up my youngest sister, Jean, who also lives here in Fredericksburg, to ask if she wants to make dumplings called *pirohy*. We make double batches at her house. I keep half and she keeps half. She doesn't know how to make them on her own. Maybe she thinks she'll mess them up, so she just mashes the potatoes and cheese and pinches the dough to close them. When Jean says, "Tom is hungry for pirohy"—Tom is her son—I know what she's saying. She's saying, "Come over and help me." But I don't mind. I enjoy it.

When my children come to visit, especially on the holidays, I make *holubky*, stuffed cabbage rolls, and *pirohy*, which are on the top of the menu. My children love Czech food but they have never actually made the food themselves.

I would like my children to know how to make the recipes that were passed to me, but they've got to start learning. Food is the only Czech tradition left in my family, and I want them to learn because I hope the tradition carries on.

▫ I have my mother's cookbook which was passed to me by my father. It is an anniversary edition of a Slovak-American cookbook that first came out in 1892. My mother's sister-in-law gave the book, which is dedicated to mothers and grandmothers of the Catholic Slovak Ladies Union, to my mom in 1954.

My mother had many recipes of her own and from friends written in pencil on the blank pages. Some of the recipes call for "half a pound of lard" or "half a pound of lard and half a pound of shortening." Yikes! I don't fix my food this way; I try to make it a little bit healthier.

### KOLACKY
#### Slovak Nut Roll

| | |
|---|---|
| 2 | envelopes dry yeast |
| 1/2 | cup warm milk |
| 6 | cups flour, sifted |
| 1 | cup butter |
| 1 | cup sour cream |
| 3 | eggs, beaten |
| 3 | Tbsp. sugar |
| 1 | tsp. salt |

nut filling:

| | |
|---|---|
| 2 | lbs. ground walnuts |
| 3/4 | cup sugar |
| 3/4 | cup warm milk |
| 1 | Tbsp. honey |
| 1 | Tbsp. lemon juice |
| 1 | tsp. vanilla extract |
| 2 | Tbsp. butter, melted |

Prepare nut filling. Combine all ingredients except butter; mix well. Divide into 8 parts; set aside.

Dissolve yeast in milk. Set aside.

In a separate bowl, combine flour, butter, sour cream, eggs, sugar, and salt. Add yeast and milk mixture; mix well. Knead until smooth.

Divide dough into 8 parts. Roll each about 1/4 inch thick. Spread nut mixture over each dough. Roll and tuck in ends. Place on greased cookie sheets; cover with cloth and let rise for 1 hour. Bake at 350° for 35 minutes. Spread melted butter on top while rolls are still warm.

*8 rolls*

▫ *Holubky* and *kolacky* are prepared as a holiday tradition in my family on Easter and Christmas.

### HOLUBKY
#### Stuffed Cabbage Rolls

| | |
|---|---|
| 1 | large cabbage |
| 1 | medium onion, chopped |
| 3 | celery stalks, chopped |
| 2 | Tbsp. butter |
| 2 | lbs. ground beef |
| 1/2 | cup rice, partially cooked |
| 1 | egg |
| 1 | tsp. salt |
| 1/2 | tsp. black pepper |
| 1 | 10.75 oz. can tomato soup |
| 1 | quart tomato juice |

Cut core from cabbage. Boil until slightly cooked. Separate leaves; set aside.

Cook onion and celery in butter over medium heat until golden brown. Combine with meat, rice, egg, salt, and pepper; mix well. Spoon mixture onto larger ends of cabbage leaves. Roll up, tucking in ends to prevent mixture from coming out. Layer cabbage rolls in a roasting pan.

Cook tomato soup and tomato juice over medium heat until smooth. Pour over cabbage rolls. Bake at 325° for 2 hours or until brown and tender.

*6 to 8 servings*

*"Vecina, aqui viene la marchanta...con cilantro fresco, tomate, repello!"*

**Early in the morning** the *marchantas* in the Dominican Republic holler as they go through the streets, "Neighbor, here is your *marchanta*..with fresh cilantro, tomatoes, and cabbage!" *Marchantas* are the traditional way of selling vegetables and other merchandise to the people in the country. The *marchantas* come really early in the morning. Many people wake up with their hollering in the neighborhood.

Usually the *marchantas* are women. Some men sell also, but the men carry what they are selling with a donkey or a wheelbarrow. The women carry big, round wicker baskets, about two feet across, either in front of them like a pregnant lady or on top of their heads. The baskets are normally set on a cloth donut or towel to give support to the basket. Sometimes the women even carry their babies in one of their hands. Most of them don't have a lot of money, so they have to take their babies with them while they make their living selling vegetables or flowers on the street.

*If the roosters didn't wake us up, the marchantas did. I wished the marchantas would have come later!*

If we want what they are selling, we'd just holler back to stop at the house. The *marchanta* basically knows what a person buys, so she may just knock on the door and ask, "You need anything today?" There are three or four *marchantas* who come around the same neighborhood. I guess they gathered themselves to make different routes. They must have their own sections or streets so they can all make money because they sell the same things.

Almost everything is sold on the street in the Dominican Republic. They sell cilantro, carrots, potatoes, avocados—every single ingredient that is needed to make a meal is sold from their baskets. Some sell flowers; some sell pastries. It depends on the time of day. Instead of going out of the house to buy, the *marchantas* bring the goods to us, and we can have everything early.

In the morning they sell the vegetables because we have our main meal at noon. Meals take hours to prepare because the food is made from scratch; nothing is from a can. Rice needs to be cleaned. It's thrown on a table and picked through for rocks, husks, or other unwanted material. Beans need to be softened by soaking them overnight, then they are cooked for one hour to one and a half hours. This is why we have to wake up early!

People from the Dominican Republic buy their meat and vegetables from the *marchantas* on a daily basis because many people do not have refrigeration. It is a waste of time. Here I can buy a whole cabbage and it will last me a week in the refrigerator, and I don't have to sort through rice because it is already selected. I am so used to having the conveniences in America. I think it would be so hard for me to go back to the Dominican Republic and get used to that kind of life again.

❑  We use wooden *pilons,* or mortars, all the time for garlic and different spices.  Most people will have two *pilons*: one for crushing garlic and a smaller one for sweet spices like cinnamon and cloves.

### CARNE RIPADA
**Shredded Beef in Tomato Sauce**

| | |
|---|---|
| 2 | lbs. chuck roast, cubed |
| 1 | whole head of garlic, crushed |
| 1 | tsp. oregano |
| 1 | tsp. salt |
| 2 | Tbsp. vinegar |
| 1 | large onion, halved |
| 1 | green pepper, sliced |
| 1 | red pepper, sliced |
| 3 | Tbsp. olive oil |
| 2 | small chicken bouillon cubes |
| 1 | 8 oz. can tomato sauce |

Boil or cook roast in a pressure cooker.  Remove meat; reserve water.  Shred and set aside.

In a mortar, crush garlic; sprinkle oregano and salt while pounding.  Add vinegar.  Cook garlic mixture, onion, green and red peppers in oil over medium heat in a covered pan for 3 to 5 minutes.

Add bouillon and tomato sauce; cook until vegetables are soft.  Add meat and enough reserved water to cover beef.  Cook, covered, for 10 to 15 minutes.  Serve with rice, boiled yucca, or boiled plantains.
*4 to 6 servings*

❑  *Morir soñado* translates into "dying dreaming." I guess the drink is called this because it is so delicious!  I make it for my children as a special treat.

Two pitchers are needed to mix the drink. The drink must be mixed quickly or the lemon will sour the milk.

### MORIR SOÑADO
**Dying Dreaming**

| | |
|---|---|
| 5 | Tbsp. sugar or to taste |
| 2 | cups milk |
| 1/2 | tsp. vanilla extract |
| 2 | cups ice |
| | juice of 1 lemon |

In one pitcher, dissolve sugar in milk.  Add vanilla. In another pitcher, squeeze lemon over ice.  Mix contents back and forth between pitchers quickly.
*2 to 3 servings*

❑  A *tostonera* is made from two pieces of wood hinged together.  It is used to flatten plantains when making *plátanos fritos* or *tostones*, or fried plantains.

Back home, when someone says, "Someone had an accident, and the car looked like a *tostone*," that meant that the car looked like a smashed plantain; so the car was in really bad shape.

### PLÁTANOS FRITOS or TOSTONES
**Fried Plantains**

| | |
|---|---|
| 2 | plantains |
| | oil for frying |

Cut plantains into 1-inch slices.  Cook both sides in oil over medium heat until a fork easily pierces plantains.  Remove; flatten in tostonera or with an unbreakable mug.  Cook again until golden brown.

Many people eat tostones like French fries with ketchup or with chili sauce.  We eat ours with the main dish.
*4 servings*

**Mama Chayo** always told me that if I saw someone at the market buying the same thing as I was—say a cabbage—wait and see if that person will pay full price or try to bargain. If that person gets the cabbage for less, I *better be sure* to get it for the same price.

People in the markets in El Salvador are always trying to sell their merchandise for two or three times more than what they normally should. I know from experience how much they paid before going to the market because I was born on a farm and we grew all the vegetables. So my grandmother, Mama Chayo, told me I had to learn how to bargain.

For example, when I buy plantains I usually buy one or two dozens to last the week. First, I ask, "How much is a dozen?"

The merchant may say, "3 colones." Colones is the money unit in El Salvador.

So I ask, "If I buy more, will you sell them for less?"

"Well, I can give them to you for 2.50."

Cecilia (far left).

*We lived in a small village, and no one had a camera. One day a man came into town, offering to take pictures. We put on our best clothes because having a picture taken was a big deal. Two months later, we received this photo.*

"No, I'll pay 1.35," and that's just to start with.

He says, "What about 1.90?"

If I was willing to go up to 1.90, "Okay, 1.90 sounds good."

All the markets are open with lots of vendors and tables. I have to stop at one table and buy a cabbage, stop at another table and buy a mango, and so on until I finish my shopping. At each table, I need to bargain or at the end of the day I will have spent too much money. I can offer the merchant up to a certain amount. If I still don't like the price after bargaining, there is always another person selling the same thing further down. Sometimes, the merchant will yell to me that he will take my price before I even take ten steps away.

There are no price tags, so if they hear someone speak just the tiniest word in English, that person is lost! When I brought my six-year-old son to El Salvador, I told him to just keep his mouth shut. He was whispering, "Why aren't you paying full price?" I had to explain to him how to deal in the market. Even though I try to dress poorly when I go to the market and I am El Salvadoran, I still do not look like I am from there. My hair looks shinier and my skin is lighter because I don't stay in the sun too much. But if I know how to bargain, I can still get what I want at a local person's price.

The merchants don't even think twice before they try to charge you double. El Salvadorans are on a tight budget and they have to stretch their money. Trying to charge more is one way of making more money. Bargaining is just a way of life.

□ My mother made it a point to bring the family to visit Mama Chayo, but it wasn't every day because Mama Chayo lived ten miles from us, and we had to walk to see her. We walked and walked and walked...forever.

Mama Chayo made the best marmalade around and the whole time I was walking I'd think, "Oh, what kind of marmalade is she having this time?" Her marmalade was the only thing that kept me walking.

When we arrived, I'd look for the marmalade. She always had it in a small clay pot, hiding it from us so we didn't just take what we wanted. I remember always tugging on my mother's skirt, begging her to ask Mama Chayo if I could have some marmalade. If I asked, Mama Chayo would tell me to wait until after dinner; if my mother asked—it was different—Mama Chayo would say yes.

### MERMELADA DE MANGO
### Whole Mango Marmalade

| | |
|---|---|
| 6 | large mangoes, peeled |
| 2 | cups brown sugar |
| 2 | large cinnamon sticks |
| 3 | cups water |
| 6 | whole cloves |

Cook mangoes, sugar, cinnamon, and water over low heat for 1 hour. Add cloves; cook over medium heat for 20 minutes. Store in the refrigerator for three days for better flavor, but it can be eaten immediately.
*6 servings*

□ The prisoners in El Salvador work, and they work very hard. They make beautiful wood carvings for bowls, plates, candle holders, and wall hangings. The design may be a house, a village, flowers, anything they can think of. They carve serving and individual bowls with the same design and sell them as a set.

The prison has a shop which is open to the public two times a month. I've heard that the prisoners get to keep a certain percentage of the money; maybe they send it to the family or keep an account.

These carvings are seen in rich people's houses and no one would ever think they were made by prisoners. I have a couple of wall hangings that show the Native Indian tribes and a container with a lid that keeps tortillas warm.

### POLLO GUISADO
### Chicken with Tomato Sauce

| | |
|---|---|
| 1 | cinnamon stick |
| 1 | tsp. black pepper |
| 2 | whole cloves |
| 1/2 | tsp. oregano |
| 3 | garlic cloves |
| 1/4 | tsp. paprika |
| 1/2 | large onion, sliced |
| 5 | tomatillos |
| 4 | lbs. tomatoes or equivalent in can |
| 1 | whole chicken, cut into pieces |
| | salt to taste |
| | oil |
| 1 | large onion, cut into rings |
| 2 | Tbsp. cornmeal or corn flour |
| 1/2 | cup water |

Mix cinnamon, pepper, cloves, oregano, garlic, paprika, sliced onion, tomatillos, and tomatoes in a blender. Salt chicken; cook in $^1/_2$ inch oil over medium heat until half done.

In a separate pan, heat 1 tablespoon oil and add sauce from blender. Add chicken; cook, covered, over medium heat for 30 minutes. Mix cornmeal and water; add to chicken. Add onion rings; cook for 20 minutes. Serve with sliced avocados, rice, and warm tortillas.
*6 to 8 servings*

**If you go** to a store in El Salvador, you will make friends right there while waiting in line. The people of El Salvador are warm and friendly. You can start a conversation with anyone. El Salvadorans are very family-oriented and socialize frequently with friends. Families and friends are always coming together. This is what I miss.

We were used to visiting without a previous call. If we went to someone's house and the person was not there, well okay; if the person was there, then it was a surprise. Family and friends get together just to talk. I remember when I came home from the university some weekends, my friends, cousins, and family would come over just to talk and be together with me. It's not like here where life is so programmed. If we want to visit friends, we have to call to tell them we're coming. There is no surprise; it's not the same.

El Salvadorans are also always looking for an excuse for a party. My family had big

*A romantic part of life in El Salvador is when a boy courts a girl with* serenatas, *or serenades, around midnight. If the parents approve of him, they will open the door and let him in. My mom was so strict. She said that if he was not my fiancé, he could not come in. I had many* serenatas!

parties with mariachis. Sometimes we made parties with just a couple of people coming over. Other times the parties were planned, like wedding showers.

When I was getting married, everyone gave me wedding showers because, like I said, we're always looking for reasons to get together. I had about twenty showers! They said, "I want to give you a wedding shower." Then I gave them a list of people to invite. They found a different theme from each of my parties so I wouldn't receive the same gifts. My favorite gifts were El Salvadoran items because I was moving to the United States.

The wedding showers may have typical El Salvadoran food like *pupusas*, *tamales*, *caldo de pata*, a soup of pig's feet, and especially fried beans called *casa miento*, representing marriage because it's like a marriage or mixture of rice and beans.

My family also spent time together going to the beach. Beaches are close to the city, thirty-five to forty minutes away, so we could go and come back in the same day. I remember when we went to the beach, people would run up to the car, trying to sell different foods. If they didn't have what we wanted—say they were selling mangoes, and we wanted *jocotes*, a fruit from El Salvador—they would start yelling and screaming to their cousins to get us what we wanted. The vendors try to please the people, and they would call their whole family just to get what the people wanted. The vendors are making a living, but their finding what people want is typical of how El Salvadorans are always trying to help.

I miss El Salvador. Everybody here is living his or her life and doesn't have much time for others. Life goes fast: go to work, come home, do a little bit at the house, go to bed, and the next day it's the same story. But in El Salvador family, friendships, and the union of people are very special, and we made sure we spent time together.

If you have a chance to visit El Salvador, I know you will love it because of the friendly nature of its people.

El Salvador has many poor people. The class structure is like a triangle: the poor on the bottom, the largest part of the triangle; the middle class in the middle; and the wealthy on the small peak.

When you pass the little houses of the poor people in El Salvador, you will always see corn, rice, and beans planted next to the houses. People make their own dough for tortillas by grinding the corn with water. *Pupusas*, tortillas stuffed with cheese, beans, and/or sausage, originated from the poor people, but every class enjoys them.

### PUPUSAS
### Stuffed Tortillas

| | |
|---|---|
| 2 | cups corn flour |
| | water |
| 1 | cup shredded mozzarella or Monterey Jack cheese |
| | crumbled sausage (optional) |
| | beans (optional) |

Mix corn flour with small amounts of water until dough does not stick to hands. Cut off 2-inch balls; flatten each between the palms. Place cheese or other fillings in center; fold and flatten again into a pancake. Repeat with remaining dough.

Cook on a griddle or pan without oil over medium-high heat until brown on both sides.
*6 servings*

Many people who go to the beach stop their cars to buy from the vendors who sell different typical snacks of El Salvador. Many of the vendors are just children. Sometimes if you have your window down, they will stick their arm right inside your car!

Mangos, sliced watermelon, and turtle eggs are some of the food they sell. The mangos, cut into pieces, are sold in little plastic bags with salt, lemon, and chili. Because they're not yet ripe, they are tart and sour. In town the vendors sell soda in plastic bags. They will tie the bag with the straw that you use to sip the drink.

*Buñuelos de viento* are another typical El Salvadoran snack. They are like donuts, but they're puffy. My mother made them for us as dessert.

### BUÑUELOS DE VIENTO
### Salvadoran Puffs

| | |
|---|---|
| 2 | cups water |
| 1 | cup margarine |
| 2 | cups flour, sifted twice |
| 1/4 | tsp. salt |
| 6 | eggs |
| | oil for frying |

Bring water to boil. Add margarine; heat until melted. Add flour and salt at once, stirring constantly and quickly until dough forms a ball. Remove from heat; cool. Add eggs individually, stirring well after each. Mix dough until soft.

Heat 2 inches oil over medium-high heat. Drop 2 to 4 spoonfuls of dough at a time. Cook until golden. Remove with slotted spoon; drain on paper towel. Place in serving bowls and drizzle with honey. Serve with fried plantains.
*6 servings*

I would like to tell a story about the celebration of the city of San Salvador, the capital of El Salvador. *El Salvador* means "The Savior" in Spanish, and the city honors El Salvador del Mundo, Patron of the Republic, from August 1 to August 6. The celebration is mainly religious, but it includes entertainment for adults and children.

The excitement and the anticipation of the festivities are overwhelming. Everyone wears a new outfit either bought or homemade; young people are preparing themselves for dances and new acquaintances; and older people are busy making sure that nobody forgets that this is a religious event. My grandmother, who went to church every day and made sure everyone was at church, was busy working on the religious preparations. I was raised in a Catholic school so I always looked forward to this celebration.

August 5 is *el dia del Salvador del Mundo,* the Day of the Savior of the World. Hundreds of volunteers prepare a float that symbolizes Jesus Christ's coming to this world. The float

Jose (front, far right) with family and friends.

*My culture is family-oriented as is shown in this Christmas gathering.*

resembles an obelisk about fifty feet tall with a world on top. The procession, led by the archbishop of San Salvador, moves slowly from the *Iglesia del Calvario,* Church of the Calvary. Along its path, people pray and sing religious songs and the children play around the procession. The way I remember the whole thing when I was younger is that I went to the procession to meet girls!

The procession moves through the main streets of the city, which otherwise are completely dead. The banks, stores, and government offices are closed for the entire week. The procession ends in front of the cathedral with the solemn ceremony called the *Transfiguracion of the El Salvador del Mundo,* or the Transfiguration of the Savior of the World. Jesus Christ, dressed up on top of the world, descends into the world and disappears. A few minutes later, Jesus emerges from the world dressed in different clothes, hence the transfiguration.

The procession ends around five-thirty in the evening, then people go to the amusement park installed for the occasion in one of the larger parks in San Salvador. In the park, people sell all kinds of typical Salvadoran food: *pupusas, tostadas, chilate, pasteles, enchiladas, nuegados, chicharras, atol de elote, tamales,* typical fruit drinks, and, of course, *Pilsener,* the famous Salvadoran beer. The *pupusas,* the most known Salvadoran meal, is comparable in popularity to the hamburgers in the United States.

In the earlier part of the day, I was at home with my family. After the procession, with my commitment to the family finished, I would find my friends and have fun at the dances and amusement park until one o'clock to two o'clock in the morning.

# Jose Osegueda

Atol de elote is usually served at parties called atoladas in semi-rural or rural environments. These parties are attended by family, relatives, and friends of all ages; this is the Latin customary way to throw parties. The parties are an opportunity for groups to gather and catch up on news of newlyweds, newborns, graduations, boyfriends or girlfriends, and people who had travelled out of the country or just come back.

You can buy atol de elote from vendors scattered in the capital city or mostly from street vendors in small towns outside the metropolitan areas. The drink is typically served in guacal de morro, the shell of the fruit from a morro tree. The thin, hard shell, which is about the size of a coconut, is cut in half to make a sort of organic bowl.

Elote means green corn; atol is a corn flour drink.

### ATOL DE ELOTE
#### Sweet Corn Flour Drink

| | |
|---|---|
| 5 | cups unripe corn |
| 12 | cups water |
| 9 | cups milk |
| 3-5 | cinnamon sticks |
| 1 | Tbsp. salt |
| 3$^1$/4 | cups sugar |

Grind corn to a paste. Place corn in cheesecloth over a large pot. Gradually add water, straining the water and liquid of the corn into the pot.

In a separate pot, cook milk and cinnamon over low heat for 15 minutes; stir constantly.

Discard corn after straining; add salt and sugar to liquid. Cook over low heat for 1 hour, stirring constantly. When atol is ready, add milk; cook for 10 minutes. Serve hot.

about 10 servings

Sweet corn is planted in May at the beginning of the rainy season, then the young corn will be ready for recipes such as tamales de elote and atol de elote in August and September. Tamales de elote is a typical meal made of cornmeal with various ingredients wrapped in corn husks.

### TAMALES DE ELOTE
#### Cheese and Crackling Tamales

| | |
|---|---|
| $^1$/2 | lb. cream cheese |
| $^1$/2 | lb. ground crackling |
| 3 | oz. melted pork fat |
| 6 | cups ground young corn |
| 2 | Tbsp. salt |
| $^1$/2 | cup sugar |
| | corn husks |

Grind cheese, crackling, and fat to a paste. Mix paste with corn; add salt and sugar to taste. Place a small amount of mixture onto 1 to 2 corn husks. Wrap by overlapping leaves lengthwise, then folding ends up. Make wrapping 4 to 5 inches long and 1$^1$/2 to 2 inches wide.

Place a few corn husks on the bottom of a large pot. Carefully place tamales, seam side down, into pot. Add enough water to fill $^1$/4 of the pot. Cook over medium heat for about 40 minutes. Serve with fried beans, cream cheese, and sour cream to make a complete atolada.

4 to 6 servings

**My grandfather**, Joseph Francis Roser, was the first member of the family to be born in the United States. His father, Harry Roser, born in Brighton in Sussex, England, had immigrated to the United States on the day the Brooklyn Bridge opened in May of 1883. He always told people that he thought the flags and decorations and celebrations were in honor of his arrival.

Harry Roser came to this country to find a better economic life for his family. He emigrated from Brixton, which today is one of the worst slums in London and in 1883 was a poor working class section. His father, Richard, had been a coachman and servant, and his family had been migrant agricultural workers in the southeast of England.

Though the family history goes back generations in England, an old family story says that the Rosers fled Alsace when the French revoked the Edict of Nantes and began a new round of religious persecutions. I found the same story in a history of a Roser family from the Rhineland in Germany.

In the England of the late 18th and early 19th century, debtors were the responsibility of the parish of their birth. In 1816, when Richard Roser was just four, his father, John, and the entire family were ordered "removed" from Ringmer in Sussex back to Lingfield in Surrey because they were a burden to the welfare establishment. England was suffering from severe economic dislocations after the end of the Napoleonic Wars. A copy of this document is hanging in my home.

A number of English traditions have remained with the family, though some are now just memories and stories. At Christmas time, the family would have chocolate bread pudding with hard sauce, a white, very sweet and sugary topping. Another recipe passed down was for Welsh rarebit or rabbit, a meal made of melted cheddar cheese and mustard cooked in either milk or beer and served over toast with Worcestershire sauce. The main tradition for special occasions and the presence of honored guests was to serve English roast beef with Yorkshire pudding.

All the women who marry into our family, whether like my wife and mother from the American South or my grandmother Roser, nee Hutchins, who was part Iroquois Indian from upstate New York, have had to learn these recipes. Hopefully, it is a tradition that will continue.

Harry Roser
1849-1914

*My great-grandfather was a railroad signal fitter. Family history tells us that he designed the signals still in use in the New York subway system.*

❑ The roast beef served on special occasions would be carved by the father with the "outside cut" going to the father or the honored guest as this was the most succulent part of the beef. In those days, the father was always served first.

When serving the beef, the father has to ask, "Who wants the Napoleon Cut? That's the 'boneypart.'" And everyone groans.

## ROAST BEEF

*standing rib roast*
*salt and pepper to taste*

Cook at 500° for 20 minutes. Decrease temperature to 350°; cook for 20 minutes per pound to desired doneness. The only seasoning is salt and pepper.

❑ Unlike the Christmas pudding which is chocolate and sweet, Yorkshire pudding is a bread dish cooked in the drippings from the roast beef until it puffs up a golden brown.

## YORKSHIRE PUDDING

| | |
|---|---|
| 1 | cup flour |
| 2 | eggs |
| 1 | cup milk |
| 1/2 | tsp. salt |

Blend all ingredients with a beater. Refrigerate for at least 1 hour. After roast is cooked, remove all but 2 tablespoons of drippings from pan. Replace pan into oven and increase temperature to 400°. After oven has reached 400° and drippings are smoking, stir and spread batter evenly into pan. Cook for about 20 minutes or until batter has risen and turned golden brown. Cut into squares and serve with the roast beef and gravy.
*4 to 6 servings*

When I am homesick and I decide to go back to England, for the two weeks before I leave, I am not thinking about the clothes I need to bring, I am thinking about what I am going to eat when I get there.

In England we have breakfast, lunch, which is a large meal like dinner in America, tea, and maybe a light supper. On the weekends we have a mixed grill for breakfast: kidney, sausage, tomatoes. We also have fried eggs, fried bread, and toast. Breakfast can be a big meal.

For lunch we usually have beef or lamb and vegetables. If it is Sunday, our lunch would be roast beef, Yorkshire pudding, and Brussels sprouts. There is nothing as good as sweet Brussels sprouts that have been picked after the frost, and there is nothing worse than the smell of a field of rotting Brussels sprouts after the frost.

*To say I miss England and the food is an understatement.*

For tea on Sundays, my grandmother used to buy prawns, mussels, or winkles from a man who went around London with his cart. He was not a fishmonger because everything he had was cooked. We would have a bit of what he sold with just bread and butter. Supper was light; maybe fish or soup or leftovers from lunch. Tea time was always my favorite so I never ate much supper.

I try to go to England every other year, but I have been lucky because I have been back to England every year for the past six years. I don't mind because I love the food. Usually my sister picks me up at the airport, and on the way home to my mother's house, we stop by the bakery where they have the freshly baked cottage loaf. This homemade bread looks like a thatched cottage with its big, round bottom and little, round top.

On the first day I'm there, we always go out for lunch at *Pisces*, a fish and chips shop. Every fish and chips shop in England has haddock, cod, and rock. The fish to have is the rock. It's actually eel from the North Sea, but people think of it as fish. It's cut into half and splayed open, and it has one chewable bone down the middle. It's really thick and delicious. When the fish and chips are served, they are first wrapped in grease-proof paper, then in newspaper. Newspaper is a marvelous insulator and keeps the fish and chips warm.

Then there's cream tea. Two years ago my mother, sister, and I stayed in the south coast of Dorset in southern England where there are delicious cream teas. As we drove through the little village, we saw little cafés with cream teas. "Cream tea" is the whole meal. We'd have a pot of tea, salmon, cucumber or watercress sandwiches, and cakes served on a tier. There were also scones with raspberry jam and clotted cream. Clotted cream is used like butter. I put a quarter to a half an inch of cream and jam on top of a scone, and it is to die for!

To say I miss England and the food is an understatement. My sister even has one kitchen cabinet set aside for me. It has foods that I like to eat when I'm in England. I have things in there like fish paste, cream sherry, pickled onions, and malt loaf. My cabinet is like a kid's candy jar; it's my goodie cabinet! I have been in the United States for thirty-four years, but I am still British and I still love British food.

◻ I once had a boyfriend with a motorcycle. After he got off work, we would ride down to a pub called Six Bells in Ruislip. Every pub has an outside garden area; we'd sit out in the garden and eat pork pies, pickled onions about two inches across, and drink lager and lime. They were delicious!

## RAISED PORK PIE

| 3 | cups flour |
| $1/2$ | tsp. salt |
| 5 | oz. water |
| $1/4$ | cup lard or shortening |
| $1/4$ | cup butter |

**filling:**

| 1 | lb. lean pork, cubed |
| $1/2$ | lb. pork sausage |
| $1/2$ | lb. unsmoked bacon |
| | salt and pepper to taste |
| 2 | hard-boiled eggs |
| 1 | egg, beaten |
| 1 | Tbsp. powdered gelatin or $1/2$ oz. |
| 5 | oz. apple juice |

Sift flour and salt. Boil water, lard, and butter until lard and butter are melted; add to flour. Mix with wooden spoon until dough is cool enough to handle. Knead on a lightly floured surface until soft and pliable. Cover with oiled plastic wrap.

Prepare filling. Mince pork, sausage, and bacon in food processor; season with salt and pepper. Press $2/3$ dough into the bottom and sides of a lightly greased 9-inch gamepie tin or a 7-inch springform pan. Make a channel along outer edge with finger to avoid a thick border of pastry.

Spread $1/2$ filling into pan. Add eggs; spread remaining filling. Roll out remaining dough; place over pie, forming a lid. Make a slit in top; brush with beaten egg. Bake in a 325° preheated oven for $2^1/2$ hours. Remove outside of tin and bake another 30 minutes.

Cool pie completely. Dissolve gelatin in apple juice. Using a funnel, pour gelatin into slit on top of pie. Cover and cool in refrigerator. Serve with salad and pickled onions.
*1 pie*

◻ Pickled onions are eaten just like dill or sweet pickles. Serve the onions with a cold cut sandwich or fish and chips.

## PICKLED ONIONS

| 5 | cups spiced vinegar (see below) |
| 1 | cup salt |
| $7^1/2$ | cups hot water |
| 2 | lbs. pickling onions, peeled |
| 1 | Tbsp. whole peppercorns |

**spiced vinegar:**

| 5 | cups malt vinegar |
| 2 | cinnamon sticks |
| 1 | Tbsp. cloves |
| 1 | Tbsp. mace |
| 1 | Tbsp. whole allspice |
| | dash of cayenne |

Prepare spiced vinegar. Bring vinegar and spices to a boil in a covered pan. Remove from heat; cool and strain.

Dissolve salt in hot water; cool. Submerge onions in salt water for 24 hours; drain. Pack into a large jar. Pour spiced vinegar over onions. Cover and seal jars. Only use metal lids if they are plastic coated. Store for 3 months before eating.

## LAGER AND LIME

Pour about 3 tablespoons Rose's® sweetened lime juice in a 10 oz. glass. Top with lager.

◻ The British really love their coffee and tea. One time my family and I were riding the barges from Surry to London. The barges stopped along the bridges and someone would call out the stop.

The day was really cold; we could just die for a cup of coffee or tea when suddenly a bloke in the back yelled, "Anyone for coffee?"

I asked, "Oh, can we have it up here in the front?" Everyone just looked at me.

The bloke said, "What did you think I said, Love?"

I said, "Anyone for coffee?"

He said, "No, I said, 'Anyone for Putney?'" We had stopped at Putney Bridge! One man missed his stop at Putney because he was laughing so much to "Anyone for coffee?"

**Ethiopia is** a very rich country. The news media misrepresents it. There is no lack of food in Ethiopia; there is plenty. The starvation that took place at the Ethiopian and Somalian border occurred because there was war in that area, and in the provinces of Aritrea and Tigra there have been conflicts between guerillas and the Ethiopian government. Because of these conflicts, the people could not farm and could not raise their animals, so starvation happened in very small areas.

Most of the land is farmland which grows wheat, barley, oats, garlic, and many other agricultural products. Coffee originated from the province of Kaffa in Ethiopia, and it is one of the country's largest exports. The agriculture changes with the climate because Ethiopia has six climatic regions ranging from *wirch*, the extreme cold, to *bereha*, the extreme hot.

Everybody has at least a little plot of land, chickens, lambs, cows, and a donkey or a horse. Even in the desert, Ethiopians can raise sheep and goat. There is a special kind of sheep called *ye adal beg*, translated as "the sheep of the Adals." The Adals are a nomadic ethnic group who live in the desert. Machinery is the only thing an Ethiopian would probably need to buy.

*It has been a long time since I have returned to Ethiopia. Just before I departed my country in 1974, this photo was taken of me with my sister, niece, and mother.*

In Ethiopia, food is eaten with respect. It is eaten sitting down after prayer and is not to be wasted. I was told that God was my sufficiency. If He did not provide, I would starve. God is the one who supplies energy to enhance the land that enables the people to produce food. Mealtime was a very peaceful time. My family talked very little while we ate. We never ate in a rush or while standing. Children were constantly reminded to "sit down and eat, sit down and eat." The only foods we ate were cereal, poultry, hens, and chickens, but never the rooster. We also ate beef and mutton but not pork.

The longer I stay away from Ethiopia, the more difficult it is to go back. I have become more detached from Ethiopian culture and more attached to American culture. If I went home, I'd like to go to the places I knew when I was growing up. I have an interest in the land because it is so rich in culture. When I stop working here in America, I plan to return to the place where I grew up: Ethiopia.

❑ Authentic Ethiopian ingredients can be found in African or Indian specialty stores. Seasoned butter is flavored with a seasoning salt, put in a big pot, and set aside for a while to age. The flavor is entirely different, but regular butter can be substituted. Cajun seasoning is the closest substitute for Ethiopian red pepper.

When I was growing up, a whole chicken was always cut into twenty-one pieces. Cutting a chicken into this many pieces was also a test for a girl to become a bride. If she could not cut the chicken into twenty-one parts, she failed and could not get married.

### DORO WAT
### Stewed Chicken

| | |
|---|---|
| 3 | cups diced Bermuda or red onion |
| 1 | cup seasoned butter |
| 1/4 | cup seasoned Ethiopian red pepper or Cajun pepper |
| 1 | cup water |
| 1 | whole chicken, cut into 21 parts |
| 5 | hard-boiled eggs |

Cook onions in butter over medium heat until almost soft. Add pepper and water; bring to a boil. Add chicken; cook until tender, adding water as needed. Stir occasionally. Make a slice halfway through each egg and add to chicken during the last 30 minutes.
*5 servings*

❑ I was brought up in a Christian family, and when I was little, I spent a lot of time with my grandmother. While cooking stew one day, she remarked, "We are like stew in a pot. The country we live in is the stew; the countries that surround us is the pot."

On the map, Ethiopia is surrounded by almost all Islamic countries; it was the only country that was Christian at the time my grandmother made her remark. Ethiopia is known in history as the island of Christianity and this is what my grandmother was referring to. Although she did not have a formal education and did not read or write, she was accurate in her succinct explanation. She did not waste words, and she left a lasting impression in my mind.

My grandmother was cooking *firfir* when she was comparing Ethiopia to her stew. In fact, it remains as one of my favorite foods today. It's quick to cook, very filling, and nutritious.

*Firfir*, which is similar to stuffing, can be made with pumpkins, mushrooms, lentil or split pea soup, or any kind of stew such as *doro wat* or beef stew. *Injera* is a large flat bread that looks like a crêpe. It is made from *teff*, a small grain which only grows in Ethiopia.

### FIRFIR
### Ethiopian Stuffing

| | |
|---|---|
| 2 | cups doro wat or any stew or soup |
| 2 | injera, broken into pieces* |

Cook doro wat or stew over medium heat, stirring occasionally. When stew begins to boil, add injera; mix well.
*2 servings*

**I started to get involved** in cooking during World War II. My father was part of the resistance in Albertville in Savoie. He hid families who were sought by the Nazis. Sometimes he picked up American parachutists coming down the Alps. He brought them home, bought them civilian clothes, and took them wherever they needed to go. My parents performed miracles to feed all of them.

My father had a friend named Teddy who owned a restaurant in the village of Venthon, about three miles from Albertville. The restaurant was still open, and people paid with food coupons. Teddy was also part of the resistance; he and my father worked together. Sometimes I even helped.

Children were involved with war then. I was very young—about twelve years old. I would ride my blue bicycle and bring messages from the English radio to Teddy on little pieces of paper rolled up and tucked into my hair. Having the radio was very dangerous because the Nazi were supposed to have taken the radio.

*I like to prepare delicious food for family and friends because good food warms the heart and makes people happy.*

Sometimes I brought parachutists to him because my parents couldn't bring them by car. Teddy was in the mountains, so it was not as risky for the people to stay at his place as in town. If the curfew at nightfall came before I returned home, I had to spend the night because it would have been dangerous for me to return.

When I went to Teddy's I had to go to the kitchen to find him. It was during these times that I began learning how to cook. He made the most delicious food. He was very good at preparing trout with fresh cream and *ris de veau*, or sweetbreads. Once he showed me how to make a *brioche*, a pastry eaten with a little butter. It was very special because although we were not too short on cows, cheese, or meat in Savoie, flour was difficult to get during the war. He made me make the *brioche* and take it home. I was so proud! Teddy liked me very much. He didn't have kids and considered me as a daughter.

Later in life, I became more involved in cooking through my father-in-law, whose presentations of dishes were gorgeous, and from learning on my own. I had many well-known people at my table when I was a newspaper correspondent for *France-Soir* in St. Paul, so I bought a giant professional cookbook by the great masters of French cooking. I didn't want to lose face, especially because my father-in-law was such a great cook.

I believe cooking is an international language. Like painting and music, food touches people's hearts and brings them together. The way to make people happy is to make their palates happy.

When the French get together, there must always be food. Food and French are two words that cannot be disassociated.

I created this appetizer for some friends who came to visit me when I lived in St. Paul, France. I had to improvise with what I had in my refrigerator. You don't need expensive ingredients to make something good; just add a few herbs and also your heart.

### PAMPLEMOUSSES AU CRABE
**Grapefruit with Crab Meat**

| | |
|---|---|
| 3 | grapefruits, halved |
| 1/2 | lb. crab meat |
| 1/2 | celery stalk, chopped |
| 2 | Tbsp. chopped fresh parsley |
| | romaine or escarole, chopped |
| | mayonnaise to taste (see below) |

**mayonnaise:**

| | |
|---|---|
| 1 | Tbsp. Maille® mustard |
| 1 | egg yolk |
| 1 | cup olive oil |
| | salt and pepper to taste |
| | dash of lemon or vinegar |

Remove insides of grapefruit; keep grapefruit shells, but discard membrane. Cut grapefruit into small pieces; drain in colander. Set aside shells and grapefruit pieces in refrigerator.

Prepare mayonnaise. Spread mustard on the bottom of small bowl. Add yolk; mix well with fork or mixer. Drizzle oil while beating until mixture thickens; add or reduce oil accordingly. Add salt, pepper, and lemon or vinegar; mix well.

Combine grapefruit pieces, crab, celery, parsley, romaine, and mayonnaise; mix well. Fill shells with mixture. Serve on a plate or platter lined with romaine.

*6 servings*

When I moved to Nice I became a partner in the restaurant *Porta Fino*. I never told my partner I could even cook an egg or he would have put me in the kitchen! I enjoy cooking for friends, but it is not fun to cook for a lot of people. When my friends come over, they only want French food. I think I will never learn how to cook American.

*Dame blanche* can be found in many French cookbooks. I have changed the dessert a bit; this is my recipe.

### DAME BLANCHE
**White Lady**

| | |
|---|---|
| 6 | egg whites |
| 1/2 | cup sugar |
| | peel of 1 lemon |
| | butter |

**vanilla cream sauce:**

| | |
|---|---|
| 3 | cups milk |
| 1/2 | cup sugar |
| 1 | tsp. vanilla extract |
| 6 | egg yolks, beaten |

Beat egg whites until firm. Gently add sugar and lemon peel. Pour into buttered mold; place mold in a larger pan with water (a bath). Bake at 350° for 30 minutes. Cool in bath.

Prepare cream sauce. Bring milk, sugar, and vanilla to a boil. Add mixture to eggs, whisking constantly. Cook in double broiler until thick, stirring constantly. Do not boil. Pour sauce around the "white lady" just before serving.

*4 to 6 servings*

**The Christmas room** was special. It was locked for many weeks before Christmas. As a child, I wanted to know what was behind the doors because it was such a secret. There were little keyholes on every door in the house, but something was always hung in front of this door so I couldn't peek through the keyhole.

Behind the doors, Mutti and Vati—my affectionate way of saying "Mom and Dad"—were setting up the Christmas tree and putting up my doll house and my brother's train set. My parents made all the Christmases very special for me. My memories about Meerane, the city where I was born in Saxon, Germany, go back to Christmas when I still had Mutti and Vati.

I finally got to go into the room on Christmas Eve. Mutti or Vati would ring a bell, and that was the moment when I could come into the room. But I always imagined that the person ringing the bell was *Weinacts Mann*, the person like America's Santa Claus.

*I cherish all special moments because they remind me of my childhood in Germany with Mutti and Vati.*

I remember waiting anxiously for the bell. And when the doors were opened, it was almost like magic. The Christmas tree was as tall as the eight-foot ceiling and was lit with many candles. Vati even needed a handle to light the candles and another stick to put the lights out. My dollhouse was on one side of the room; my brother's train was on the other side.

The dollhouse was huge with a first and second floor and an attic. It almost reached the ceiling. I could stand in front of it and play. It was electric, so I had electric lights. Vati built an elevator for it, too. Besides the elevator, there was a little bathroom on each floor. Many rooms had furniture that was exactly like ours in the house. One of my father's friend had made the furniture.

Vati had built the dollhouse for my sister when she was little, and I inherited it. They put it up for me every Christmas. It had to be put together section by section; this is why I could only have it up for Christmas. I loved my dollhouse.

Preparations for the holiday were overwhelming. So much baking was going on, and there were many smells in the house. Mutti worked so hard making cookies and *stollen,* a German fruit bread. Oh, the cookies in Germany are very special butter cookies made into stars and the different shapes of Christmas! But the *stollen* was made especially for Christmas, and the smell of its baking came weeks before Christmas.

When I moved to Chesapeake, Virginia, my mother-in-law was very interested in my upbringing. She encouraged me to carry on my German traditions. So through the years, I put my foot down that Christmas here was going to be a lot like mine was in Germany.

# Isolde Barbara Myers

❑ When I came to the U.S. I met a bunch of German girls, and we'd all get together for coffee and cake at least once a week. Each of us got really special about our cakes, and each made whatever she was really good at. I was the one who made cakes with apples or whatever fruit was in season. But once I started making *stollen*, it became my specialty.

*Stollen* is baked many weeks before Christmas because it does not taste good fresh. It must lay at least a week before eating it.

## SÄCHSISCHER CHRISTSTOLLEN
### German Fruit Bread

| | |
|---|---|
| 4 | cups flour, sifted |
| 2 | packages dry yeast or 2 cubes |
| $^3/_4$ | cup warm milk |
| $^1/_2$ | cup sugar |
| $1^1/_2$ | cups butter or 3 sticks |
| 2 | eggs |
| $^1/_4$ | tsp. grated fresh lemon peel |
| | dash of cardamom |
| | dash of cinnamon |
| | dash of ground cloves |
| | dash of nutmeg |
| | dash of salt |
| 1 | cup slivered almonds |
| 1 | oz. almond extract |
| $1^1/_2$ | cups raisins |
| 1 | cup currants |
| 1 | tub candied orange peel, chopped |
| 1 | tub candied lemon peel, chopped |
| 2 | $^5/_{16}$ oz. packages vanilla sugar |

All ingredients must be at a warm temperature while preparing.

Soak raisins and currants in rum for one week before preparing. Drain; dust with flour.

In a large bowl, make a well in flour. Pour milk and 1 teaspoon sugar in well. If using yeast cubes, dissolve in milk first; otherwise, sprinkle dry yeast in well. In the center, mix only part of the flour into a dough, leaving loose flour around the bowl.

Sprinkle remaining sugar over loose flour. Slice 2 sticks of butter and drop around bowl. Place in a 150° preheated oven until dough doubles in size. Add eggs, grated lemon peel, cardamom, cinnamon, cloves, nutmeg, and salt. Work dough with a wooden spoon outwardly from the center until dough pulls from bowl.

Place in oven until dough doubles in size. Grind almonds and mix with extract. Add almond mixture, raisins, currants, orange and lemon peels to dough; knead only until mixed evenly. Place in oven again; let rise for 45 minutes.

Divide dough into 2 parts. Shape into circle. Fold over $^3/_4$ of the way, pushing edge down gently. Repeat with other loaf. Place on greased cookie sheet. Let rise again for about 10 minutes. Bake at 350° for 30 to 35 minutes or until light brown.

After removing from oven, melt 1 stick of butter over both loaves and sprinkle with vanilla sugar. Cool; store in zip-lock bags and place in an airtight container for at least one week. Sprinkle with powdered sugar before serving.
*2 loaves*

❑ When I lived with my sister, I remember she made *früchte bowle*, an adults' fruit punch, for special occasions and family gatherings. After the parties were over, I used to eat all the fruit left behind in the bowl. The fruit was even better than the drink!

## FRÜCHTE BOWLE
### Fruit Punch

| | |
|---|---|
| 1 | lb. fresh strawberries, peaches, or any fruit |
| 1 | cup sugar |
| 2 | cups cognac |
| 2 | bottles white wine |
| 1 | bottle champagne |

Prepare 2 hours before serving. Combine fruit, sugar, and cognac; set aside for 2 hours. Add wine and champagne just before serving.

**Many people who** meet Mom for the first time usually ask where she is from. Although she has lived in America most of her life, she still has her German accent.

My mother was born and raised in Plauen-Vogtl, East Germany. Her family life had been filled with many hardships and difficulties. Her mother died when she was only eight years old, and soon after, a strict stepmother came into her life. Yet in her childhood memories, there are also recollections of many happy times and a loving family. She had aunts, uncles, two older sisters, and many friends who were very close to her—even to this day.

Mom is one of the most generous, hard-working people I have ever known. Perhaps a lot of that has to do with her day-to-day struggles to survive during World War II. Mom experienced much tragedy during this time as a young woman.

Her home was destroyed. Her father died from malaria. When my aunt begged Mom to bring my cousin to another town, Mom and my cousin travelled by train for three days without food, only ration cards. Many times they had to leave the train to take shelter from the air raids and bombs, but they finally arrived safely in Zittau. To feed her sisters, her niece, and herself, Mom went out on a bicycle during black-outs to find kindling for cooking. Often she had to take potatoes from farmers' fields.

Giving food has also been an important part of how Mom shows her love to her own family. She can never bear the thought of one of her five children, fourteen grandchildren, or seven great-grandchildren going without food or proper meals. Sometimes we almost

Mom with my sister.

*My mother, Hanna Strobel Sciascia, is very special. She has made her family's life sweet and strong because she gave us her heart, faith, and love all these years.*

don't want to let her know we're coming because she will have a bag of groceries, sandwiches with all the trimmings, cakes, rolls, or even an entire meal for us to take back home.

When guests come to my parents' home, Mom welcomes them with coffee and freshly baked cakes. She is an excellent cook, perhaps because she puts so much of her heart into the food she prepares and serves. She always gives a part of herself through her cakes, rolls and meals.

The path as a wife and mother has had its share of heartaches along the way, but Mom is a rare example of unselfishness, perseverance, and talent. She could have been many things in her life: a nurse, a ballet dancer, or even a model. However, she chose to be a devoted wife, mother, and grandmother. Mom was lovely in her youth and still is at the age of seventy-two.

❑ Germans are well-known for enjoying large quantities of good food. In the afternoon, Germans usually have a snack of fancy pastries. *Apfel kuchen,* or apple cake, is wonderful with a cup of freshly brewed coffee or a glass of cold milk.

### APFEL KUCHEN
### Apple Cake

| | |
|---|---|
| 1/2 | cup lukewarm water |
| 2 | cakes or packages yeast |
| 1/2 | cup sugar |
| 4 1/2 | cups flour |
| 1/2 | cup butter or margarine, melted |
| 2 | eggs, beaten |
| 2/3 | cup milk, scalded and cooled |
| 1 | tsp. salt |
| 1 | tsp. grated lemon rind |
| 1/2 | tsp. mace or ground cardamom |
| | sliced apples, peaches, pears, or plums for topping |

**streusel:**

| | |
|---|---|
| 6 | Tbsp. flour |
| 4 | Tbsp. sugar |
| 1 | tsp. cinnamon |
| 4 | Tbsp. butter |

Combine water, yeast, and 1 teaspoon sugar; set aside until foamy.

Place flour in a separate bowl. Make a well in center. Pour yeast mixture into well. Keeping to sides of bowl, add remaining sugar, butter, eggs, milk, salt, lemon rind, and mace or cardamom. Mix dough until stiff. Knead on a floured surface until smooth and elastic.

Place dough in greased bowl. Cover with a warm, damp towel; let rise until doubled in size. Punch down; set aside a few minutes. Divide in half and roll each half into a 12- to 14-inch circle on a lightly floured surface; set aside.

Prepare streusel. Combine flour, sugar, and cinnamon. Cut in butter until coarse crumbs form. Layer fruit on top of dough and sprinkle streusel over fruit. Bake at 350° for 25 to 28 minutes or until brown.

*2 cakes*

❑ Potatoes are one of Germany's main vegetables, along with beets, carrots, onions, turnips, and cabbage. This potato salad is always requested by the whole family when we have our get-togethers.

### DEUTSCHEN KARTOFFELSALAT
### German Potato Salad

| | |
|---|---|
| 2 | lbs. small red potatoes, cleaned but not peeled |
| 1 | medium onion, thinly sliced |
| 2 | bread & butter or dill pickles, thinly sliced |
| 1/4 | cup vinegar |
| 1/2 | cup vegetable oil |
| | dash of salt |
| 3-5 | bacon slices, cooked crisp and crumbled |
| 2-3 | hard-boiled eggs, sliced |

Boil potatoes until almost tender; drain and rinse. Cool in refrigerator, then peel. Combine onion, pickles, vinegar, oil, and salt; mix well. Gradually add potatoes to mixture, mixing gently after each addition. Top with bacon and eggs. Refrigerate until serving.

*6 to 8 servings*

**My daughter** has beautiful blue eyes. Once a woman asked, "Where did you get such beautiful blue eyes?" My daughter said, "From the milkman."

The milkman was Walter Stein—my husband. I met him while I was working as a cook for a family in Georgetown in Washington D.C.

The regular milkman used to come and bring milk, cheese, and other dairy products. I didn't know many people in Washington, so I asked him if he got around to the German embassy or if he knew any German girls I could meet. He said, "Not really. We have this German guy at the dairy, but he's too old for you." And that was the end of the conversation.

One Saturday another milkman came. I said, "Oh, we have a new milkman." He came in without saying anything, then left to get some butter out of the truck. When he came back he started to talk in German. I thought I'd die because he came in to look me over before ever saying anything!

*My sister and I (right) have always been close. I remember the time I cut off her beautiful hair just before she was going on a date. She was quite mad!*

Well, we got married in September; we only met in April. I guess he thought I would take off. I never dreamed of being married in this country. He wrote to my mother in Germany asking her if he could marry me. She wrote him back saying I was old enough to know what I wanted. Yeah, he was really old-fashioned. He even got on his knees and proposed.

He came from a different part of Germany than where I came from. He was from Baden Baden, a resort in the Black Forest; I was from Bremen in the north. His dialect was a little different, and I couldn't understand him. If I talked in my own German, he couldn't understand me so we talked in High German, or Deutsch.

I had an idea that Germans were different when I lived in Munich for six months. I remember getting off the train at the railroad station at Munich; I thought I was in a strange country because I couldn't understand the Bavarian language.

Where he comes from they also cook differently from the way we do in the northern part. They eat more meat such as *rouladen,* beef rolls; *wiener schnitzel,* veal cutlets; *sauerbraten,* marinated meat; and more noodles. He also liked *spätzle,* noodles with goulash. I never had it until we went to his mother's in Germany.

In Bremen, we eat a lot of *geflügel,* fowl such as chicken, geese, or turkey; *kohl and pinkel,* kale and sausage; and *schweinebraten,* pork. But I learned how to cook his food. He cooked most of the meat, and I did the rest.

We celebrated common traditions like Christmas, Advent Week, and Easter in the German fashion. His father was Catholic and his mother was a Lutheran, but he became a Protestant. I was raised a Lutheran. When I came here I saw so many different churches on every corner. I had thought there were only Catholics and Protestants. There are so many denominations here. It's so funny when you think there is only one God.

I didn't realize that Germans could be so different. Walter and I had our own languages, but we spoke a common language. We had different food, but he taught me some recipes from his home town, and I taught him some of mine. We got along nicely.

□ My father told me that if I had a chance to see the world, grab it. So in 1953 when the family I was working for in Germany transferred to America, I did.

I stayed with the family for two and a half years, then went back to Germany. I didn't like Germany anymore. I stayed five months and came back to America. The freedom here was so much better, and the people were nicer.

I'm still here, and I still cook German food. Here is a recipe for *rouladen* which we had on special occasions in the northern part of Germany.

## ROULADEN
### Braised Stuffed Beef Rolls

| | |
|---|---|
| 3 | lbs. top round steak, sliced $^1/_2$ inch thick |
| | salt and pepper to taste |
| $^1/_2$ | cup spicy brown mustard |
| 2 | Tbsp. sugar |
| 3 | medium onions, thinly sliced |
| | bacon |
| | bread & butter or dill pickles, thinly sliced |
| 3-4 | Tbsp. oil |
| 1 | envelope ox tail or beef soup mix |

Spread slices of meat; sprinkle with salt and pepper. Combine mustard and sugar; mix well. Spread lightly over meat. Place onions, bacon, and pickles in the middle of meat. Roll up and tie with string.

Cook in oil over medium heat until evenly brown. Place in a deep pot; cover with water. Combine soup mix with a small amount of water; add to meat. Bring to a boil; reduce to low-medium heat. Cook for 2 hours or until done.

Remove meat. Thicken gravy with about 2 tablespoons flour mixed with water. Serve rouladen with red cabbage and dumplings with the gravy on the side.
*6 servings*

□ After church there was always bread left over from communion. Some was to be thrown away, so I took it home because it's a sin to throw food away. I dried the bread in the oven and crumbled it in the food processor. I used to use a mallet, but now the food processor is much easier.

Plain noodles served with the veal look a little naked. To make them look better, I cook some bread crumbs in butter and toss them with the noodles. *Wiener schnitzel* is very easy to make, and it's scrumptious.

## WIENER SCHNITZEL
### Veal Cutlet

| | |
|---|---|
| 4 | veal cutlets |
| | salt to taste |
| | flour |
| 1 | egg, beaten |
| | fine bread crumbs |
| | butter for frying |

With a mallet, pound cutlets until thin; sprinkle with salt. Dredge in flour and dip in egg. Dredge with crumbs. Cook in butter over medium heat until golden brown. Serve with noodles.
*4 servings*

**In my childhood,** I lived a very sheltered home life. It was the time before Hitler took over and the time when my father was the mayor of Hadamar, our small town in Germany. My mother's only job was to raise her three little girls and teach them a good cultural upbringing. We had two servants at home, and when I think back, we had servants just so my mother could be with her children day and night.

Our holidays were always marked by traditions. Before Lent started, we had *Fastnacht,* a festival when the children "turned" into ghosts, clowns, and other creatures, like on Halloween. Once Lent began, *Fastnacht* was over and the next holiday was Easter. On Easter everyone went to church and the children hunted for the Easter Bunny's goodies. We had bunnies made of hard plastic that my mother always filled with jelly beans each year. After Easter they disappeared, and on Easter the next year, they were filled up again.

But most outstanding was the preparation for the Christmas holidays. It started on December 6 with St. Nicholas, our Santa Claus. He would go to all the schools and homes to visit. If we were well-behaved throughout the past year, we children would put our plates and shoes outside so he could leave goodies. The goodies were not like the ones children have in America; we were given just an apple, orange, cookies, or candy.

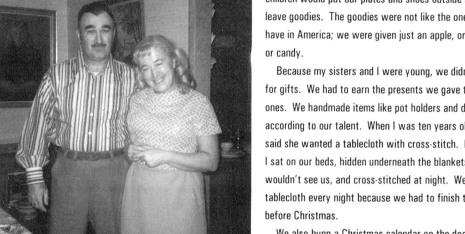

*My husband of fifty years enjoys the German holidays. I am sentimental about them and I make these times very special. I still cook quite a few Old World recipes, and he loves my German cooking.*

Because my sisters and I were young, we didn't have money for gifts. We had to earn the presents we gave to our loved ones. We handmade items like pot holders and decorated them according to our talent. When I was ten years old, my mother said she wanted a tablecloth with cross-stitch. My sisters and I sat on our beds, hidden underneath the blankets so our mother wouldn't see us, and cross-stitched at night. We worked on the tablecloth every night because we had to finish the tablecloth before Christmas.

We also hung a Christmas calendar on the door in anticipation of the holiday. A German Christmas calendar is only for the month of December, up to the 24th, and each day has a door with candy behind it. Every day during December, we opened a door to count the days left before Christmas. Then we ate the candy. The rest of the days and weeks were marked by celebrations. We looked forward to Christmas Eve and Christmas Day.

When Christmas Eve finally came, my mother would make us come to the family room to pray and sing. My little sister and I played the piano while my older sister played the violin. We were not so good, but Mother's wish had to be done! When a bell rang, Mother would say that the Christ child was there. The doors of our dining room, which was only used for special occasions, were opened, and for the first time, we saw the Christmas tree and the nativity stable, a must in every Christian home. Our gifts were second place to the glorious tree and nativity.

My mother always made every holiday special. I will never forget the holiness and love which came with our German traditions, especially Christmas.

❑ We always had a goose for our German Christmas dinner. The goose is prepared the same way as a turkey, but the fillings—potatoes, sage and chestnut stuffing, and rice with raisins and apples—are different.

Most of these recipes are old and were passed down in the family. Christmas dinner usually included salads, Brussels sprouts, red cabbage, and dumplings with gravy.

### VANIALLA SÜSSPEISE
#### Vanilla Pudding

| | |
|---|---|
| 1 | package vanilla pudding powder |
| 3 | Tbsp. sugar |
| 2 | eggs, separated |
| 2 | cups milk |
| 4-6 | biscotti |
| 2 | Tbsp. apricot brandy |

Combine pudding powder, sugar, egg yolks, and 6 tablespoons milk; mix well. Bring remaining milk to a boil; remove from heat. Stir in pudding powder mixture. Bring to a boil again. Cook for a few seconds; remove from heat. Whisk egg whites until stiff. Fold egg whites into pudding. Pour hot pudding over biscotti dipped in brandy.
*4 to 6 servings*

### RÔTKRAUT
#### Red Cabbage

| | |
|---|---|
| 1 | red cabbage, quartered and thinly sliced |
| 1 | large onion, sliced |
| 3 | apples, quartered |
| 1/2 | cup water |
| 1/2 | cup lard or drippings |
| 3 | Tbsp. vinegar |
| 1 | bay leaf |
| | salt to taste |
| | sugar to taste |
| | cornstarch |

In a large pot, combine all ingredients except cornstarch; cook over low-medium heat for 1 to 1$\frac{1}{2}$ hours. Thicken with cornstarch when cabbage is tender.
*4 to 6 servings*

❑ Particularly for Christmas dinner, *kartoffelsalat warm* is served as a small vegetable side dish.

### KARTOFFELSALAT WARM
#### Warm Potato Salad

| | |
|---|---|
| 3 | lbs. potatoes |
| 1/4 | lb. bacon, cooked and crumbled |
| 3 | Tbsp. bacon drippings |
| 1/2 | cup hot water |
| 2 | Tbsp. vinegar |
| 1 | small onion, chopped |
| | salt and pepper to taste |

Boil potatoes with skin until done; peel and slice. Set aside.
Combine remaining ingredients; cook over medium heat for about 5 minutes. Pour over hot potatoes. Serve warm.
*4 to 6 servings*

**I come from Ghana**, a country where when a child is born, there is a big celebration. As it is universally known, everyone is happy and relieved when a birth happens.

When the child is a week old, the parents, maternal and fraternal grandparents, close friends, and relatives meet in the home of the father's parents around five o'clock in the morning. The fraternal grandparents and relatives gather in one place, and the maternal grandparents and relatives gather in another place so they are facing each other. The child's parents sit together, usually in the center, with the mother holding the child. Everyone, including relatives and friends, dresses in white or white-based clothing. In my culture, white is the celebration of life.

An elder and a spokesperson are chosen in advance. Peace and quiet are ordered by saying, "Agooo." Every time this is said, it means everyone must be quiet and attentive. The spokesperson tells of the reason for the meeting and introduces the parents, relatives, and friends from each side.

*My husband and I love Ghana. We intend to retire in our country.*

A bottle of schnapps, a bottle of water, two glasses, a pencil, paper, and a plate are gathered. The schnapps, water, and glasses are placed on a small, short table; the pencil, paper, and plate are placed on another table. The pencil and paper are used to write the addresses of people who give gifts. Traditionally, gifts are given in cash form to begin a savings for the child. The plate is used for collecting the money.

Schnapps is poured half-full into one glass; water is poured half-full into the other glass. The table is placed in front of the elder, who is usually chosen from the father's side. The mother gives the child to the elder. Again the spokesperson announces, "Agooo." Everyone becomes quiet again.

The father of the child is called to give the name of the newborn. He chooses the name of the child, usually naming the child after his mother, father, or grandparents. The father tells the name to the spokesperson, and the spokesperson tells the name to the elder. The elder tells the child how the name was chosen and after whom he or she is named.

Afterwards the elder dips his right middle finger, already washed with soap and water thoroughly, into the schnapps and places the schnapps on the child's tongue. He does this three times, each time repeating, "If it is alcohol, it is alcohol." He then dips the same finger into the water and places the water on the child's tongue. He does this three times, each time repeating, "If it is water, it is water." This ceremony is done to let the child know from the beginning to differentiate right from wrong or truth from lies.

The child is then shown to the relatives and friends, and the name is announced to everyone so that the child will be called by his or her proper name, not "hi" or "he who." The schnapps is passed around for tasting, everyone using the same glass. The child is passed around for everyone to recognize. Then the celebration with food starts.

In my country, goat soup or stew is cooked in large quantities for big celebrations. We buy a whole goat, using the fat, legs, and head for the soup and the meat for the stew.

*Apokye floe*, or goat stew, is usually cooked for the celebration of a newborn. There are a lot of people for this occasion so a whole goat is needed. This recipe is for a smaller quantity.

### APOKYE FLOE
### Goat Stew

| 5 | lbs. goat meat |
|---|---|
| 2-3 | large onions, diced |
| 1/2 | cup coconut oil or any oil |
| 1-2 | jalapenos, ground in blender |
| 2 | tomatoes, diced |
| 1 | 8 oz. can tomato paste |
| 2 | Tbsp. cornstarch |
| 1 | Tbsp. curry |
| | salt to taste |

Pressure cook meat for 5 to 10 minutes after bringing to a boil. If cooking on stove, cook over medium heat 1 to 1 1/2 hours or until done. Drain meat; set aside.

Cook onions in 1/4 cup oil over medium-high heat for 5 minutes. Add jalapenos; cook for 5 minutes. Add tomatoes; cook for 5 minutes. Add tomato paste and cornstarch; cook for 5 to 10 minutes. Stir in curry.

In another pan, cook meat in remaining oil over medium heat until lightly brown. Add to mixture, sprinkling salt. Cook for 15 to 20 minutes. Serve with white rice with beans.

*12 to 14 servings*

In Ghana when a girl leaves childhood and enters womanhood, the family—and sometimes the whole village—has a celebration. The celebration may start with just the family, but as it was, the neighbors, seeing and hearing the dancing and music, would come; then the whole village would know about it. Maybe it was embarrassing to the girl, but it was routine.

The girl is perfumed and dressed up in gold and beads by her mother. She wears beads around the wrists, neck, as earrings, and sometimes on the legs and waist. All the siblings are around, and the old person of the family sits the girl down and tells her about life.

On this day the girl doesn't do anything; she is the girl of the hour. The family cooks traditional meals like goat soup and stew and *fufu* for the celebration. *Fufu* is boiled cassava and/or plantains pounded until very soft and shaped into balls. After the family cooks, she is the first to eat. The celebration lasts for about half a day, then afterwards the girl can get married.

The recipe for goat stew is above, but *nam nkotobre floe* can be eaten as an everyday meal. For a vegetarian variation, omit beef and salt fish and add cheddar cheese.

### NAM NKOTOBRE FLOE
### Beef with Spinach

| 1 | lb. stewing beef |
|---|---|
| 1 | large onion, diced |
| 2 | medium tomatoes, diced |
| | freshly ground red pepper to taste |
| 1/2 | cup oil |
| 1 | small piece dried salt fish |
| 1 | 8 oz. can tomato paste |
| 1 | bunch fresh spinach or 2 boxes frozen |

Boil beef until tender; set aside. Chop 1/2 of salt fish in blender; set aside.

Cook onions, tomatoes, and pepper in oil over medium heat until onions are tender. Add chopped salt fish and tomato paste; cook for 5 to 10 minutes. Add beef and remaining salt fish; cook for 10 to 15 minutes or until done. Stir in spinach. Serve with boiled yellow plantains or white rice.

*5 to 7 servings*

I grew up in *sterea elada*, or central Greece, in a village that was not too big, maybe 200 houses. The people of my village, Klisorevmata, cared for and helped one another because most were family. They also worked very hard for themselves.

My father was a fisherman. The rest of my family—there were eight kids, plus my mother—worked on the land. Starting in February, we planted the tobacco seeds. After the seedlings grew, we picked them up and went to the field to plant each one. It was done by hand back then; now machinery is used. When the leaves were big enough to be sewn together, we picked the tobacco. We would start around five o'clock in the morning. The leaves were hung to dry under a tent which protected the leaves from the rain.

Most people owned a one- to two-acre plot of land, and they planted on it year-round. One crop was tobacco; the other was olive trees. Everyone had his own trees for olive oil. When

it was time to pick the olives, we'd bang the trees with sticks and pick the fallen olives off the ground, one by one. They were brought to a local factory which had the machinery to extract the oil. Back then we didn't pay the person to make the oil. If he made two cans of oil from our olives, he would keep one of the cans for payment. The olive oil was always enough to last for a whole year until it was time to pick again. Any extra was sold.

We never bought milk because we had goats. We never bought fish because my father kept some fish for the family—although we really didn't like fish—instead of selling all

*Greeks work to live, not live to work. Life is not routine. Almost every day is a holiday. There is much to celebrate and we really enjoy life.*

of it. We never bought eggs because we had chickens. If my mother wanted to cook a chicken, she had to slaughter it herself. I remember watching my mother cut off a chicken's head. She had put the chicken in the hot water, but it got away and was flying all over with no head! I had a hard time eating chicken because of that.

On all the major holidays and *Panagia* on August 15, the whole village celebrated together. *Panagia*, a holiday commemorating the death of the Virgin Mary, is a big three-day festival for the village. There are bands and music with different cultural dances, the most popular being *syrto* and *kalamatiano*.

Everyone helped out for the festival. The person who owned the land where the festival took place built a tavern. He also provided the food and wine. There was not too much food, just lamb, cheese, bread, tomatoes, and olives. It's not like here where everyone brings something to the celebration. We all helped out preparing the food, together.

So for three days, the people of the village forgot about the olives and the tobacco because work stopped during the holidays. In the morning, everyone went to church and relaxed for the rest of the day. In the evening, they met at the tavern, mostly to drink and dance.

Living in a small village took a lot of work, but I liked that everyone knew each other. When I took my daughter to my village, I never had to worry about her if she wanted to come home late. The people of the village knew who she was even though she had never met most of them. In my village in Greece, the people just care about each other.

◻ After laying the foundation for a new house, some Greeks will slaughter a rooster and pour its blood around the foundation for good luck. It symbolizes a way to keep the house or family together. Afterwards, the rooster is cooked, and the family and builders will celebrate with food and wine.

In Greece, to this day, if you hired a person to work—for example, picking olives or building a house—you would feed them. Even if a man worked far away from the house, like on a farm, the woman of the house would prepare a meal and bring it to the worker.

*Kotopoulo me patataes,* or roasted chicken with potatoes, is a typical Greek dish.

### KOTOPOULO ME PATATAES
### Roasted Chicken with Potatoes

| | |
|---|---|
| 1 | whole chicken |
| 4-6 | potatoes, halved or quartered |
| 1/2 | cup water |
| 1 | Tbsp. oregano |
| | salt and pepper to taste |
| 3/4 | cup olive oil |

Place chicken, potatoes, and water in roasting pan. Sprinkle with oregano, salt and pepper. Drizzle oil over chicken and potatoes. Bake, covered, at 350° for 50 to 60 minutes or until done. Uncover and cook until golden.
*4 to 6 servings*

◻ Marriages in Greece are not really arranged—they're persuaded. The parents are like matchmakers, but if the couple doesn't like each other, they are not forced to marry. Once a couple is married, there is no divorce. They would rather suffer than divorce because it looks very bad.

Sometimes the parents arrange a meeting in which neither person being matched knows about the other. The parents just want to see how the couple will react. After a few hours of talking, each is pulled aside and asked, "So, do you like him?" or "Do you like her?" If they say yes, *proksenio,* a toast of wine, ouzo, or any liquor is made, then the families will arrange the engagement. The arrangement must finish right there at the first introduction or forget it.

At the engagement party, the wedding band, not an engagement ring, is placed on the left hand. When the couple marries, the priest will put the ring on the right hand. Before the marriage the couple can meet for dinner at their parents' homes, but they can never go out together alone.

When Greeks have a big party or celebration, they always have roasted whole lambs. The more lambs, the more people in the village and surrounding villages will talk, "Oh! They had ten lambs!" It was a big deal if there were many lambs. The rest of the food is just like food on a regular day. *Karidopita* can be served at a big party or just as an everyday dessert.

### KARIDOPITA
### Walnut Cake

| | |
|---|---|
| 8 | eggs, separated |
| 2 | cups sugar |
| 1 | cup milk |
| 2 | cups bread crumbs |
| 2 | cups walnuts, chopped |
| 1 | cup flour |
| 2 | Tbsp. cinnamon |
| 2 | tsp. baking powder |
| 1 | tsp. baking soda |

**syrup:**

| | |
|---|---|
| 2 1/2 | cups water |
| 2 | cups sugar |
| | juice of 1/2 lemon |

With a mixer, beat egg whites until foamy. Add sugar, beating constantly. Then add milk. Add remaining ingredients; mix well. Pour into a 9 x 15 pan. Bake at 350° for 45 to 50 minutes or until a toothpick comes out clean. Cool. Prepare syrup. Combine syrup ingredients; boil for 15 minutes. Cut cake into diamonds. Pour syrup over cake.
*1 cake*

**At my mother's home**, you are greeted at the door first with her smile, then with the aroma of food cooking. Someone would always say, "Oh, that smell reminds me of when I was a kid!" It is an aroma-memory that we have all experienced. Whenever I visit my mother and she is cooking chicken soup, my aroma-memory reminds me of meeting my grandparents for the first time in Greece.

One day I noticed that my cousin, Stephanie, had her Grandma and Grandpa—Baba and Deddo in Macedonian—living in the same town that we did. I asked my mother about my Baba and Deddo, "Where are they? Where do they live? When can I see them?" She told me they lived across the ocean in a country called Greece. That is when she decided to take me over the ocean to meet them. We boarded the Queen Mary and sailed off to Greece.

I was privileged, at only eight years old, to step on the grounds of my roots in the village of Skopia in Florina, Greece. My feet took off to Uncle Vello's house, Aunt Tsilla's house, the vineyard, and anywhere else I could find a new adventure. Of course, there was food at each visit.

Needless to say, my adventures were too much in one day for an eight-year-old. That night the fever came. As a child you might have had those fevers: one minute, I was larger than the bed; next minute, I felt flea size—a shape shifter before Odo's time. The next thing I knew, the village "medicine woman" was taking me down to the creek. What! Was I hallucinating too? A swim now? But I just wanted chicken soup! There I was, naked, standing in the stream. She doused me with some icy cold water and chanted some good spirits over my head to get rid of the nasty fever. Well, it worked! I felt great, the size of an eight-year-old, and I was ready to eat again. That evening I had soup—thick, lemony, chicken soup.

*I recall when I was entering the first grade the kids could not pronounce my Macedonian birth name, Nevenka. So I was dubbed "Nancy," and it is still my alias.*

In grasping for all the memories of that trip, only a few stand out, like the slaughtering of the pig for a pig roast. It wasn't to my liking, and it frightened me as it would any eight-year-old unaccustomed to watching a slaughtering. I remember someone made the sign of the cross on my forehead with the blood of the pig. It was not a part of a ritual; it was placed there as a symbol to comfort me. We were in Macedonia for two months. Although I do not remember everything, being so young, I came home with happy feelings that I visited Macedonia, and I knew my Baba and Deddo, too.

◻ Macedonia is a northern region of Greece with its own language. My first words spoken were Macedonian. Although our language is unique, our foods are quite the same but are prepared to suit our own tastes. *Manja* is a traditional stew. It always consists of a meat and vegetable, meat and vegetable, meat and vegetable...you get the picture.

### SVEENSKO MESO SUS ZELKA MANJA
**Pork and Cabbage Stew**

| | |
|---|---|
| 2 | lbs. boneless pork loin roast, cubed |
| | olive oil |
| 1 | large cabbage, chopped |
| 1 | 6 oz. can tomato paste |
| 1 | 28 oz. can crushed tomatoes |
| 1 | 14.5 oz. can stewed tomatoes |
| 1 | garlic clove, chopped |
| 1 | small hot banana pepper (optional) |
| | long shake of Greek seasoning |
| | salt and pepper to taste |

In a large pan, cook pork in oil over medium heat until brown. Add enough water to cover meat; cook until meat is tender. Add remaining ingredients; mix well. Cook until cabbage is tender, stirring often to prevent cabbage from burning on bottom. Add water as needed. Manja is tastier when made earlier in the day and allowed to stand.
*4 to 6 servings*

◻ I cannot guarantee that bringing your children to a stream and splashing them with cold water will remove fevers, but this soup certainly will help them feel better.

### KOKOSHKA SOUPA
**Lemon Chicken Soup**

| | |
|---|---|
| 6-8 | skinless chicken breasts and thighs |
| 1 | 14.5 oz. can chicken broth |
| | extra fine soup noodles |
| | long shake of Greek seasoning |
| | dash of garlic powder |
| | salt and pepper to taste |
| 1 | large onion, chopped |
| 2 | celery stocks with leaves, chopped |
| 1-2 | Tbsp. butter |
| | juice of 2 lemons |
| 3 | eggs |

In a large pot, cover chicken with water; bring to boil over medium-high heat. Cook until tender, adding water as needed. Remove bones from chicken; add broth and bring to a boil. Add noodles, Greek seasoning, garlic, salt and pepper.

In a separate pan, cook onion and celery in butter over medium-high heat; add to pot. In a bowl, beat lemon juice and eggs for 2 minutes or until frothy. Gradually add a ladle of broth to egg mixture, stirring constantly to prevent curdling. Gradually pour egg sauce into pot, stirring constantly. Season to taste.
*4 to 6 servings*

**I took my children** to Guatemala because I wanted them to appreciate exactly how life is in the country where I grew up. Here in America, my children have their own bedrooms, their own bathroom, their own television. Before we left, they kept asking me, "Mami, do they have cars? Mami, do they have television?" I just kept telling them "no" because I wanted them to understand that we didn't have everything.

Guatemala is very Americanized, but there are still many differences—for example, transportation. Suburban buses are always packed with hundreds of people. There is not a single space left. But they will still squeeze a person on anywhere and take off.

We went to Livingston, one of the places where I grew up. Livingston is on a peninsula where one can see a lake, a river, and the Caribbean all together. Most of the residents fish for a living, but the town itself thrives off tourism. Tourists pass through Livingston on their way to the castle at the tip of the peninsula. King Philip of Spain built a castle there in the 1600's to keep an eye on the English pirates. This was my children's first experience going to a castle.

*While I was showing my children Guatemala, I decided to treat myself. Along the river in Livingston, there are hot springs. Many people believe that if you get into these springs, you will become younger. Of course, I got into the springs and it worked!*

They really enjoyed going underground and exploring it.

Before leaving for the castle, we stopped at one of the outdoor seafood restaurants in Livingston to order what we wanted to eat. It is a local custom to tell the restaurant two to three hours ahead of when we want to eat so they can fish and prepare the food. After visiting the castle, we came back to the restaurant and ate. The food was delicious because it was so fresh.

It had been so long since I'd been to Guatemala, I'd forgotten about the birthday customs. Around five o'clock in the morning, my cousins and all of his children, my aunts and everybody lit these firecrackers. Needless to say, I jumped out of bed. My oldest son was screaming, "The guerillas are attacking us!" He had no idea that one of the customs back home is to wake up the birthday person—me—with firecrackers. After the fireworks, they sang the traditional birthday song, *Las Mañanitas*, which is about a prince singing to a princess on her birthday. They took pictures of us. My hair was going in all different directions! We laughed about the firecrackers, but they did scare the daylights out of me.

Everyone went back to sleep and around noon all the family came to eat and drink. We barbecued pork chops and chicken, but we normally would roast a whole pig. There were different salads and a lot of *Gallo*, a Guatemalan beer. We had a big party. All the relatives were there and it was a lot of fun.

My immediate family have all moved from Guatemala. Guatemala has many political problems. Students take years to finish their education because the government and students are constantly in conflict over political issues. The government will just shut down the universities as a way to stop protests. My mother did not want that for us. I finished school in New York, married, and had children. Now my eldest is in college, but before he went I wanted him to see Guatemala and understand how I had grown up. He was surprised. He asked, "Mami, how could you have lived here?" But that is the way life is in Guatemala.

◻ The women in Guatemala have to go to the market in the morning before breakfast and again in the afternoon before dinner for the daily meals. I kept arguing with one of my family, "Why don't you just buy everything and stick it in the refrigerator, then go again in a week?" But that's not the way it works there. The men like everything fresh, and the women are obligated to do this daily chore.

## HILACHAS
### Spicy Beef with Tomatoes

| | |
|---|---|
| 1 | lb. beef roast |
| 8 | Roma tomatoes |
| 1 | red pepper |
| 1/2 | tsp. chopped pasa hot pepper |
| 1/2 | tsp. chopped guaque hot pepper |
| 2 | garlic cloves |
| 1/2 | cup chopped onions |
| 1/2 | tsp. cumin |
| 3-4 | uncooked tortillas |
| 4 | cups water |
| | salt and pepper to taste |
| 2 | carrots, sliced |
| 3 | small potatoes, halved |

In a large pot, combine all ingredients except carrots and potatoes; cook over medium heat until meat is done. Remove meat and chop into small pieces; set aside.

Purée remaining ingredients from pot in a blender; return to pot. Bring to a boil over medium heat; add carrots and potatoes. Stir in meat when potatoes and carrots are tender. Serve with rice.
*3 to 5 servings*

◻ Lunch, consisting of soup, salad, and a main course, is the largest meal of the day in Guatemala. Soup is the number one item no matter if it is a hot or cold day. Potato soup, beef soup, soup with milk—it was all homemade.

I remember being at school at seven o'clock in the morning, then walking back home for lunch. Back then it seemed like twenty miles, but it is really only a little more than a mile walk. By the time I got home, I was really hungry! My mom would have a big meal ready, and after lunch I had to walk back to school and stay until five o'clock.

## JOCON
### Tomatillo Chicken

| | |
|---|---|
| 1 | whole chicken, cut into pieces |
| 1 | small onion, halved |
| 8 | tomatillos |
| 2 | scallions, chopped |
| 1 | garlic clove, crushed |
| 1 | green pepper |
| 1/4 | bunch cilantro, chopped |
| | salt and pepper to taste |
| 4 | cups water |

In a large pot, combine all ingredients; cook over medium heat until chicken is done. Remove chicken and shred; set aside.

Purée remaining ingredients from pot in a blender; return to pot. Bring to a boil over medium heat. Stir in chicken. Serve with rice.
*4 to 6 servings*

**I was my father's tester** for his music. He would call me and whistle his new song. When I said it was beautiful, he would say, "Okay, I will bring it to them. Come on with me, Alma. We go and visit my friends."

His best friends were the musicians he had once played with. Later, he changed his occupation, but he still loved and wrote music. He shared his music with his friends, and they played it together in the studio. I would sit down and watch them play. He never wanted recognition. He had no interest in having his name on the music. He just enjoyed making it.

My father played the marimba, an authentic instrument of our Guatemalan heritage. He inherited his passion for music from his father, a soloist flute player. The marimba is similar to the xylophone, but it is larger and made from a special wood called "hormigo." The sound of the marimba is also softer and more harmonious than the xylophone. Marimbas are always played in pairs: a small one for the high tones; a larger one for the deep tones. The musicians play with two drumsticks tipped with rubber.

Alma with her
brother, Ramiro.

*In my home, you will find
the hospitality and cordiality
of the Guatemalan people.
We freely open our arms to
visitors and give them a
warm welcome!*

When I was a little, each year my father had a big celebration with the great musicians who were his friends. We had the celebration in our home after my mother finished the *novena*. The *novena* is a nine-day prayer time to Jesus. People, especially women, came to our home to sing and read from a book of prayers. While we sang, we played maracas and plastic whistles shaped like birds. We also used an empty tortoise shell as an instrument. We turned it on its back and played it with a stick.

The final day of the *novena* was a big party. My mother first served cookies and *ponche*, a punch made from pineapple, sugar, cinnamon, and dried fruit. Afterwards, the marimba players started playing. Everybody was dancing and having a good time. The musicians played all night, taking shifts from playing when they grew tired. The music went on and on throughout the night.

My mother made chicken sandwiches and coffee, so everyone could stay awake longer. My father's friends would say to him, "Ramiro, we are not leaving your home until you kick us out!" My father would say, "Then you can stay all night!"

They really enjoyed being at our home because they did not see my father often. When morning came and they were still there, my mother made breakfast for them.

We did not have this celebration because we were rich and could afford the best marimbas and great musicians. No, it was because my father loved music. He rented the best marimbas. Fortunately, the musicians, who were his friends, played for free.

This kind of music only came into the neighborhood once a year. When my father had this celebration, it was a very special occasion for my family and the whole neighborhood. Our neighborhood had an atmosphere of excitement because the people delighted with the melodies and harmonious music. The neighbors always asked my mother, "When is the next party?" But the next party wouldn't happen until the following year.

These memories still live in my heart. I can still feel my father's love and the vibrating sounds of the marimbas.

❑ I was born in a country full of history and color. Guatemala is called "The Land of Eternal Spring" because the temperature is always warm—between 60 to 75 degrees—all year long. We have a diversity of panoramas, from the golden sand beaches full of the tropical sun to the majestic heights of the beautiful volcanoes. The *cordilleras*, or mountain ranges, add a wonderful touch to the landscape.

Our rivers and lakes are precious and offer us the serenity and sweetness of their clear water. On Sundays, my father would take us to a lake or river because he loved nature. He loved music and poetry, and he enjoyed them along with the panoramic landscape of Guatemala.

We would stay at the lake or river all day. My mother would prepare a picnic for lunch or dinner near the water. We brought most of our food from home because typical Guatemalan food usually takes a long time to prepare, like *frijoles*, or refried beans.

## FRIJOLES
### Refried Beans

| | |
|---|---|
| 1 | lb. black beans, soaked |
| 1 | whole head of garlic |
| 2 | tsp. salt |
| 1 | large onion, chopped |
| 4-6 | Tbsp. oil |

Combine beans, garlic, and salt in a slow cooker; cover with water. Cook for 5 to 6 hours. If using a pressure cooker, cook for 1 hour. When beans are tender, remove and discard garlic. Mix beans in a blender.

In a separate pan, cook onion in 2 to 3 tablespoons oil over medium heat; remove and discard onions when dark brown. Add beans and 2 to 3 tablespoons oil; cook until consistency is like a soft dough. Stir constantly. Shape into a roll. Serve on small platter as a side dish.
*8 to 10 servings*

❑ As a result of our pre-Columbian and colonial past heritage, we have living representatives of the age-old Mayan civilization. They live their lives true to their traditions, beliefs, and heritage. Both *tortillas de maiz,* or corn tortillas, and *frijoles* are basic foods of the Mayan.

These have become very typical foods of Guatemala. If you go into any home, rich or poor, you will find these two foods. In Guatemala there are people who make the tortillas and bring them to your home at lunch time. We never had to make them. I learned how to make tortillas in the States!

## TORTILLAS DE MAIZ
### Corn Tortillas

| | |
|---|---|
| 2 | cups masarina or maseca (instant corn masa mix)* |
| 1½ | cups warm water |

In a large bowl, combine masarina and water; mix well until a firm dough forms. Add a small amount of water if too dry. Divide dough into 16 balls. Cover with damp cloth.

Place each ball between waxed paper; press or roll until 6 to 8 inches in diameter. Heat pan over high heat. Cook tortillas, without oil, for about 30 seconds on each side. Cook first side again for 30 seconds. Wrap in cloth once cooked. Serve instead of bread or rice with beef.
*6 to 8 servings*

**Because Hong Kong** was once a part of mainland China, it has different styles of Chinese food depending on where the Chinese came from. Beijing, Sichuan, and Cantonese are the most well-known styles around the world. Coming from Hong Kong with a Cantonese background, I know more about the Cantonese style.

The Cantonese are good at preparing soups. When different herbs are boiled with the bones of beef, chicken, or other animals, this kind of soup can give great benefits to the organs of human beings. Different organs or parts of chickens or pigs can also give benefits. For example, the Cantonese think that the leg of a chicken, mixed with herbs in a soup, can help a person who has something wrong with his foot. We don't say that the person will completely recover, but the soup is good for those parts involved.

Good things come from bones also, like calcium and vitamins. If a bone is chosen to make soup, it should be boiled a little longer to force benefits out of the bone and into the water. Pregnant women who need calcium buy ox bones because these bones have more calcium. Unfortunately, ox bones are not very tasty, but the women must have them for calcium.

Stephen with his wife and two children.

*My family and I moved from Hong Kong because Hong Kong is returning to Chinese rule. We didn't want to move, but like many people from Hong Kong, we felt forced to leave because we wanted to keep our freedom and democracy.*

After the soup has boiled for a long time and is ready to serve, salt and other spices are added, but it is very important not to boil the soup again. For the western people, they think that food can be served for only one meal; the Chinese don't think so. Soup can keep in the refrigerator, but if the soup dries up a bit, do not dilute with more water because the body had gotten used to the benefits.

There is a secret to making soup. My mother told me this way. She said when the water boils, add all the raw materials. Keep boiling for ten to fifteen minutes, then reduce the temperature to low-medium heat.

The Chinese also believe that drinking Korean ginseng is powerful for older people. We like to have ginseng, but real ginseng is very expensive. There are also many imitations, so unless the person is an expert, it is very difficult to find real ginseng. People can get other benefits from basic vegetables like tomatoes, cabbage, or any kind, with some herbs. But herbs will not work alone; they should be combined with meat.

Sometimes the Cantonese eat meat which is not very popular in America like snake, rabbit, tortoise. They all can be bought at the markets. Snake, rabbit, and sheep, believed to give more energy and warmth, are very popular during the winter. Snake is made into a delicious, creamy soup. These animals are thought to give people more power to their health.

Hong Kong offers the best in food: poultry, pork, fish, vegetables, no matter what kind. Because Hong Kong is a modern city, many tradesmen want to trade with China. Many VIP's settle in Hong Kong while trading with China, and many famous chefs from different countries go to Hong Kong to serve these important people. This raises the level of catering for the western and oriental people.

All food is imported to Hong Kong from China. With the food come the beliefs and customs in its preparation. For thousands of years, the Chinese have believed in their ways of getting the benefits out of different foods, and they still do.

❑ The Cantonese like to steam only saltwater fish because it is more delicious than freshwater fish. It is a custom, and we trust the ancient people who said it was much better this way, so we just follow.

It is very, very important not to overcook fish. The Chinese do not have clocks in the kitchen. They understand the duration for cooking. All seafood must be served hot. If it gets cold, just give up; it's rubbish. Also, the next time a Chinese friend comes to visit, do not serve him white wine with his fish. This is a western custom. If you serve these together to a Chinese, he will not enjoy his meal.

Here is a recipe for steamed fish called *ching yue*. Before steaming the whole fish, it must be dried off. This is very important. Pouring the boiling oil over the fish is the secret in this recipe.

### CHING YUE
### Cantonese Steamed Fish

| | |
|---|---|
| 1 | 2 to 5 lb. whole fish, cleaned and dried |
| 1/2 | bunch parsley |
| | 1-inch piece of ginger, sliced |
| | soy sauce |
| 1/3 | cup oil, boiling |

In a steamer, place fish on top of 3 to 4 pieces parsley. Steam fish until done; time depends upon size. Remove fish and place in platter. Spread parsley and ginger over fish; sprinkle with soy sauce. Carefully pour boiling oil over fish.
*3 to 5 servings*

❑ After I came to America, people told me that chickens here are made to grow up as quickly as they can. That's not good; it's terrible, terrible! In Canton, we feed and keep the chicken in a free-style manner. We let the chickens walk around and just eat normally like a human—breakfast, lunch, and dinner.

Chicken is probably the most popular meat for the Cantonese because it is good for health. For example, after a woman gives birth, the woman's mother will advise her to eat more chicken because it is good for her. The mother will make chicken soup and tell her daughter to eat it all. Every daughter will follow her mother's instructions, and she will pass the advice down, too.

When the Cantonese serve steamed chicken, we eat it with a dip, which is like a dressing, made from ginger and parsley. This recipe is a secret for delicious and tender chicken. I learned it from a chef in Hong Kong.

### PAK CHIK KAI
### Steamed Chicken

| | |
|---|---|
| 1 | 2 to 3 lb. whole chicken |

| | dip: |
|---|---|
| 1 | tsp. chopped ginger |
| 2 | Tbsp. chopped parsley |
| | salt to taste |
| 1/2 | cup oil |

Bring a large pot of water to a hard boil. Add whole chicken; cook, covered, for 30 to 45 minutes or until done. Remove from pot and spray with tap water for 10 minutes.

Prepare dip. Combine ginger, parsley, and salt; stir in oil.
*4 to 6 servings*

For me and certainly for my parents and grandparents, the biggest social organization was the church in the city that my grandparents immigrated to when they left Hungary. All the people who went there were friends, and the church was a central place for them. As I remember growing up, everything my family did—picnics, dances, and social groups—was related to the church.

Picnics were held behind the church in a pavilion. People enjoyed themselves with food, drink, and music. *Kolbasz*, which is essentially a pork, garlic, salt and pepper sausage, was always sold at the picnics as a sandwich on crusty rye bread with sauerkraut. Typically we had *kolbasz* for New Year's; we weren't allowed to have chicken because the chicken would scratch bad luck or something like that. *Töttöte kaposzta*, stuffed cabbage, and *hurka*, a kind of rice and liver dish, were usually served at the picnics, too. My parents used to tell me *hurka* was liver, but I have a feeling it was mostly anything else.

*As I remember growing up, everything my family did—picnics, dances, and social groups—was related to the church.*

Besides food I seem to remember music at all kinds of events. Gypsy bands with one or two violins and a clarinet were always at picnics. At other events popular dance music was played, including traditional folk dance music like for *csardas,* a Hungarian dance similar to the polka.

Although these events were all connected to the church, there was always liquor and beer. Someone was always getting drunk or getting into a fight or breaking glass at the gatherings, particularly at the dances. It was like a normal course of event. These people were blue collar folks, and this was their big night out. I am sure that it still happens, but at that time, it was not desirable.

A couple of social events that stick in my mind are mock weddings and funerals. People, dressed like a bride and groom, would go through town in a hay wagon. Going through the community was the way newlyweds celebrated their wedding in Hungary. I imagine this sort of festival of a wedding was to tie in children with their cultural identity.

During funerals, a ladies group or club in the church would sing the night before the burial at the casket, especially if the person were one of the group. It was poignant to hear these older women singing hymns for someone who was gone. Hungarians sing slowly and drawn out, and if it was anything that the folks had emotion for, it was very moving. The church cemetery was about two to three blocks from the funeral home. The casket was driven from the funeral to the church, and the folks walked along the street.

A funeral back then was a total experience. I guess, thinking back on it now and being older, it shows a real kind of caring for the members for the group. Most of them didn't know each other growing up because they were all immigrants, yet they formed this kind of identity with each other.

I see from these picnics, dances, funerals, and social groups a close community that had strong national and religious ties. These immigrants continued or reinforced their language, their cultural beliefs, and their cultural habits through the church. I had a really good feeling from these folks, and I have always felt a part of that community.

❑ The Hungarian food I grew up on was very much peasant-type food with a lot of meat. We'd use every part of the animal. When my grandmother made chicken soup, for some reason I always got the gizzard and my brother got the feet, but he loved chicken feet. The skin was even put in biscuits.

We also ate *solona,* or raw fat. We'd hold a piece of fat over a fire until it began to drip, then we'd slice off pieces and eat it on rye bread with a couple onion slices and salt. It was like we were in heaven.

My wife, Lynn, and I don't really cook traditionally Hungarian. Food like *solona* is terrible for cholesterol. We try not to have creams and sauces, and those are absolute in Hungarian food. Hungarians also cook mostly with lard.

We just cook differently. Lynn is a vegetarian and I'm an at-home vegetarian. When our boys were home, we cooked more and ate meat. Now we prepare food like stuffed cabbage without meat, which is totally removed from Hungarian cooking, and crêpes called *palacsinta* for breakfast.

### PALACSINTA
### Crêpes

| | |
|---|---|
| 3 | eggs |
| 1¹/₂ | cups milk |
| 1 | tsp. honey |
| ¹/₂ | tsp. vanilla extract |
| ¹/₄ | tsp. salt |
| ¹/₂ | cup flour |
| | butter |
| | cottage cheese |
| | jelly |

Combine eggs, milk, honey, vanilla, salt, and flour. Begin with ¹/₂ cup flour, adding more until batter spreads easily but is thick enough to hold together. Mix well; let batter stand for at least 1 hour.

Melt about 1 teaspoon butter in a 10-inch pan. Add a small amount of batter; spread by tilting pan. Cook until bubbles form. Flip and cook other side. Spread 1 tablespoon cottage cheese and 1 teaspoon jelly over crêpe and roll up.
*4 to 6 servings*

❑ My family was fairly matriarchal, at least with family relationships. The men were supposed to represent the folks to society, but we would say that we're going to my grandmother's house even though my grandfather was there as well. The women were very much in control.

On Sunday we'd go to church with my grandparents, then have dinner at my grandmother's house. Dinner was never formal or quiet at all. Folks could go off on any topic. If someone felt they wanted to yell at someone else, that was all right. Go right ahead.

Typically, Hungarian goulash is like a stew but in a broader sense. I've seen goulashes with thin or thick sauce; I've seen it with noodles or dumplings. This is just one recipe from my mother.

### SZEKELY GYLAS
### Hungarian Goulash

| | |
|---|---|
| 1 | lb. lean pork, cut into strips |
| 2-3 | Tbsp. oil |
| 1 | Tbsp. paprika |
| 1 | tsp. salt |
| 1 | tsp. black pepper |
| 1 | Tbsp. flour |
| 1 | cup sour cream |
| 1 | lb. sauerkraut |

Cook pork in oil, seasoning with paprika, salt, and pepper over medium heat until done. Stir in flour and sour cream. Add sauerkraut.
*4 to 6 servings*

Family heritage has been instilled in me since childhood. My grandfather always told me to be proud of who I am and to never forget where I came from. My great-grandparents, like many other immigrants, were so obsessed with being American. Their native language and culture were not practiced much at home and are now virtually lost. But I do remember that when Nuge Mama and Nuge Pappa were mad, they said their bad words in Hungarian so my brother and I couldn't understand them.

Naturally, the few Hungarian traditions I have are very important, those being family gatherings and cooking. Any time there is a cause for celebration, the family joins together for food and fellowship. Weddings, funerals, and holidays are just some of the celebrations with the best food.

Nuge Mama, whose recipes have been passed down through family and friends, was a wonderful cook. Not only did she cook for her large family, she worked in the kitchen of a zinc mining company. When we went to visit her, her house always had the most wonderful aromas. She was always baking some sort of bread, using her pottery mixing bowl and the flour sifter with the green handle. Sometimes she would let me help.

Although Nuge Mama and Nuge Pappa are gone now, I still have memories of them with me. Nuge Mama kept her recipes in large black ring binders which are still in our family. To this

Michelle (front right) with her family.

*It's difficult for all of us to get together often because we live far from each other. When we do, it's for special occasions, like on Dad's birthday.*

day, my family prepares her recipes, especially the Hungarian filled cookies called *kiflis*. Kiflis have become the official Christmas cookie of the Rapole family. We even use her mixing bowl and pastry knife as part of the tradition. Making the cookies is part of a two-day family get-together. The dough is made one day, refrigerated overnight, then cooked the next day.

We usually make several batches of the cookies to include them with fruit, nuts, and other homemade goodies in holiday gift baskets for family and friends. They are also quite addictive; no one can just eat one. They are holiday cookies, therefore I splurge a little bit.

When the holidays draw near, I am reminded of one January when it was the first family celebration in my new home. We had to reschedule Christmas for January because a record-breaking snowstorm at the end of December prevented my family from getting together. My sisters, father, and I were having a discussion of how the *kiflis* should be made. This was nothing unusual because it happens every year. Everyone has his or her own idea of how to make the perfect *kifli*.

Picture this: a small kitchen, a table covered with baking flour in the center, and four or more people covered in flour arguing on how thick the dough needs to be rolled, how large to cut the squares, how much filling to use, and, of course, which filling *should* be used. Sometimes, looking back at those moments, I am surprised that Nuge Mama didn't appear in the fog of baking flour, pick up her baking utensils, and settle the discussion right there.

# Michelle Rapole-Lyons

❑ The fillings used during my great-grandmother's time were fruit and nut based because they were readily available. Now store bought fillings can be used. All-fruit spreads work best. Do not buy pie fillings or jams and jellies. Jams and jellies tend to run because of their high sugar content.

❑ Most Hungarians had small land plots to plant gardens. Everyday dishes were mainly vegetable based, and meat was limited to what was readily available. Paprika, a typical Hungarian spice, grew in every garden. Today it is one of the largest agricultural exports of Hungry.

### KIFLIS
### Hungarian Filled Cookies

| | |
|---|---|
| 2 | cups butter |
| 1 | lb. flour |
| 3 | eggs, separated |
| $^1/_4$ | tsp. salt |
| 1 | cup sour cream |
| | fillings (see below) |

In a large bowl, crumble butter and flour together with by hand. Add yolks, salt, and sour cream; work into a smooth dough. Chill overnight.

Roll out dough thinly on a floured surface. Cut dough into 2- to 3-inch squares. Place $^1/_2$ teaspoon filling in center. Bring up opposite corners and pinch together. Brush with egg whites. Bake at 400° for 25 to 30 minutes or until golden brown on top.
*about 65 cookies*

### LEKVAR FILLING
### Prune Filling

| | |
|---|---|
| $^1/_2$ | lb. prunes, chopped |
| 1 | tsp. vanilla extract |
| 2 | Tbsp. sugar |

Combine all ingredients; mix well.

### Nut Filling

| | |
|---|---|
| $^1/_2$ | lb. chopped walnuts |
| $^1/_2$ | cup sugar |
| 1 | tsp. vanilla or almond extract |
| 2 | Tbsp. sweet cream |
| 1 | medium apple, grated |

Combine all ingredients; mix well.

### PAPRIKAS CSIRKE
### Paprika Chicken

| | |
|---|---|
| 1 | onion, chopped |
| $^1/_2$ | Tbsp. shortening |
| 1 | tsp. black pepper |
| 2 | tsp. salt |
| 1 | tsp. paprika |
| 1 | 3 to 4 lb. chicken, cut into pieces |
| $^1/_2$ | cup water |
| 1 | cup sour cream |
| 1 | tsp. flour |

Cook onions in shortening until brown. Add seasonings and chicken; cook for 10 minutes. Add water; cook, covered, until tender. Remove chicken. Combine sour cream and flour; mix well. Add to drippings in pan; mix well. Add chicken after sauce thickens.
*4 to 6 servings*

**Lifestyles of the Rajputs**, the ruling royal families in India, were naturally very different from the rest of the Indians. The Rajputs were accustomed to many people working for them. The rajas, or rulers, had ancestral lands that the working class worked on. The working class worked the land, but the rajas would give them just enough to live on and the rest would be put into the rajas' pockets. I am a Rajput, and I have never seen a raja physically work.

Not all royal families taxed the people for money. Many Rajputs were enterprising and went into business, especially where I lived. Some owned huge orchards and made money from selling the fruit all over India and even Europe.

But after 1947 with independence and democracy, lifestyles changed. The rajas did not have much power any longer. Many could not afford to keep their land because they had to pay taxes now, so they sold it. Some rajas resorted to renting their palaces or got into different businesses. They just could not afford to live the extravagant lifestyles they had lived before.

Bandhana (front left) and her family.

*The only person smiling is my daughter who was born in America. Usually no one smiles because family portraits are very formal in India.*

The working class realized that they didn't have to do what the rajas wanted them to do. Many sent their children away to school so the children could get jobs and not live as their parents. Because of this, people were not staying in the villages anymore.

My father had told me stories of the rajas before everything changed. It was a time when the men-folk would gather in each other's palaces for entertainment while the women, who were strictly prohibited from joining them, stayed in the women's quarter elsewhere in the palace. The rooms where the men entertained did not have chairs or sofas; all the men sat on embroidered silk cushions on the floor, which was covered with Persian rugs. *Nautch* girls in their colorful dresses called *ghagra* sang and danced to classical and folk music while the men drank and smoked hookahs. It was a very male-oriented atmosphere, and sometimes these parties lasted into the morning.

Of course, there was a lot of food and many kinds of meat done in different recipes. A whole goat, wild boar, or lamb would be roasted. Households of the Rajputs serve meat whereas in other houses meat is rarely served. Servants, dressed in traditional wear, came to serve or there was a buffet. Back then, the meal was served on shallow bowls called *thalis*. The *thalis* were made of silver or gold, depending on how rich the raja was.

Marriages of the rajas were also very different from the working class. The rajas, as well as people in the other castes, did not marry out of caste. There may have been a few exceptions, but as a rule Indians stayed within their caste. The female of the raja class brought in a great deal of money and jewelry. Jewelry was given literally by the kilos for dowry. After all these years, the Rajputs are basically inbred because the royal caste is not that large. For example, my husband's uncle is married to my aunt; my husband's youngest uncle is married to my cousin. Somehow, everyone is always related to both sides of the family!

The royal families that exist today are leaving the traditional ways and mainstreaming themselves. The Rajputs do not have the political power that they once had, but they still have the respect and love from the people.

My father loves hunting; it's his stress breaker. He would go hunting every week with his friends. In Punjab, he hunted for partridges. He would wake up at four o'clock in the morning, get into his jeep and go. He would come back with thirteen to fifteen partridges. Partridges are very small, so he needed to shoot quite a lot to feed a family of five.

My mother makes the best partridge I have ever tasted in my life. This is her own marinade for partridge, but it can also be used for any poultry.

### PARTRIDGE MARINADE

| | |
|---|---|
| 2 | whole heads of garlic |
| 3 | Tbsp. ginger |
| 1 | tsp. garam masala* |
| | ground red pepper to taste |
| | salt and pepper to taste |
| 5-6 | Tbsp. lemon juice or vinegar |
| 1/2 | cup plain yoghurt |
| | partridge or poultry |

In a mortar, pound garlic and ginger to a paste. Add garam masala, red pepper, salt and pepper; mix well. Combine paste with lemon juice and yoghurt. Marinate partridge or other poultry. Grill on skewers.
*marinates 13 to 15 partridges*

Divali, a festival of lights of the Hindu religion, celebrates the homecoming of Rama, the incarnation of Lord Vishnu, after fourteen years of exile. Rama's stepmother sent him away because she wanted her son to be king, but her son did not share her ambitions. He followed Rama, telling him to return. Rama sent his stepbrother back, asking him to look after the kingdom until he returned.

Divali is the day that Rama returns to his kingdom. Every house is lit with candles and lamps to show the way home to the king. Candles and lights are lit all over the house and burned from the evening to the morning. The festival always falls on the darkest night in October.

Divali is like Christmas but without the presents. The family, wearing their new clothes, spends time together during the festival. Usually they say a prayer at home and do a little gambling with cards. The gambling is done only in the family with hopes that Laxmi, the goddess of money, will visit the house. There are tons of food, particularly lots of sweets and a black *dal*, or lentils. The *dal* brings good luck; it is auspicious to eat it on this day.

Traditionally, *dal* is made in Himachal, the state where I come from. Other parts of India may make a different dish.

### DAL
### Lentil Stew

| | |
|---|---|
| 1 | cup black lentils |
| 3 | cups water |
| 4-5 | garlic cloves, crushed |
| 1 | medium onion, chopped |
| 1 | Tbsp. grated ginger |
| 2 | tsp. ground coriander |
| 2 | tsp. cumin |
| 1/2 | tsp. turmeric |
| 1 | tomato, chopped |
| 2 | Tbsp. ghee* or clarified butter |

Boil lentils in water until tender; do not drain. In another pan, cook garlic and onions. Add ginger, coriander, cumin, and turmeric; cook for 2 to 3 minutes. Stir in tomato. Pour mixture into lentils; cook for 10 minutes. Add ghee. Dal should not be thin. Pour over rice.
*6 servings*

**People must realize** today that family values are most important. The construction of the Hindu society is that if you go to the small villages in India, you will find examples of strong family values. Families are living together; they are sharing gifts; and they are enjoying themselves with each other. When they live together, they are bound.

In my family, there were thirty-two people living under one roof. We had a big house. One may ask, "Oh, how did you have thirty-two bedrooms?" But there were not thirty-two bedrooms. Those who were married had their own room. The rest, boys and girls separated, slept on cotton mats on the floor. We slept, talked, and made jokes together; we were very close.

Someone was always home to take care of the children, which was very important. While some adults worked, others gave the children proper training and education. Parents and family gave the best quality of life.

My mother, who prepared the meals, was very clever. For example, she knew that I liked

pizza, so on one day she made pizza for everybody. That day the meal was my choice. The next day was someone else's choice. I may not have liked his choice, but I knew that I had my choice the previous day.

Not all thirty-two of us ate at the same time during the day because people were at home at different times. But during the evening, we ate together as a family unless someone was out of town. We ate in two groups: first, the children, then the adults.

Living this way not only made the family closer, it was also economical. Suppose there were five brothers and five sisters. If they were living separately, they would need separate houses and separate everything. They would end up spending a lot of money. By living together, each can become stronger by saving money. Because my country is one of the poorest, the government does not give social assistance like food stamps or social security. That means from the very beginning we are trained to save money and help each other in the family.

*My father's theory on life was simple. He would tell me if you can help, help; if you can't, don't. Just don't harm anybody, not just human life but any life. If no one harms anybody, life is beautiful.*

When I came to America in 1981, I had only six dollars that I got at the exchange, but I was happy that I made my life on my own. Of course, all my relatives helped me in the beginning. When I started my business, I didn't have money. I asked my brother, sister-in-law, and brother-in-law to help me with contributions. I returned all of their money. Now I am working in my own business.

In Hinduism, round is most important. The universe is round, the earth is round. If you go all the way around, you end up at the same place. Whatever you do, you will get the same result. It's the Karma theory. If you do good things, you will get good returns; if you do bad things, you will get bad returns. So it is with family also. When my family was living together, we all took care of each other. My father took care of my grandfather, I took care of my father, and I know someone will take care of me. In life, such family value means security.

❑ Right now in India, beef is prohibited. There are many philosophies behind the prohibition. One is that the Hindu religion believes in nonviolence. Because of this, the cow is not killed.

The main reason for not killing the cow is not because of religion, but because of economy. The cow is like our mother because it links us to the land. Because of the cow, we produce bulls. Because of the bulls, we are able to farm. Because of the farm, we have different foods.

The cow not only supplies us with bulls, milk, and cheese, but it provides manure for the vegetables. Manure is also used as fuel for the poor people. They dry the manure in the sun on the roofs, then burn it for fuel.

To convince the people not to kill the cow, there are two ways. One way is to say, "Don't kill the cow." But people who are not educated will not understand the economic principle of not killing the cow. People are very religious in India, so if they are told not to kill the cow for religious reasons, they will believe. They still believe this now.

*Jalebi*, made with yoghurt, is a typical Indian sweet.

## JALEBI
### Batter Coils in Syrup

| | |
|---|---|
| 1¹/₂ | cups flour |
| ¹/₂ | cup gram flour, lightly toasted* |
| ¹/₃ | cup yoghurt |
| ¹/₂ | yeast cake |
| | water |

**syrup:**

| | |
|---|---|
| 1¹/₄ | cups water |
| 1 | cup sugar |
| ¹/₂ | tsp. saffron powder |
| ¹/₂ | tsp. ground cardamom seeds |
| | oil for frying |

Combine flours, yoghurt, yeast. Add small amounts of water until batter is thick and creamy. Set aside for 2 hours. Mix again before using.

Prepare syrup. Combine water and sugar; bring to a gentle boil over low-medium heat. When sugar dissolves, add saffron and cardamom.

Heat oil over medium-high heat. Pour a thin stream of batter into oil, forming coils. Cook for 30 seconds. Turn over; cook other side for 30 seconds or until golden and crisp.

Drain on absorbent paper. Immerse in syrup for 3 minutes. Remove and serve hot.
*4 servings*

❑ In arranged marriages in India, parents are looking for quality in family and character in a match. The definition of character in my country means a person's whole life: his family relations and social relations, not just his personality or good looks.

My wife and I met only once we were engaged. We didn't "date." One way that is good; one way that is bad. It seems that the meaning of dating in other countries is to understand each other: my thoughts, your thoughts; my choice, your choice.

But I feel that marriage is a part of life. There should also be no "My," only an "Ours." Marriage is a mutual understanding that each must sacrifice something. Did I think my wife was 100% perfect? No. Did she think I was 100% perfect? No. Marriage means two bodies but one soul.

*Suli halwa* is a sweet my wife prepares. It is another typical dessert in India.

## SULI HALWA
### Semolina Sweet

| | |
|---|---|
| ³/₄ | cup ghee* or clarified butter |
| 1 | cup fine semolina |
| ²/₃ | cup water |
| ¹/₃ | cup raisins |
| ¹/₃ | cup shredded coconut (optional) |
| ¹/₄ | cup almonds, shredded |
| 1 | tsp. ground cardamom seeds |
| ¹/₂ | cup sugar |

Melt ghee over low heat. Add semolina; cook for 10 minutes, stirring constantly. Add water, raisins, coconut (optional), ¹/₂ of almonds, and ¹/₂ of cardamom. When water is absorbed, stir in sugar.

Remove from heat. Sprinkle with remaining almonds and cardamom. Serve hot.
*6 servings*

**A special tray**, symbolizing what families wish for, can be found in every Iranian family's home on *Norooz*, or New Year's Day. The tray is called *haft seen*. *Haft* means seven; *seen* is a letter of the alphabet like "s." *Haft seen* is a big tray with seven items that start with an "s." Traditionally, each of the seven items has a special meaning that is important to Iranian families.

*Sekeh* is money. All Iranian families wish for money or financial ability. We ask God to give us more money for the year that is just starting.

*Seeb* is an apple. A red apple is chosen because it is so beautiful. Red is the color of being fine and healthy, so we choose an apple as a sign of good food and health in the coming year.

*Samanue* is a very special burgundy-colored sauce or pudding. It signifies togetherness because every member of the family has to come and stir the pudding in the pot. The family also sits and talks. The *samanue* must be mixed; the more it's mixed, the better it becomes. It's made with special Iranian spices and ingredients that cannot be found in this country.

*Serkei* is vinegar. Vinegar is used to save apples or different vegetables in the winter. So *serkei* is put on the tray as a sign that things are saved, not wasted.

*Somogh* is like a medicinal spice and has health significance. The Iranians believe that when we eat *somogh*, it takes the high cholesterol out and clarifies the blood. Many Iranian foods are fried, so this is one way of cutting the oil. *Somogh* is also put on salads or on rice to give it a red color.

*Senjed* is a fruit that looks like a date and is shaped like a jelly bean. Iranians put it on the tray to wish for more food during the year.

*Sonbol* is a flower with different colors on top. *Sonbol* is put as a hope for flowers and good things in life.

A bowl of water with a small red fish is also placed on the tray. The water is a sign of the soul being as clear as water when there is no darkness or dishonesty. The fish is a sign that life moves instead of being stable. Death to Iranian people means no motions. Immediately opposite of that is life. Fish never rest; they are all the time moving, so they symbolize hope for improvement and a better life.

*Persia is the old name of Iran. Coming from the Persian word "areya," "Iran" means the "place of kind people."*

New Year's Day in Iran, which is on the first day of spring, means that everything is new. Every family tries to buy new clothes, and a week or two before the new year begins the house is cleaned. Not only is it the start of a new year, but on that day everything shines. The people shine and their places shine.

The streets are crowded because New Year's is a special occasion when families get together and visit the oldest member of the family. That oldest member puts money in the Koran for good luck and gives gifts or money for New Year's. After the oldest member gives the gifts and the rest of the family kisses his or her hand or face, then the food from the tray can be eaten. Of course, the basic seven items are not touched, but there are cookies, candies, and different sauces and Iranian desserts. Iranians really eat on this day!

New Year's is a very happy occasion. Iranians don't want anyone to cry on this day. We say that if you cry on this day, you will cry for the rest of the year. If you have a disagreement with someone, you don't bring it up that day. We just want a day of peace and happiness for the New Year.

❑ My mother inherited her tray from my grandmother. It was huge, about five feet in diameter, with Persian designs all over it, and it was made in my hometown. My mother is so attached to the tray because we have celebrated New Year's with it for so many years.

Iranian families cook special foods for New Year's because we want to complete our happiness with sitting around the table, having a good time, and really enjoying what they are eating. Many Iranians like to cook these recipes on New Year's.

## CELLO KABOB
### Beef Kebab with Persian Rice

**rice:**

| | |
|---|---|
| 2¹/₂ | cups rice |
| ¹/₂ | cup salt |
| 3-6 | Tbsp. olive oil |
| 1 | tortilla or any thin bread |

**kebab:**

| | |
|---|---|
| 2 | large white onions |
| 2 | lbs. ground beef |
| ¹/₄ | tsp. turmeric |
| ¹/₄ | tsp. salt |
| ¹/₄ | tsp. black pepper |
| ¹/₄ | tsp. saffron |
| | tomatoes (optional) |
| | green chili peppers (optional) |

Prepare rice. In a large bowl, wash rice several times to remove starch. Add water to cover and salt; set aside for 4 to 5 hours or overnight. After soaking, wash again 2 to 3 times. Bring half a pot of water and 3 tablespoons oil to a boil; add rice, stirring constantly. Cook until rice is a little soft when squeezed between the fingers. Do not overcook. Drain; rinse with running hot water.

Grease bottom of large pot. Cover bottom with tortilla. Spread rice on tortilla with a slotted spoon, shaping rice into a large cone. Make 4 large holes in rice. Sprinkle 1 to 3 tablespoons oil and salt to taste. Cover tightly; cook over low-medium heat for 30 to 45 minutes.

Prepare kebabs while rice is cooking. In a food processor or blender, purée onions. Combine onions, meat, turmeric, salt, pepper, and saffron; mix well by hand. Firmly squeeze a handful of mixture onto greased skewers. Broil in oven over low heat or on grill. Turn every 5 minutes until meat is done. Serve with rice and grilled tomatoes and chili peppers, if desired.

*4 servings*

❑ On New Year's Day, each Iranian family cooks food that our ancestors made and passed down as a tradition. *Cello kabob* and *ghormeh sabzee* are two recipes prepared as part of my family's tradition. Other families' selections may be different.

## GHORMEH SABZEE
### Vegetable Stew with Rice

| | |
|---|---|
| | rice |
| ¹/₂ | lb. stewing beef |
| 2 | bunches parsley, leaves only |
| 1 | bunch green onions |
| 3 | bunches spinach |
| 1 | bunch dill leaves |
| 2 | bunches cilantro |
| ¹/₂ | cup oil |
| 1 | cup water |
| | juice of 1 to 2 limes |
| 1 | 15.5 oz. can kidney beans |
| ¹/₄ | tsp. salt |
| ¹/₄ | tsp. black pepper |
| ¹/₄ | tsp. turmeric |

Cook rice according to instructions above. Boil meat separately until done; set aside.

Chop parsley, onions, spinach, dill, and cilantro in food processor or blender, but do not liquefy. Cook vegetables in oil over low heat. Combine vegetables, meat, and remaining ingredients; cook over low-medium heat until reduced to very little liquid. Serve over rice.

*4 servings*

**It is no joke** that potatoes were a staple in the Irish diet. Many of our families came here between 1845 and 1849 during the Irish potato famine, "When our potatoes ceased to grow, we came in search of Idaho." History now records that there are more Irish people in America than there are in Ireland.

I was raised on a cattle farm as the oldest of ten kids in an Irish family. Except for meals like chili and spaghetti, there were always potatoes on the table in one form or another. Potatoes went with breakfast, lunch, dinner, and sometimes dessert. I was well-grown and gone the first time I actually saw my father eat rice. A meal was not a meal without the prithees on the plate. There are literally hundreds of ways to cook and eat potatoes.

Along with a dietary dependence on potatoes, I also inherited other ways from my Irish blood. Irish people saw patterns in their lives that found their expressions in many art-forms. We are known for our wit. I still have a great appreciation for the well-turned phrase or a comment with a double-edge placed just so. We love a good story. Our history and stories were passed from generation to generation by way of songs and music committed to memory.

Our music is distinctive. Sometimes light and energetic, sometimes haunting or sad, but always the patterns are there for the ear to savor. Music drove and motivated our warriors and sang praise to our chiefs. Music reflected the complexity of the patterns we used to decorate our simple tools and our fine jewels.

The patterns remind us that we do not go through life alone. Everything we do or say touches many other lives and, eventually, makes its way back to us where it started. For us, life does not end with death, but simply begins a new pattern—never ending.

We celebrate this in Halloween and in our stories of fairies and "The Little People." The Little People began as dim memories of enemies long ago defeated, but their spirits remain with us. Halloween is our New Year's Celebration, a time when the veil between the worlds is thin and the spirits can pass among us; the beginning of "the dark days":

*I am well-known for being stubborn. It comes with the blood and is stuck with the family. My great-great-grandmother used to say that it was the Irishman who taught the mule how to be stubborn.*

> *"As the oak begins in the dark of the seed,*
> *As the lamb begins in the dark of the womb,*
> *So the New Year begins in the dark of the old."*

Who has to wait for St. Patrick's Day to show they are Irish?

*Where did it begin?*
*Where does it end?*

◻ My mother loved anything that could be made in one pot. When dinner was ready she just moved the pot from the stove straight to the center of the table. *Colcannan* can be cooked and served from the same kettle and is warm and welcome on a cold night. It is inexpensive, stores well, and handles a microwave like a champ. Mom called *colcannan* "Old World Slop-in-a-Pot," but we loved it all the same.

There aren't precise measurements for *colcannan*. It's made out of leftovers and garden findings. Corned beef and rye bread are also close Irish associates, so enjoy a tour through Irish history in a kettle.

## COLCANNAN

| | |
|---|---|
| $1/2$ | kettle of mashed potatoes; milk, salt and pepper to taste |
| 1 | skillet of sautéed cabbage with onions |
| 1 | lb. corned beef, sliced and chopped |

Combine all ingredients; mix well. Serve over rye bread.

Variations: Add caraway seeds to potatoes while cooking or top with Cheddar cheese.

◻ Homemade potato sponge bread is not like the store bought one; it's heavy, moist, and very delicious. And it ain't yellow!

## POTATO SPONGE BREAD

| | |
|---|---|
| 1 | cake of yeast |
| $1/2$ | cup warm water |
| 2 | cups mashed potatoes; without milk, salt or pepper |
| 2 | Tbsp. sugar |
| 1 | Tbsp. salt |
| 4 | cups flour |

Dissolve yeast in water. Add sugar, salt, and dissolved yeast to mashed potatoes; mix well. Stir in flour, adding more as needed until dough is soft. Knead well. Let rise overnight in a warm place. Divide dough into 2 parts. Dough can be placed in bread pans or raised once again before baking. Bake at 350° for 45 to 50 minutes.
*2 loaves*

◻ There were so many kids in my family—ten—that my mother had a griddle built right in the middle of the kitchen. She also had to cook for the many men who stayed at our farm over the weekends to put up the hay during the hay season. My mother was just used to cooking for these armies.

Potato pancakes are a breakfast assembly-line food. Mom had bacon, eggs, and potato pancakes on the griddle, and we kids or the men would just come around in a line while she filled our plates.

## POTATO PANCAKES

| | |
|---|---|
| 1 | lb. potatoes, peeled and grated |
| $1^1/2$ | cups flour |
| $1/2$ | cup milk |
| $1^1/2$ | tsp. salt |
| $1/2$ | tsp. baking powder |
| 4 | Tbsp. oil |
| | butter |

Combine potatoes, flour, milk salt, and baking powder; mix well. Cook in oil over medium heat until brown on both sides. Butter and serve hot.
*4 to 6 servings*

**My wife,** Corita, and I are from Irish backgrounds. My parents and Corita's grandparents came from Ireland. When we married, we thought it would be an ideal honeymoon trip to go back to our roots in Ireland, which we did in the spring of 1979.

We toured most of the island during a two-week trip. Because there was a postal communication strike in Ireland at the time, we were unable to previously make connection with Corita's relatives who live near Waterford. However, we ventured out one day into a section where we knew some of Corita's distant relatives lived and asked people if they knew the family of relatives.

At one stop a dairy farmer tending to his cows told us, surprisingly, that he was indeed one of that family. He was emotionally taken back by our unannounced arrival at his dairy farm. In any event, he gathered himself and said he would contact the rest of the family and that we should come back the next day for a little family gathering.

The following day we met all the relatives at one of their houses. We were hospitably accepted by them and swapped stories of who resembled whom in the family. We had an enjoyable meal, and were impressed by the freshness of the dairy products and hams. We also noticed that in these modest farmhouses, there were fine collections of crystal Waterford on display!

Hugh with his family.

*I maintain my proud Irish heritage as president of the Irish group, the Ancient Order of Hibernians.*

We visited the elderly Aunt Katie's pub and other relatives who also had a dairy farm. We were somewhat surprised to find the family very interested in American television shows, especially a new show that my wife and I weren't too familiar with it: *Dallas*.

After a delightful time with these friends and family, we pushed on to Belfast after a brief stop in Dublin. In Belfast we stayed with a cousin of mine named Alice. Alice had previously lived with my family for nearly a decade in the 1950's. She saved enough money to return to Ireland and establish her own business as a hairdresser.

Alice treated us like the long-lost relatives that we were. She took us to a rural section where there were small farms and showed us an old, modest stone house which was in great disrepair. She pointed out that this was where my grandfather had reared eight kids. I was stunned by the humbleness of it and imagined how crowded it must have been for my father and his siblings so many years ago.

As it happens, most of those children lived to adulthood and immigrated to America. I was deeply moved by the thought that these were the origins of my parents. After having heard my parents' stories of their early years, I had an appreciation of the hardships they had endured. I admire their being able to rise out of them and establish a better life in America.

❑ I acknowledge that Irish cuisine has taken a back burner in the public image to its continental cousins; I really don't expect to see a "Gaelic Gourmet" program on the Food Channel any time soon. Nevertheless, there are certainly many Irish dishes to delight the palate, ranging from salmon steaks to Irish stew.

The selection I offer here, however, is a simpler fare. Harking back to the adage that bread is the staff of life, I present two favorite recipes of this food group: one for Irish skillet bread, a treat which my wife prepares, and the other for Irish soda bread.

### IRISH SKILLET BREAD

| | |
|---|---|
| 3 | cups flour |
| 3/4 | cup sugar |
| 1 | tsp. salt |
| 3 | heaping tsp. baking powder |
| 1 | egg, slightly beaten |
| 2 | cups milk |
| 1/2 | cup margarine, melted |
| 1/2 | cup raisins |
| 1 | tsp. butter |

Combine flour, sugar, salt, and baking powder. Mix well and set aside.

In a separate bowl, mix egg and milk. Add margarine; combine with flour mixture. Gently mix into a wet dough. Stir in raisins.

Melt butter in 9-inch iron skillet, spreading butter over bottom. Lightly dust with flour. Spread dough in pan; lightly dust top with flour. Without cutting through dough, score center with back of knife; scoring prevents top from bursting. Bake in a 300° preheated oven for 1 hour. Increase heat to 325° if bread does not evenly brown. Cut into wedges. Serve with butter, jam, and tea.
*1 loaf*

❑ Irish soda bread is a pleasing comestible from the oven of a friend, Ann Cunningham, who often serves it at meetings of our Irish organization, the Ancient Order of Hibernians.

May I suggest that you combine either of these breads with a well-brewed cup of Irish breakfast tea or Irish coffee. It just might warm the cockles—and even the muscles—of your heart. Alive, alive-Oh!

### IRISH SODA BREAD

| | |
|---|---|
| 3 | cups flour |
| 1/2 | cup sugar |
| 3 | tsp. baking powder |
| 1/2 | tsp. salt |
| 1 | tsp. caraway seeds |
| 1/2 | box raisins, rinsed |
| 6 | Tbsp. butter, melted |
| 3 | eggs |
| 2/3 | cup milk |
| | melted butter for top of dough |

Combine all dry ingredients and raisins; set aside.

In a separate bowl, combine eggs, 6 tablespoons butter, and milk; mix well. Add 1/2 of mixture at a time to dry ingredients, mixing into a heavy dough. Place dough on floured surface without kneading. Divide and shape into 2 balls. Place in buttered pans and flatten slightly.

Rub melted butter on top. Make a cross on top with knife. Bake at 345° for 40 to 45 minutes or until a toothpick comes out clean.
*2 loaves*

**"I'm bored."** These words were never heard when I was a child in Ireland. The days were never long enough; we had plenty to do. Part of the day was to do the work on the farm. As a family and a community, we—young and old—shared many interests in our social life. My rural experiences were pleasant.

I grew up on a mountain farm that had some erratic fencing around our home, but for the most part it was sprawled and unhindered towards a peak of the Sperrin Mountains in Northern Ireland. My family lived just outside of the village Draperstown. We had about 500 sheep and 100 cattle, and we had the right to graze on 400 acres near the peak of the mountains. The land wasn't the most fertile area of Ireland, but it was arable. It could be plowed and tilled for potatoes, corn, and hay.

As a child, I wandered, bare-footed, many a mile through the mountains in search of a stray cow or sheep. I also herded the cattle from the lowland to the upland, depending on the season. It was kind of fun. I remember my brother and I—he was about seven and I was eleven—with just a dog to help us, running through the village street with 100 head of cattle. We were bringing them to the McBride's farm on the other side of Draperstown. My father paid McBride so the cattle could graze there.

I also remember the first time I was taken to the top of our mountain by my father. I was five. After what seemed like days of walking, we crested over the mountain. We could see the six northern counties of Northern Ireland, the patchwork of fields, peaks and mountains, and the green fields all coming up to Lough Neagh, the largest fresh water lake in the British Isles. The view was amazing.

My father took me up there for no inspirational reason. He couldn't read or write; he was just fun to be with. Mostly we talked about the sheep and shared worries. He told me stories about when he was young and wild and ran around. His family had been there for generations; he grew up there.

Seamus and his mother.

*Wander into any pub in Ireland and you'll notice that young and old participate vigorously in conversation. You will soon realize there is no such thing as a stranger in an Irish pub. For that matter, there is no such thing as a stranger in Ireland.*

Besides work, there were lots of social activities going on: boxing, bridge, parties, and dances at other parishes. The area was identified really by parish than town. With six boys and five girls, my family literally could entertain ourselves. We read, sang, played charades, delivered recitations; there were no televisions, electronic entertainment, or telephones. Our entertainment was creative and challenging. For example, if someone mastered the English language, drama, or music, it was considered a tremendous gift, even more than money.

When parties were arranged, someone had to pick up the older people living on their own and drive them to the parties. There weren't many cars, but if someone had a car, it was your car also. It was at your disposal. Bringing the older people out into the social setting was a social responsibility. This was the whole idea of sharing within the community.

I went back one time and some young kid walked up to me the dark, "Where are you going, Seamus?" and he jumped into my car. He put like fifty dollars worth of gas in the car—gas is so expensive there—and until this day, I don't know who he is. I must have been pals with his dad. But there was a sense that we knew each other although I hadn't been back for a while and he was much younger than I. There was just something eternal about where I grew up.

◻ We raised sheep and cattle as well as the usual clutter of hens, ducks, and the occasional pig. My mother could neatly and efficiently dispatch any chicken that was too lazy to lay and have it ready for the pot within a half hour. We were not squeamish as children.

The sheep and cattle escaped the ignominy of being butchered at home to feed our family. The pig, however, was ceremoniously killed, cut up, and neatly packed with salt in a tea chest for consumption during the winter. This was considered a man's job.

Although typically Irish, these recipes have been adapted to the American palate by my wife, Caroline.

### PORK AND APPLE STEW

| | |
|---|---|
| 4 | medium onions, thinly sliced |
| 4 | medium cooking apples, peeled and thinly sliced |
| 6 | pork chops |
| $1^1/2$ | Tbsp. brown sugar |
| | salt and pepper to taste |
| 1 | Tbsp. water |

Spread $^1/2$ of onions on bottom of casserole dish. Spread $^1/2$ of apples. Add pork chops, sprinkling with $^1/2$ of sugar, salt and pepper. Repeat layering with remaining ingredients. Sprinkle water over dish. Bake, covered, in a 350° preheated oven for 1 hour. Reduce heat to 250° and cook 1 hour. This can also be cooked at 250° for 3 hours or in a slow cooker. Serve with mashed potatoes.
*6 servings*

◻ During the early days of summer, we walked about five miles to the peat bog to dig out the "turf." The turf was used as fuel for heating and cooking throughout the whole year. Before it is harvested, the peat resembled cold, black, softened butter. It was so cold that we kept our bottles of milk or sweet tea naturally refrigerated by placing the bottles underneath.

Digging out turf was hard work, so was working the hay later in the summer. Tractors and machinery were still fairly rare during this time. A large slab of gingerbread cake, along with milk or tea, was just the thing to keep a young boy or a grown man supplied with the energy to keep going through a long Irish summer's day.

### GINGERBREAD CAKE

| | |
|---|---|
| $2^1/4$ | sticks butter, softened |
| 2 | cups sugar |
| 3 | eggs |
| 1 | cup molasses |
| $^1/2$ | cup peeled and finely chopped ginger |
| | grated rind of 2 oranges or lemons |
| 1 | tsp. cinnamon |
| $^1/2$ | tsp. ground cloves |
| 1 | tsp. baking soda |
| 1 | Tbsp. vinegar |
| $3^1/3$ | cups flour, sifted |
| 1 | cup milk |

Beat butter with mixer until light and fluffy. Gradually add sugar while mixing. Beat in eggs. Add molasses, ginger, rind, cinnamon, and cloves; mix well. In a separate bowl, combine baking soda and vinegar; blend into mixture.

Add $^1/3$ of flour; mix lightly. Add $^1/3$ of milk; mix lightly. Add remaining flour and milk alternately until blended well. Pour into a greased and floured 9 x 13 pan. Bake in a 375° preheated oven for 55 to 60 minutes or until toothpick comes out clean and cake pulls away sides of pan. Cool in pan.
*1 cake*

**One of the best** parts of growing up Italian was waking up on Sunday morning. In fact, we did not wake up but rather rose from our pillows as if the aromas from the kitchen were grabbing us by our nostrils and were actually pulling up our heads.

Our first-generation American parents were up early, browning fresh garlic in olive oil. They could have gone no further and the house would have smelled fine all day, but the sausage with fennel, the pre-made bracciole and the secret-formula meatballs (that mysteriously appeared from the refrigerator under the cover of a dishtowel) met with the same fate.

Well, the day was shot from there. All we could do was wander around the house, breathing deep, looking baleful, waiting for company from somewhere in Brooklyn (the smell reached all the way there). We also sharpened our skills at dodging the wooden spoon as we lunged for that cooling meatball. We could rip off the end of an Italian bread and dip it into the sauce without ever breaking stride. It was expected that all we could filch would be considered our breakfast.

Peter (right) with friends in Sicily.

*You're never alone in Sicily.*

The pasta, all nice and snug in its red blanket of sauce, became the first course of the weekly feast that featured a salad that could only fit in a small swimming pool and a meat course of succulent lamb or an eye round directly from God. Another bowl, full of fruit, graced the table along with coffee, cake, and various liquors. I recently asked my family, "Who ate all that food?" and, of course, everyone simultaneously pointed to the other.

Adolescence being what it is and the bounty being what it was, the inevitable eating contests sprung up just as sure as Aunt Jenny was going to take a doggie-bag when she went back to Brooklyn. It started out with the pasta. One bowl was great, but two were GREATER! Two just wasn't a big enough number, so we moved to meatballs. Mom's were heavy from all the cheese and stuffing, and although younger, my brother, Phil, was a consummate pig. Two bowls of pasta and five meatballs made him the winner.

When the competition switched venues to my Parina's, my cousin, Big Pete, boasted an impressive two bowls and eight meatballs. He was later disqualified when we discovered that Parina's meatballs weighed in at a mere half the weight of Mom's. Ravioli was served at that meal, and a new event was born. These were not the small ones, mind you. Our German Shepherd, Hugo, had trouble gulping these two and one-half-inch jumbos.

Phil was doing the Bellmore Scelfo's proud at twelve ravioli, but Babylon's Albie finished up at fifteen. Peter Boy—that's me—looked like a sure winner at an amazing eighteen, when "outta nowheres," eleven-year-old, sixty-five-pound Josephine popped another two to make twenty, the winning number. This made me look like a complete fool—losing to a skinny girl. I still say it didn't count because she is Parina's niece's daughter and no relation to me.

To this day, nobody but nobody can touch my all-time record of nine of Mom's eggplant parmigiana. Maybe I shouldn't say that so fast. Cousin Steve ate half of a huge watermelon at someone's funeral and given Steve's spectacular projectile-vomiting distance scores, we all considered his performance right up there with my holding *down* nine parmigiana. Steve was weird anyway, but that's another story.

◻ I'm giving Mom's eggplant parmigiana recipe, but forget it, you won't make it as good as she; nobody can. If you down more than nine, you better have a video with a clock behind you so you can prove it's true. All cutlets less than four inches in diameter don't count! Bon Appetito!

## EGGPLANT PARMIGIANA

| | |
|---|---|
| 2 | large eggplants, peeled (optional) and cut into $1/4$-inch slices |
| | salt |
| 1 | cup milk |
| 4 | eggs, beaten |
| 2 | cups seasoned bread crumbs |
| 2 | jars tomato sauce |
| 1 | cup Locatelli® Parmesan cheese |
| 8 | oz. part-skim mozzarella cheese |

Very lightly salt and layer eggplant in a colander. Place a heavy plate on cutlets; set aside for about 2 hours. Rinse off salt.

Combine milk and eggs. Dip eggplant into milk mixture, then dredge in bread crumbs. Bake at 450° to 500° on a greased cookie sheet until brown.

Layer eggplant, sauce, and Parmesan cheese, ending with a generous amount of sauce. Top with mozzarella. Bake at 350° for 30 minutes.
*6 to 8 servings*

◻ I remember this one dinner when "Aunt Grace's Denture Soup" stepped into culinary history. Prior to this amazing evening it had been known as "Spinach and Tortellini Soup." Dad and Aunt Grace were in the kitchen waiting for a ride to the hospital to visit my cousin Jackie, Aunt Grace's daughter.

Italians are well-known for talking with their hands, especially when they are upset. Aunt Grace was really upset; the soup she was tasting was flying out of her spoon. She had the enviable quality of being able to continue any conversation despite what her hands were saying or what was in her mouth. This time Aunt Grace was too upset, and the soup undoubtedly made its presence known to her windpipe.

Dad must have thought this was a sympathy

episode for Jackie, so he did what all good Italian brothers do for their sisters—he yelled at her! Aunt Grace started yelling back, but all the yelling and choking was too much. Dad backed off and gave her the old pounding-on-the-back treatment. This always makes matters worse, but back then, who knew?

You guessed it, though, the pounding made Aunt Grace's lower denture want to make a statement by itself, and, smiling all the while, it made a very quick and graceful denture-dive into the pot of soup.

I'm still laughing about it, but we didn't see much of Aunt Grace after that. My dad ate most of the soup anyway, mumbling about boiling it extra long and the stuff he had to eat during World War II, but I wouldn't touch it. It took me twenty years to overcome the obvious, and now I'm glad I did. It is wonderful!

## SPINACH AND TORTELLINI SOUP

| | |
|---|---|
| 1 | package refrigerated tortellini |
| 1 | lb. package spinach |
| $1/2$ | medium onion, chopped |
| $1/2$ | celery stick, chopped |
| 1 | Tbsp. butter |
| 1 | Tbsp. chopped fresh parsley |
| 1 | tsp. Italian herbs |
| 2 | 10.5 oz. cans chicken broth |
| 2 | 10.5 oz. cans water |
| 1 | Tbsp. chicken base |
| 1 | 11.5 oz. can V-8® vegetable juice |
| | grated Romano cheese |

Prepare tortellini according to package instructions; set aside.

Clean spinach and remove stems; set aside

Cook onion and celery in butter over medium-high heat until transparent. Add remaining ingredients except tortellini, spinach, and Romano cheese. Bring to a boil. Reduce to medium heat; cook for 20 minutes, seasoning to taste.

Fill bowls with a serving of cut spinach. Sprinkle with Romano cheese. Add tortellini; cover with hot broth. Serve with hot Italian bread.
*6 to 8 servings*

**We had a little farm** in Panni, a hilltop town in the province of Foggia. My father was in the States most of the time. Only my two sisters, brother, mother, and I lived on our farm in Italy. We did not cultivate the land; there was a man who cultivated it. When harvest came, we divided the harvest, half and half. We did pick the olives from the trees to make our own olive oil.

Around November, my mother and I had to pick the olives. We put a big sheet around the bottom of the tree, climbed into the tree and shook it. Some came down on the sheet; others had to be picked by hand. After picking all the olives, we brought them home on the donkey. We had to have a donkey—everyone had to have a donkey—there were no automobiles that we could use because this was in the late 1920's to early 1930's.

There were only two places in town where we could crush the olives. We went to the one close to the house. The owner of the olive oil place gave us a certain day when we could bring our olives in to make the oil. We dumped the olives into a large cement "tub" to be crushed by three stone wheels, about eight to nine inches wide and two feet high, set equally apart. One wheel crushed the olives around the outside of the tub; one crushed in the middle; and one crushed on the inside.

Joe and his wife, Kitty.

*When I left Panni and came to America, I was sixteen years old, so I already knew about Italy and where I came from.*

Each of the wheels was attached to a horizontal shaft that was connected to a vertical shaft in the middle of the tub. One more shaft for a mule or donkey was connected to the centerpiece. The mule would go around and around, turning the center shaft that moved all the wheels at the same time to crush the olives.

After the olives were crushed, they were put into containers made of coiled rope that acted as sieves. These containers were stacked up high. A plate on top pressed down all the containers, squeezing the water and oil from the olives. The water and oil ran into a four-inch deep plate on the bottom which had an opening like a spigot. The liquid was caught in buckets and put in wide wooden barrels.

After filling the barrels, they were left for five to six hours so the oil would rise from the water. The oil was then scooped from the top—pure, dark green olive oil. That's the way we used to make olive oil. My mother put the oil in five-gallon bottles. She never sold the oil; we kept it all to last us for the rest of the year.

The people still make olive oil in Panni, but now everything is electric. They even purify the oil, and it's made quicker and cleaner. But the olives still need to be picked by hand. They can't get away from that!

# Joseph Mastrangelo

◻ Joe makes *frittatas* which he learned how to cook by watching his mother. Every time he makes the omelettes, they're different, but he makes good ones. He doesn't really have a recipe; he just uses whatever is in the refrigerator. He has been known to put wine in them, too!

—Kitty Mastrangelo

## FRITTATA
### Italian Sausage Omelette

| | |
|---|---|
| 2-3 | Tbsp. olive oil |
| 3 | garlic cloves, sliced |
| 4 | Italian sausage links, cut into 1-inch slices |
| 2-3 | green peppers, cut into wedges |
| 1 | small onion, cut into wedges |
| 2 | fresh tomatoes, cut into wedges |
| | mushrooms (optional) |
| | carrots (optional) |
| | fresh basil (optional) |
| 1/2 | cup red wine |
| 3 | eggs, beaten |

In a 12-inch pan, cook garlic in oil over medium-high heat until golden. Add sausage; cook over medium heat until almost done. Add vegetables and wine. Cook, covered, for 3 to 5 minutes. Add eggs; cook for about 1 minute.

Carefully flip frittata onto a plate which is larger than the pan. Wear a cooking mitt on the hand holding the plate. Slide frittata back into pan; cook other side or place pan under broiler without flipping.
*4 to 6 servings*

◻ *Ragu* is a tomato pasta sauce that I also learned to cook from watching my mother. I call it "gravy."

## RAGU CON CARNE
### Tomato Pasta Sauce with Meat

| | |
|---|---|
| 2-3 | garlic cloves, sliced |
| 1/2 | small onion, sliced |
| 3 | Tbsp. olive oil |
| 1/2 | lb. pork chops or ribs |
| 1/2 | lb. round steak, cut into chunks |
| | salt and pepper to taste |
| | basil to taste |
| 2 | 28 oz. cans crushed tomatoes |

Cook garlic and onions in oil over medium heat until brown; discard garlic and onions, leaving only oil. Add meat and cook until brown. Add salt, pepper, and basil. Remove meat and add tomatoes. Bring to a boil over medium heat; reduce heat to low. Return meat to pan. Cover loosely and cook for 40 minutes, stirring occasionally. Serve over pasta.
*6 to 8 servings*

**Mom,** the former Lorenza Marie Cartelli, was born in Sortino, a small—and do I ever mean small—town in the mountains of southeastern Sicily. She came to America when she was fourteen years old. Even though she spoke, dressed, and on the surface looked like a "regular" American, Mom has always been a Sicilian at heart.

Mom keeps her heritage alive through her fantastic cooking. My sister, Alessandra (Sandy) Marie Stagnato, and I have followed Mom's lead. I love to cook and I love to eat. It's really good when the two go together. Sandy and I turned out to be pretty decent cooks, and my boys, Guy and Dean, can whip up a meal that will have people asking for seconds. Dad, on the other hand, was born in England of an English mother and a Danish father. My English grandmother was not the best cook in the world, but my Grandpa Jensen was a excellent cook and taught Mom some great Scandinavian Dishes.

On the Italian side, there were so many wonderful cooks that I just don't know where to start. My Grandma Cartelli could do more with a "roasta fresha chicken" than anyone I know.

*I come by my love of food honestly. My mother is a fantastic cook. I love to cook, I love to eat, and I love cooking shows. Just ask my grandchildren, and they will tell you that next to Grandpa, I love Jeff Smith, the Frugal Gourmet.*

With Grandma, it didn't matter if it was a stewing chicken or a fryer; to her, it was always a "roasta fresha chicken." Mom and Grandma made great Italian tomato sauce. Today, it is fashionable to serve some sort of fancy pasta sauce: pesto, cream or butter sauces, or a variety of other clever toppings for pasta. But when we were growing up, it was just good old macaroni and tomato sauce.

Dinner was a time of celebration in my family. Company always came for Sunday dinner, bringing with them wonderful tales and yarns. Mom and Dad could keep an audience enthralled with recollections of life and family history in Europe and the "Great Trip to America." Everyone participated. Children, no matter how young, were never ignored or excluded from the conversations.

With this in my blood, I have come to associate good food with interesting situations. Most of the foods we eat have fascinating memories accompanying them. Even though most of the "old bunch" is gone now, my cousins and I get together periodically to reminisce about the past and enjoy the present.

▫ In Sortino, there was very little meat but plenty of pheasants. After coming to America, Grandma Cartelli switched from pheasants to chicken. When we were growing up, Sunday dinner began with spaghetti. Next came salad served with meatballs, then Grandma's "roasta fresha chicken" served with a bitter green such as mustard greens or broccoli. A large round loaf of crusty bread, covered with butter, and, of course, a glass or two of red wine, or grape soda for the kids, were also part of the dinner. Dessert consisted of fresh fruit and cheese, but on special occasions we would have Italian pastries such as *connolis* and *sfogliatelle*.

### ROASTED CHICKEN AND SAUSAGE

| | |
|---|---|
| 1 | whole chicken, cut into pieces |
| 1 | lb. Italian sausage links, hot or mild |
| 8 | medium potatoes, quartered |
| 4 | medium onions, quartered |
| | olive oil |
| | garlic powder |
| | oregano |
| | paprika |

Arrange chicken in a large roasting pan; place sausage links between chicken pieces. If links are large, cut into half. Add potatoes and onions; drizzle with olive oil. Sprinkle garlic powder, oregano, and paprika. Bake in a 350° preheated oven for 1 hour or until chicken is golden and potatoes are tender.
*4 to 6 servings*

▫ Grandma Cartelli used to say that you had to come from Sortino to know how to make *arancine*, but you had to be a Cartelli to make great *arancine*. This recipe for rice balls has been in my family for many, many years and was brought to the New World when my family emigrated from Sicily.

Arancine was the specialty of my Commare Ciccia, or Aunt Frances. Commare Ciccia could do so much with a cup of rice. When I was a little girl, I loved visiting her because she always had a big plate of *arancine* ready and waiting for us to snack on as soon as we finished with the hugs and the "How are you doing's?" *Arancine* means "little oranges."

### ARANCINE
#### Sicilian Rice Balls

| | |
|---|---|
| 2 | cups rice |
| 4 | cups water |
| 1/4 | lb. ground round or chuck |
| 4-5 | cups Italian style tomato sauce |
| 2-3 | cups shredded mozzarella cheese |
| 1 | cup Ricotta cheese |
| 2 | eggs, beaten with 1 Tbsp. water |
| | seasoned bread crumbs |
| | oil for frying |

Cook rice in water for 20 to 25 minutes. Fluff with fork; set aside to cool.

Cook meat over medium-high heat; drain on paper towel.

Mix rice with 2 to 3 tablespoons tomato sauce, using only enough to dampen rice. Add mozzarella; mix well. Shape into balls the size of a medium orange. Make a large hole in the center with finger; stuff with Ricotta cheese and meat. Close hole and dip into beaten egg. Roll in bread crumbs. Deep-fry until golden. Serve with extra tomato sauce.
*12 to 14 balls*

**Let's go back** about thirty years to February 14, St. Valentino's day, in my home town of Bussolengo, Italy. St. Valentino is the patron saint of Bussolengo, and there is big town celebration every year. Thirty years ago, when my sister got married, she and her husband started a tradition of inviting all the male members of my brother-in-law's family, our family the Biasi's, and my mother's side of the family for a get-together on St. Valentino's day.

Usually on St. Valentino's Day, all of the men in the farming community went to the agricultural fair held on this day. New bank loans, new machinery, new technology—these were the men's concerns. But after that, the men from the three families would go to my sister's house where my sister, my mother, several aunts, and I had been cooking since sun-up.

Of course, there was a great deal of food for this occasion. A typical dish for St. Valentino's is *primo piatto*, or rice and tripe, but we also prepared an array of meats and vegetables—all for the men; the women were to serve.

Maria enjoying a cigar and a cup of tea at Gargoyles Coffee Bar.

*On St. Valentino's Day, the men take their sweet time eating and enjoying themselves. They loosen their belts; they sit back and talk about politics; they moan and groan about taxes and how bad the past season was. They talk about who is getting married and who passed away. When they finish, then it's the women's turn.*

The tripe, or stomach, must be scrubbed and cleaned with lime to remove its strong smell. It is cut julienne-style, then cooked in tomato sauce, rosemary, garlic, and pepper for hours until tender. Outside, a huge pot with meat is boiling to make *brodo*, the meat stock. Prime meat, chicken, or calves' heads give more consistency to the soup. On this day the food must be perfect; not a single kernel of rice can have a blemish. All of the women sort out the rice as part of the tradition.

After the *primo piatto*, boiled meat with *pepperata*, a black pepper and nutmeg sauce used as a dip, and greens such as dandelions are served. Next is *cotechino con crauti*. *Cotechino* is a boiled pork sausage made from the stringy meat, skin, and tendons all ground up. *Cotechino* is accompanied by a side dish of *crauti*, or sauerkraut. The sausage and sauerkraut change the whole flavor of the meal. Usually guinea hen, pheasant, or duck come after the *cotechino con crauti*. A variety of cheeses are served, once again to change the flavor. Meanwhile, everything is abundantly wetted down with *Rechito* wine. *Rechito* wine, typical of the Verona region, is commonly known in the male population as the "manly wine" because it is full-bodied and high in alcohol content.

Then we arrive at the fruit and nuts and finally the *pasta frolla*. *Pasta frolla* is an extremely rich sweet made from flour, sugar, and butter; it's a type of gingerbread. *Pasta frolla* is served on a big, round, wooden dish like a cutting board. The head of the house breaks it into pieces with his fist. Everybody takes their uneven pieces and they pass around a bottle of *grappa*, a very strong spirit. *Grappa* is poured over the pieces because the *pasta frolla* is thin and hard after it is cooked. Given that these men have been eating and having their fill of wine for a few hours, the *pasta frolla* is just to top it off.

First the women take care of the men, then the women have their day to do whatever they want and get happy just like the men did. So the next day, February 15, all the women get together. Because the women had been cooking for so long and so much, there is plenty left over. The women drink but they do not get drunk. They dip their *pasta frolla* in their coffee or espresso. It is not common for women in Italy to get drunk.

Every family celebrates St. Valentino's Day, but this tradition amongst the families was a way to tie all three families closely together.

◻ My mother always made my favorite sweet, *chiacchiere,* during the winter months or Carnival time. When I make *chiacchiere,* I use the broken egg shell to measure the gin or vodka which is equivalent to about 3 tablespoons. In Italy *grappa* is used, but gin or vodka are good substitutes.

A loose translation of *chiacchiere* is "to chat." My daughter always says that these remind her of pillows.

## CHIACCHIERE
### Sweet Pillows

| | |
|---|---|
| 3 | cups flour |
| 1 | egg |
| 3 | Tbsp. gin or vodka |
| | pinch of salt |
| 1 | Tbsp. sugar |
| 1 | Tbsp. butter, melted |
| | powdered sugar |
| | oil for frying |

Make a well in flour; add egg, liquor, salt, and sugar. Knead dough until smooth and elastic; add more flour if needed until dough does not stick to hands.

Divide dough into 5 parts. Flatten each with rolling pin to about 9-inch circle. Layer dough, brushing each with butter. Flatten with pin again until as thin as possible without breaking. Cut with different shaped cookie cutters.

Heat oil over medium-high. Cook only a few at a time depending on size. Chiacchiere instantly puffs when placed in oil. Cook each side for 2 to 3 minutes; drain on paper towel. Sprinkle with powdered sugar.
*6 to 8 servings*

◻ Way back when in the hills of Rome, the poor people, who were not miners, made their own sort of "briquets" to sell. They gathered huge piles of wood to burn, but smothered the fire with dirt to make embers. Once the fire died, what was left could be sold. In Italy there are no coal mines. Coal Miner's Spaghetti is what these workers called their food, and this tradition has remained until now. *Spaghetti alla carbonara* is very popular in Italy.

I have become famous for my *spaghetti alla carbonara*. If my friends are coming over for dinner, they will tell me that I need to prepare this dish. When I pass the recipe to my friends, they say, "Maria, mine never tastes like yours!"

## SPAGHETTI ALLA CARBONARA
### Coal Miner's Spaghetti

| | |
|---|---|
| 1 | lb. spaghetti noodles |
| 4 | quarts lightly salted water |
| 1 | lb. lean smoked bacon, finely ground |
| 2 | Tbsp. olive oil |
| 5 | eggs |
| 1 | cup grated Parmesan cheese |
| | pinch of nutmeg |
| | black pepper |

Cook spaghetti in water "al dente"; drain. While spaghetti is cooking, cook bacon in oil over medium-high heat.

In a warm, large bowl, combine eggs, cheese, nutmeg, and pepper; mix well. Add spaghetti, mixing thoroughly and quickly so eggs will not "cook" from the heat of the spaghetti. Add bacon "sauce" over each serving of spaghetti.
*6 to 8 servings*

**Everything I remember** about being with my Italian family has to do with eating. Every big event centered around food. I'm not sure why. Maybe it was because my mom liked to cook. No matter the affair, it was a big event as far as time spent to make all the food.

My mother woke up really early to begin cooking. She would spend the whole day in the kitchen and do all the cooking by herself. She never allowed anyone to help her. Lasagna, baked ziti, manicotti, ravioli, stuffed shells—she always made at least five main dishes, along with the vegetables, fruit salad, antipasto, pickled vegetables, and always Jordan almonds.

When I was younger, the extended family—aunts, uncles, great-aunts and great-uncles—came, even for birthdays. There were always a lot of people, maybe forty to fifty. By the time company came, my mother would already have the food cooked and everything cleaned and put away.

All the food was put on the table, and everyone would walk down with their plates. The table was just for holding the food; there was nowhere to sit down and eat. We just sat on the floor, couch, or wherever there was space to eat.

*Family should always be together in mind and spirit, not only on holidays and special occasions.*

My grandfather never had a table big enough for the family, so in the mid-60's, he decided to make his own from a door. He made a really long table, eight to nine feet long, that folded up. He passed it to us, and we use it to this day for big gatherings.

I always looked forward to the family gatherings because it was the only time I saw my extended family together. When I was a child, once the relatives were in the door, we'd hug and kiss, and I would get out of the way. When I got older, I sat around and talked with them. I respected them and whatever they wanted to talk about was great.

I had one uncle who was a shoemaker in Italy. He talked *a lot* about shoes. But if my uncle wanted to talk about shoes, we'd talk about shoes! I had a couple of other uncles who were very Italian. They were very hard to understand; we had to listen really closely. Most Italian men are know-it-alls, so listening to them was quite interesting. Picture several Italian men talking in a room and all of them knowing everything and anything. Nevertheless, there was still a certain amount of respect that I had to show.

My family is spread out now, so we aren't together much except at Christmas, funerals, and weddings. We don't have the big family events like we used to when I was a kid. In my immediate family, my wife and I try to continue the traditional type foods around the holidays or special events. How my mother did it by herself, I don't know.

□ This recipe for *pizzellas,* Christmas time cookies, came over from Italy with my great-grandmother. My mother and father make *pizzellas* and Christmas cookies together during the holidays; it is their special thing to do. It is one of the few times that my mother allows any help.

My parents are both perfectionists. My father is in charge of stacking the *pizzellas*; he has a certain way of stacking. He also picks all the edges off after they come out of the iron. Now my family carries on the tradition of making the wafers and other cookies during the Christmas season.

Traditionally, the first *pizzella* is given to the dog or birds because the old irons had to be oiled and the first one made would absorb that oil. Definitely keep the *pizzellas* in a can or an airtight container; they absorb moisture because they are very thin.

## PIZZELLAS
### Christmas Wafers

| | |
|---|---|
| $2^1/_3$ | cups sugar |
| 1 | cup shortening |
| 1 | cup margarine |
| 4 | tsp. anise oil |
| 12 | eggs |
| 7 | cups flour |
| 4 | tsp. baking powder |

Cream sugar, shortening, and margarine. Add anise oil; mix well. Add eggs individually while mixing. Add flour and baking powder; mix well.

Drop 1 teaspoon of batter on a heated pizzella iron. Close iron; cook for 30 seconds or until light goes out. Remove; stack until cool. Store in a coffee can or cookie jar.
*12 dozen*

□ Instead of buying a frozen bag of *gnocchi*, we get together in the kitchen for a couple of hours to make these homemade potato dumplings. It rekindles our family tradition of spending time together around the food.

I remember the counter being covered all over with three-fourths-inch *gnocchi,* because the *gnocchi* must be allowed to dry for at least five hours on a floured counter.

## GNOCCHI
### Potato Dumplings

| | |
|---|---|
| 5 | Idaho potatoes, peeled |
| 1 | egg |
| 5 | cups flour |

Boil potatoes; mash well. Blend in egg. Make a well in potatoes; gradually add flour until dough is smooth. Too much flour will make gnocchi tough. Cover counter with flour. Roll out strands about the thickness of a cigar. Cut into $^3/_4$-inch pieces. Dry on a floured counter for at least 5 hours.

Bring a large pot of water to a boil. Cook enough gnocchi to cover bottom, stirring constantly to prevent sticking. When gnocchi floats, remove with slotted spoon. Serve with pasta sauce.
*5 servings*

*"God bless the wheat and the grapes, from these we eat and drink."*
—Serafino Orsini

**My grandparents,** Serafino and Valentina Orsini, emigrated from Abruzzo, Italy, to New York City in the early 1900's. They eventually settled in the predominately Italian borough of Lodi, New Jersey, or as Grandpa called it, "Godsa Country." Raising four sons in the midst of the Depression was a daily struggle for my grandparents. Nevertheless, they instilled in their four sons and grandchildren a passion for good food, good wine, and family.

Grandma made every meal an event. Her food was not only delicious, but creative. Whenever I was in Grandma's kitchen, she would tell me stories about her dishes. Looking out the window to her garden, she would reminisce.

Debra with her husband, Frank.

*Tradition is wonderful because it allows us to keep a little part of the people we love.*

One day during the Depression, she removed some flowers from the yellow squash in her garden to help the remaining flowers produce larger squash. Being careful never to waste anything, she filled her apron with the beautiful yellow squash flowers and brought them into her kitchen. She lightly breaded and fried the flowers to a golden brown and served them to her family that night. The dish was well-received, though the boys had no idea what they were eating. Fried squash flowers became one of Grandma's signature dishes. What a kick she would have today knowing that these edible flowers are now served in some of the finest gourmet restaurants.

Grandpa had a wine cellar in his basement where he produced the heavy, dry red wine indicative of his native Abruzzo. Each time we visited, he would treat us to the official tour. Keys hung from his belt as we descended the stone steps to the cool, dark basement, and after he unlocked the heavy door, we entered into Grandpa's domain.

Musky wine casks and religious calendars, some dating back thirty years, lined the walls. On my last visit with him, he led me to a special cabinet, then lovingly removed four bottles filled with the remainder of his last batch of wine. Each bottle had the name of a son. "When I die-a, eacha son geta little of my lasta wine. No tella nobody." That night at dinner, I noticed he was pouring from one of the bottles. When I asked him about it, he said, "Eh, I no die-a yet, so I drinka myself."

After we gathered around the dinner table—everyone talking at once, my uncle pouring the wine, Grandma making sure everyone has enough on their plates—Grandpa Serafino stood at the head of the table and in his broken English prayed, "We thanka God for the food anda the wine. We thanka God we are all together. I hope we can be together again."

I want my children to experience what I had experienced with my grandparents, especially the food and the togetherness we shared. When I teach them how to cook some of the traditional foods, I tell them stories of how I learned. Tradition is wonderful because it allows us to keep a little part of the people we love—even when they are no longer here. I miss you, Grandma and Grandpa.

☐ Grandma's warm, inviting kitchen was her stage; her family was her audience. She was never too busy to show her grandchildren how to make pasta by hand, put the sign of the cross in Easter bread, or hide a hard-boiled egg in the Easter pie for luck.

*Veal scalappine al marsala* is one of my family's favorite dishes. It can be prepared in under thirty minutes. Chicken can be substituted for the veal. Although the flavor will be different, it is still delicious.

## VEAL SCALAPPINE AL MARSALA

| | |
|---|---|
| 2 | lbs. veal cutlets, thinly sliced |
| 4 | Tbsp. butter or margarine |
| 3 | cups sliced mushrooms |
| 3/4 | cup marsala or sherry |
| 1 | Tbsp. flour |
| | salt and pepper to taste |

Cut veal into 6-inch squares; pound with mallet until $^1/_8$ inch thick. Dredge in flour, adding salt and pepper.

Cook mushrooms in butter over medium-high heat. Remove mushrooms; set aside.

Brown meat on both sides. Add marsala or sherry; cook for 5 minutes. Return mushrooms to pan and cook for 10 minutes. Do not overcook.
*6 to 8 servings*

☐ This garlic soup is my father's creation. The name is a little misleading. The soup has a lot of garlic, but the flavor is very mild.

## ERIC'S GARLIC SOUP

| | |
|---|---|
| 6 | large garlic cloves |
| 1 | cup chopped onions |
| 1/2 | cup chopped celery |
| 1/2 | cup chopped carrots |
| 1/2 | cup extra virgin olive oil |
| | black pepper to taste |
| 4 | cups chicken stock |
| 1 1/2 | cups Wheatsworth® cracker crumbs |
| 3 | cups finely chopped spinach |
| | sesame seeds |

Cook garlic, onions, celery, and carrots in oil over medium-high heat until soft. Season with pepper. Add chicken stock; cook over medium heat for 20 minutes. Add cracker crumbs; cook for another 10 minutes, stirring often. Cool; purée in blender or food processor. Add spinach and reheat for 10 minutes. Sprinkle each serving with sesame seeds. Soup will keep up to one week in the refrigerator or several months in the freezer.
*6 to 8 servings*

☐ Of all the wonderful dishes Grandma made, the one that Grandpa served—peaches in wine—brings back the fondest memories.

Every meal concluded with fruit. Grandpa, at the head of the table, would peel and slice a fresh peach into his wine glass then pour his homemade wine, a good red Zinfandel or Chianti, over the peaches. The peaches in wine were always a treat because Grandpa was the only one who prepared this for the family.

For an elegant presentation, serve this delicious dessert in stemmed goblets. If preferred, chill for an hour prior to serving.

Christianity and *obeah* are the two most popular belief systems or religions in Jamaica, and they are very different. *Obeah* is what most Americans refer to as "voodoo," but we never use that term.

Sometimes, religion mixes with the local belief. For example, my mother is a Christian, but if her left eye jumped, she would say that something bad was going to happen; if the right eye jumped, something good was going to happen. If she dreamt about the color green, she'd say, "No, I'm not going to that business meeting. It will be a disappointment." Sometimes, it's true; something very close to her dreams will happen. She's a very good dreamer. If a bat or a cat came into the house, she or my grandmother would say that those animals were spirits of the dead. So even the Christians may have faith elsewhere.

During New Year's, the Christians hold a Revival March that takes place mainly in Kingston. We can hear the march coming because of the noise from the drums, tambourines, and singing. The Christians, or Revivalists, wrap their heads with turbans and are dressed in full white. They march like a parade, jumping and stomping as they speak in tongues. They also sing revival songs, calling to the spectators to start a new stage and accept the Lord during this upcoming new year. People follow and march alongside, singing and humming with them as they go. Many aren't even Christians, but they can't help but to follow because it's exciting to see all the people dancing and having a good time.

For such a big festivity, there is no food for the occasion. Afterwards, we go to our own homes to eat, and much of this has to do with *obeah*.

Very often, the *obeah* workers issue potions to persons seeking their help. These people will use the potions on others to "persuade" them to do what they want. Some people may call on the *obeah* worker to do a lot of devious things.

We never were involved with this, but we know it can happen. We know it works and we hear people talking. There was a girl at school who had a sore on her ankle that wouldn't heal. She went to the doctor and he said someone had *obeahed* her. The sore had worms in it even though she and her doctor cleaned it. They said that she was so brilliant in school so someone tried to keep her down by working *obeah* on her. Maybe it was someone with a grudge.

*What do I love about Jamaica? I love picking ripe grapefruits right from the trees and eating them.*

This is why many of the Jamaicans will not eat food outside of their home or at other people's homes unless they know them very well. They fear that something may be put in their food. I was raised like that by my grandmother. Mama told me I could never eat anywhere except home. It has become part of Jamaican tradition. It was very strange coming to America and eating in other people's houses because it was just not my custom to eat from other people. It's weird, but it's a part of Jamaica.

▫ Curried goat is a traditional Jamaican dish served with cooked green bananas or rice. In Jamaica goats are not wild animals or pets; they are raised just for eating. Goat meat isn't that common in this area yet, so deer or lamb can be substituted.

### CURRIED GOAT

| | |
|---|---|
| 2 | lbs. goat, deer, or lamb, cubed |
| 3 | Tbsp. Jamaican curry powder |
| 1 | tsp. salt |
| 1 | tsp. black pepper |
| 1 | tsp. garlic powder |
| 1 | large onion, chopped |
| 2 | cups water |
| 1/2 | cup butter |
| 1 | Jamaican hot pepper |
| 1 | large potato, diced |

In a large pot, combine meat, curry, salt, pepper, garlic, and onion; marinate for 1 hour. Add water, butter, and hot pepper. Bring to a boil over high heat. Reduce heat to medium; cook until meat is tender, adding water as needed. Add potatoes; cook to a gravy consistency.
*4 to 6 servings*

▫ Jamaicans serve fish with the heads on. My father once told me about a lady tourist who ordered fish at a restaurant. She started screaming that the fish was looking at her. Tourists!

### STEAMED FISH

| | |
|---|---|
| 1 | tsp. salt |
| 1 | tsp. black pepper |
| 1 | 2 lb. snapper or perch |
| 1 | medium onion, chopped |
| 1 | medium tomato, chopped |
| 1/2 | cup butter |

Sprinkle salt and pepper over fish. Place in skillet. Cover fish with onion and tomato. Cut butter and place on top of vegetables and fish. Cook, covered, over medium heat for 20 minutes or until done. Do not turn.
*4 servings*

▫ When a person buys property in Jamaica, there are always fruit trees on the land. Even if it is property in the city, there may be a least one grapefruit, mango, or plum tree. When I came to America I wondered why people bought property with no fruits trees. The land was all bare! My mom's place in the country had grapefruit and breadfruit trees. Breadfruit is like a cantaloupe but it is larger. Mama prepared grapefruits like this as a treat.

### MAMA'S GRAPEFRUIT TREATS

| | |
|---|---|
| 5 | grapefruits, meat only |
| 1/2 | cup condensed milk |

Combine ingredients; mix well. Serve in individual bowls.
*5 servings*

*Hanabitaikai* is the name of a fireworks festival that we have in Japan. It is similar to the Fourth of July in the United States because of the fireworks, but *Hanabitaikai* is a competition for who has the best fireworks display among different groups or clubs. The festival is always during the summer time. My city, Shizuoka, has its festival at the end of July. Cities throughout Japan celebrate it during different times of the summer. Shizuoka City lights off a big, colorful display of the fireworks, and thousands of people come to celebrate because it only happens once a year.

The festival lasts for about three hours. *Taiko tataki,* the beating of the traditional Japanese drums, comes first, then the fireworks are lit. After the fireworks, there is a night fair, lit by many lights, with many vendors of foods and games.

I like the *yo-yo* store. It's completely different from the yo-yo on a string. A Japanese *yo-yo* is a small balloon with a little bit of water in it. The balloon suspends on an elastic that is tied to the finger, and it bounces against the palm of the hand.

*Messing around with my best friend, Rica, is what I miss the most when I was in Japan.*

Another favorite vendor of mine is the man who shapes *zaiku,* a soft candy, into various shapes such as animals, Disney characters, and Japanese animated characters. I can order any shape I want, and he will make it right there.

One game I enjoy playing is *kingyo sukui,* or the goldfish scoop. Each participant is given a scooper made of paper and a bowl. The object is to scoop as many fish, from a large aquarium filled with goldfish, to the bowl before the paper scooper breaks. Of course at the fair, there are also many food vendors selling typical Japanese food: broiled squid; *yakisoba* noodles; *takoyaki,* an octopus dish; and *okonomiyaki,* a seafood pancake. Some vendors sell bananas dipped in chocolate, candy apples, and snow ice.

Many of the girls—old and young—wear their *yukata,* a light-weight kimono for summer, and their *geta,* Japanese wooden sandals, to the festival. The men may also wear the male version of the *yukata*. Most people are just dressed in western clothes. I enjoy wearing my kimono because the festival is a rare time to wear it. The shoes were not comfortable; I got blisters. Still, I like dressing in a kimono. The last time I wore my kimono was to my grandparents' house. They had traditional Japanese dancing called *bonodori.* I probably wore it only twice that year.

I love *Hanabitaikai* because it is a big holiday when the whole city comes together to watch the fireworks, eat food, and talk with friends. Sometimes people go with their families, sometimes with their friends. When I was little I had to go with my family. Now that I am older, I can walk around and enjoy myself with just my friends.

▢ My father needs a license to cook *fugu,* a blowfish delicacy, because eating an improperly cooked blowfish is very dangerous. The fish has a strong poison in it. If *fugu* is not cooked properly, the person eating it will die. I have read in the newspapers about people who had died. Even with this reputation, the Japanese still eat *fugu* because it is a delicacy and is delicious.

You don't have to worry about becoming poisoned with *okinomiyaki;* I make it myself. We usually have the pancakes with a slightly sweet *okinomiyaki* sauce on top. This sauce and *bonito,* powdered fish, can be found in Asian stores.

## OKINOMIYAKI
### Seafood pancakes

| | |
|---|---|
| ¹/₄ | cup dried bonito* |
| ¹/₄ | cup sweet sake |
| 1 | cup hot water |
| ¹/₄ | cup soy sauce |
| | dash of sugar |
| 1 | yam, peeled and grated |
| 2 | cups flour |
| 4 | eggs |
| ¹/₄ | cabbage, sliced |
| 4 | green onions, sliced |
| | salt and pepper to taste |
| ¹/₄ | lb. pork, thinly sliced |
| | oil for frying |

Combine bonito, sake, water, soy sauce, and sugar; mix well. Add remaining ingredients except pork; mix well. Heat about 1 teaspoon oil for each pancake over medium-high heat. Place 3 to 5 tablespoons of mixture into pan, forming a pancake. Add pork on top. Cook both sides until golden or pork is done.
*4 to 6 servings*

▢ *Tempura* is very typical in Japan. My father cooks it often using *aji,* a small horse mackerel with soft bones. The batter is very easy to prepare, and so many foods such as onions, sweet potatoes, fish, or green peppers can be dipped into it. *Tempura* is supposed to be crunchy. Shrimp *tempura* is my favorite.

## SHRIMP TEMPURA
### Fried Shrimp

| | |
|---|---|
| 2 | eggs |
| 1¹/₂ | cups water |
| 2 | cups flour, sifted |
| | salt and pepper to taste |
| | oil for frying |
| 1-2 | lbs. shrimp |

Combine eggs, water, and flour; mix well, adding salt and pepper. Adjust water or flour until batter has a pancake batter consistency.

Heat oil over medium-high heat. Holding shrimp by the tail, dip in tempura and carefully place in oil. Cook until lightly golden. Serve with okinomiyaki sauce, soy sauce, or freshly squeezed lemon juice.
*4 to 6 servings*

My parents taught me and my brothers and sisters to do everything in a respectable way. We had to be well-behaved, and we were taught to respect our parents, elders, and people of higher positions in society.

Respect is shown to the Japanese by bowing. People have knowledge of their positions in the family and in society, and they bow accordingly. Even an older person may bow to a younger person who is in a higher position in society. If a person is really respected, people bow way down. If the person is just a friend, just a nod is done. We only bow really low to our parents during special occasions like New Year's.

When we saw our father in the morning, we would say "good morning" and bow down, just a slight bow. We also had a great deal of respect for my eldest sister because she helped bring up my brothers, sisters, and me. My eldest sister was like a mother to me.

As a sign of respect for our father, we would never eat before he ate. Sitting on our knees, we would wait for him. After he sat and started to eat, then we could begin. He had to pick up his chopsticks first, and before we began to eat, we would say "*Itadaki mas,*" which is a sign of respect for the person who had made the food for us. It is not a prayer, and it is not said by all of us together. *Itadaki mas* is said out of respect.

*To show our closeness, my sister wanted to give me a gift that was very personal. She wove material and made this kimono for me.*

Japanese show respect even with their food. Plates and rice bowls are small. Japanese plates are about the size of salad plates in America. We only put a little rice at a time in our bowls. If we put in too much rice, it will become cold or be wasted. But if we put in a little, we can finish quickly, then have more hot rice. Rice and soup are in different bowls. We never mix our food together.

We have certain foods that are served on certain plates. For example, sushi has to be served on a rectangular or round, flat plate. This is the rule, the way to respect sushi and whoever started it.

The way I was brought up is incorporated into my life today. Even now, when I meet new people or friends, I respect the ways I associate with them. If I have a friend whom I do not respect or who does not respect me, we cannot have a good relationship. It is not always like that, but it is most of the time. The new generation may show respect in different ways, but this is the way I grew up.

◻ China introduced tofu to Japan about 2,000 years ago. The Japanese eat tofu almost every day. We have it in soup, stir-fry, salads, or just by itself.

For breakfast we may have tofu soup with miso, boiled rice, just one or two of a variety of sweet pickles, and green tea. We don't have heavy breakfasts.

### MISO JIRU
### Tofu Soup with Miso

| | |
|---|---|
| 2 | cups water |
| 1 | heaping Tbsp. miso * |
| 1 | chicken or beef bouillon cube |
| 1/2 | cup tofu, cut into 1/2-inch squares |
| | pinch of chopped green onion |

Bring water to a boil over high heat. Add miso, bouillon, and tofu; return to a boil. Add green onion; remove from heat.
*2 servings*

◻ Everything we eat is pre-cut. We don't need to use a knife and fork. We use only chopsticks, therefore the food has to be cut small.

For this salad I cut the tofu with chopsticks so the sauce sticks to the rough surfaces. The firmness of the tofu is your preference. We have *hiya ya ko* as a light lunch.

### HIYA YA KO
### Tofu Salad

| | |
|---|---|
| 1 | box medium tofu |
| | chopped ginger |
| | pinch of shredded bonito * |
| | soy sauce |
| | finely chopped green onions |

Cut tofu by running chopsticks in opposite directions through the tofu. Sprinkle remaining ingredients to taste.
*2 servings*

◻ *Yaki* means "to grill." Beef teriyaki tastes better grilled than cooked in a pan. This marinade also can be used with chicken.

### NIKU TERIYAKI
### Marinated Beef

| | |
|---|---|
| 2 | lbs. sirloin, thinly sliced |
| 1 | cup soy sauce |
| 1/2 | cup wine or sake |
| 1/4 | cup sugar |
| 1 | tsp. chopped garlic |
| 1 | tsp. chopped ginger |
| 1 | Tbsp. oil |
| 3 | drops sesame oil |

Combine all ingredients; mix well. Marinate for 4 to 10 hours. Cook over grill to desired doneness.
*6 to 8 servings*

**Certain foods are forever** intertwined with important holidays and celebrations in Korean culture. One of the biggest Korean holidays is *Chusôk,* which is on August 15 on the lunar calendar. Like Thanksgiving in America, it is a day for giving thanks to family and friends. But more importantly, it is a day for all Koreans to worship their ancestors. They visit their ancestors' graves and arrange a table filled with the new crops of food such as rice, apples, pears, chestnuts, persimmons; *jujube,* a Korean fruit; and *songpyôn,* a rice cake filled with the sweet paste of sesame seed, bean, or chestnuts. The rice cakes are the main celebratory food of *Chusôk.*

Koreans also worship their ancestors on New Year's Day by preparing traditional food and performing ceremonial bows to the deceased and the elders of the families. Ceremonial bows are also done during weddings and *hangap,* a party for a person who becomes sixty-one years old. The main dish on New Year's Day is *tûkguk. Tûkguk* is a soup dish made with rice cakes which look like overgrown string cheese. The rice cakes are sliced and cooked in beef broth. Koreans are considered to be officially one year older after having this soup.

During *peabeck,* the ceremony when a bride becomes part of the groom's family, traditional food, laid on a table before the groom's parents, is part of the ceremony. First, the bride and groom bow in front of his parents to introduce the bride to the family. This is the first formal bow to the groom's family. The parents say a few good words like "Be happy together" or "Love each other forever," then

*Peabeck is a traditional wedding ceremony for Koreans. My husband is pouring rice wine which we will have as a toast to our marriage.*

they toss chestnuts or *jujube* to the couple. The chestnuts and *jujube* are tossed as a hope that the couple will have many children. The chestnuts represent having boys; the *jujube* represent having girls.

Living in America, my family has become more Americanized. The most important aspect of Korean culture that I want my children to learn is respect for elders. During holidays such as *Chusôk*, New Year's, *hangap*, and *peabeck*, Koreans show respect to their elders. I don't expect my children to do the ceremonial bows, but I hope they will learn the spirit behind the respect.

□ The main dishes served for almost every Korean meal are rice, some type of soup, and, of course, *kimchee*, pickled cabbage. Rice is always served because Koreans live on rice. There are many side dishes that cover almost all types of food. This is true of the soup that is made for the meal. There are fish soups, vegetable soups, meat and poultry soups, and combinations thereof.

All of the food is prepared with our own version of seasonings and spices. Hot pepper, soy sauce, bean paste, hot bean paste, sesame seeds, several types of fish sauces, ginger, garlic—all are typical in Korean cooking.

## KIMCHEE
### Pickled Cabbage

| | |
|---|---|
| 5 | cups salt |
| 1¹/₂ | cups water |
| 5 | napa cabbage, cut into 5-inch pieces |
| 3 | Tbsp. sweet rice powder |
| 2 | cups boiling water |
| 6 | whole heads of garlic |
| 1 | small ginger root |
| 2 | Tbsp. sugar |
| 2-3 | cups ground hot red pepper |
| 2 | radishes, thinly sliced |
| 2-3 | bunch green onions, thinly sliced |
| 1 | bunch watercress, sliced 2 to 3 inches |
| 1¹/₂ | cups oysters (optional) |
| 1¹/₂ | cups shrimp fish sauce |

Combine 2¹/₂ cups salt and water. Submerge cabbage in salted water; sprinkle remaining salt over cabbage. Soak for about 10 hours. Wash 3 to 4 times. Drain and set aside.

Mix rice powder in boiling water; set aside to cool.

Chop garlic and ginger in a blender. Combine garlic and ginger mixture and rice powder mixture. Add sugar, hot pepper, and ¹/₈ cup salt; mix well. Add radishes, green onions, and watercress; mix well. Stir in oysters (optional) and fish sauce to make a seasoning sauce. Adjust seasonings to taste.

Spread seasoning sauce between cabbage leaves. Place in large jars with tight lids. Store at room temperature for 2 to 3 days until ready to eat.
*4 to 5 gallons*

□ *Bulgogi* is Korean-style marinated meat. It can be fried on the stove but is best when grilled. If spare ribs are used then the dish is called *galbi bulgogi*.

## BULGOGI
### Korean-Style Marinated Meat

| | |
|---|---|
| 1 | medium onion |
| 6-8 | garlic cloves |
| 1 | cup soy sauce |
| 1 | cup water |
| ²/₃ | cup sesame oil |
| 1 | cup sugar |
| ¹/₂ | bunch green onion |
| | black pepper to taste |
| | sesame seed to taste |
| 5 | lbs. meat, thinly sliced or ribs |

Chop onion and garlic in a blender. In a large bowl, combine all ingredients except meat. Place meat in marinade; mix well. Marinate for at least 4 hours before cooking. If using spare ribs, clean and drain ribs before marinating. Increase marinating time to about 10 hours.
*12 to 14 servings*

It is not unusual for many members in a Korean family to live under one roof. A long time ago, my grandmother, grandfather, uncle, mother and father, my two sisters, two brothers, and I lived in one house.

Mom was the one who always took care of all the meals. She woke up very early every morning to prepare meals for everyone. Every meal always had rice and soup bowls for each person, the rice bowl being smaller than the soup bowl. The table was set with a spoon and a pair of chopsticks and different small dishes that everyone shared. There were at least six small dishes; some may be Korean pickled cabbage called *kimchee*, bean sprouts, spinach, tofu, and some kind of meat or fish dish. If we had company, a few more small dishes would be added.

Typically, each person used the spoon for the soup or rice, but used the chopsticks to pick food from the small dishes in the center and bring it to the rice bowl or to the mouth. There was not a separate plate to place your selections from the small dishes, only the rice bowl.

*When I lived in Japan, my girlfriends and I (left) always went to each other's homes to share a meal.*

Back then when we had meals, my family did not eat on a typical dining room table with chairs like here in America. We had short-legged tables called *soung* which could be either round or square and we sat on the floor. We always ate together although we had different tables. My grandfather had his own small round *soung*; my father and uncle shared a square one; and there was a big, round *soung* for my grandmother, mother, and all the children.

Although there were many of us living together, we did not have problems. We showed great respect for each other, especially my grandfather, even when we had our meals.

❑ *Mandu* are similar to egg rolls, but they are smaller and usually shaped in semi-circles or triangles. I usually make many at one time and freeze the rest. Lightly fry the *mandu* before freezing.

### MANDU
### Korean Dumplings

| | |
|---|---|
| 1 | small cabbage, chopped |
| 2-3 | carrots, chopped |
| 1/4 | lb. bean sprouts, cooked and drained |
| 1 | onion, chopped |
| 2 | garlic cloves, chopped |
| 1 | small package potato noodles* |
| 1 | lb. ground beef |
| 2 | eggs |
| | salt and pepper to taste |
| 1 | package wonton skins |
| | oil for frying |

Cook each type of vegetable separately in a small amount of oil over high heat; mix vegetables together. Drain excess juice.

In a large bowl, combine vegetables, noodles, ground beef, eggs, salt and pepper; mix well by hand. Place 1 tablespoon of mixture into each skin. Fold over, sealing edges with a small amount of water. Deep-fry in oil over medium-high heat until golden.
*8 to 10 servings*

❑ One way of showing respect to the elders is through the ceremonial bows for the deceased, done every Korean New Year. The women do all the cooking, and they set up a large beautiful table filled with special foods. Early in the morning, only the men form a line and bow once for each parent who passed away up to the great-great-grandmother and great-great-grandfather.

*Shigumchi* is a spinach salad. It is always found on the great table set on the Korean New Year.

### SHIGUMCHI
### Korean Spinach Salad

| | |
|---|---|
| 1 | bunch young spinach |
| 1 | tsp. sesame seed |
| 1 | tsp. sesame oil |
| 1 | large garlic clove, chopped |
| | msg to taste |
| | salt to taste |

Blanch spinach. Drain; rinse in cold water. Drain again, squeezing out excess water while forming into a ball. Slice spinach ball twice to make smaller pieces.

Combine spinach and remaining ingredients in a bowl; mix well. Serve as a side dish.
*4 servings*

**Korean parents** are devoted to their children. They spend lots of time with their children and help them get a good education. Parents want their children to have better jobs and better lives in the future than they did. Even though a person's work is digging in someone's yard, that person will try to put his kids through college so they don't have to make a living the same way.

Parents make sure their children graduate from a university or at least from a community college. Of course, high school is basic; almost everyone graduates. There is a very low percentage of high school dropouts. Parents invest a lot of money in the eldest son's education because he is expected to take care of the parents when they retire. They want him to get a good job and make good money so they can be comfortable when they retire. Nursing homes are very unpopular.

Koreans believe in owning their houses and cars. Not too many places have layaway, and many people don't have credit cards. If a person does not have money to buy—say a refrigerator or car—with cash, he doesn't buy. "If you can't afford it, you shouldn't have it," that's what we believe.

Because of this belief, many parents will help their children establish themselves after they marry. Newlyweds may live with their parents until they save up money to move out on their own or the parents will help by taking care of some of the costs of living. Usually the bride's parents provide furniture, and the groom's parents may lease an apartment for a year or until the newlyweds make enough money to pay their own lease. This way the couple can live comfortably without worrying about rent. The parents will give the couple their wings, and that's about it.

Another way Koreans show care and love for their children is by spending a great deal of time together as families. When I was little, I remember going as a family to the temple for Buddhafest, the celebration of Buddha's birthday. The celebration is the same concept as a church picnic; it is a feast with varieties of food. Families bring steamed, fried, or salted fish, vegetables, and many side dishes. Poultry and meat are not allowed. Everyone shares food. The food never runs out and lasts throughout the night. All the people of the temple have a good time celebrating with their families.

Han bok *is the traditional Korean clothing. It is worn for holidays, parties, graduations, or any special occasion. Sometimes colors tell of the occasion. For example, before a honeymoon, the bride will change into a pink* han bok. *People will know that she just got married. My friends and I (far left) are wearing our* han bok *for our college graduation reception.*

My family even spent time together going to the market. Every other day, Ommony, my mother, would take all four of us with her to go shopping. Often during the winter when the weather was too cold to do anything else, we would make *kimchee*, Korean pickled cabbage or radishes, and *mandu*, small egg rolls together. I remember having flour all over our faces and hands. We had fun laughing and throwing flour at each other. It was a family affair; my dad even pitched in.

My older sister, Myong, still lives very close to Ommony in Korea. She'll call me once in a while and say that she just had lunch or made *kimchee* with Ommony. I get a little jealous. I guess I'm jealous because I miss sharing Korean traditions and being close to my family.

◻ When Koreans drink coffee or tea, they must be very quiet, but when they eat *chap chae* or any kind of noodles, they make as much noise as they can. The noise is a compliment to the host or hostess; it means the food is very delicious, and the diners are enjoying it.

## CHAP CHAE
### Mixed Vegetables with Noodles

| | |
|---|---|
| 1 | 13.5 oz. package oriental starch noodles* |
| 1 | bunch spinach, cut into thirds |
| 8 | carrots, julienned |
| 6 | shiitake mushrooms, quartered |
| 1 | yellow pepper, sliced (optional) |
| 1 | green pepper, sliced (optional) |
| 1 | lb. beef, thinly sliced |
| | salt and pepper to taste |
| 1/2 | tsp. chopped garlic |
| 1/2 | cup soy sauce |
| 1/4 | cup sesame oil |
| | sesame seeds |
| | oil |

Soak noodles in warm water for 10 to 15 minutes. Bring to a boil; cook for 5 to 10 minutes. Drain; run cool water over noodles. Cut into 5-inch lengths; set aside.

Blanch spinach; squeeze out excess water. Set aside.

Cook each type of vegetable separately in oil over medium-high heat; set aside.

Cook beef over medium-high heat, adding salt, pepper, and garlic. Stir in vegetables one kind at a time. Add a small amount of noodles at a time; mix well. Add soy sauce and sesame oil; mix well. Sprinkle with sesame seeds before serving.
*6 to 8 servings*

◻ Use any leftover *chap chae* for *mandu,* Korean dumplings or egg rolls. I add a box of firm tofu and bokchoy or *kimchee,* Korean pickled cabbage, to the *chap chae,* then I finely chop the mixture. The *mandu* [see page 117] can be fried, steamed, or put into soup.

Ommony used to make her own egg roll wrappers for *mandu.* During the winter when it was too cold to go outside, we would stay inside and make the little egg rolls. Ommony would give me, my sister, and brothers jar tops and we would cut out the wrappers one by one. We were little so, of course, we took forever to make just one. The filling was always oozing out of ours! It was a lot of work, but we had fun. Now it's cheaper just to go to the market and buy wrappers, so Ommony stopped making her own wrappers.

We would make at least 100 to 200 little egg rolls. Ommony put them in the freezer. Instead of having cookies and milk as a snack, we had apples, bananas, or *mandu.* Every time we came home from school, Ommony had something waiting for us. *Kanjang* is a dipping sauce for the *mandu.*

## KANJANG
### Spicy Egg Roll Sauce

| | |
|---|---|
| 1/2 | cup soy sauce |
| 1/4 | cup sesame oil |
| 1 | tsp. hot pepper |
| 1 | Tbsp. chopped green onion |
| | toasted sesame seeds |

Combine soy sauce, oil, hot pepper, and onion; mix well. Sprinkle with sesame seeds. Keep in refrigerator.
*3/4 cup*

**Traditionally, Koreans** have a big celebration called *hangap* for a person who turns sixty-one years old. A long time ago people didn't live as long as they do now, and families celebrated when a member became sixty-one years old to show respect. It is a big affair for family and friends and a party is given, usually by the children.

When my mother had her *hangap,* I returned to Korea for the party and brought my husband and two children. My brother and I had been talking about this event for a couple of months earlier. He arranged the food, place, and invitations. About 150 people who know my parents were invited. Years ago, friends just came to the honored person's house. Now there are too many people, so a place must be rented and a buffet-style dinner of typical Korean dishes is arranged.

Because my family is Catholic, a mass was held first at the Catholic church. Then the ceremony moved to the place that was rented. A spokesperson led the affair. He told stories of my mom and her family to the guests: when and where she was born, how many children and grandchildren she has, and the history of her life.

During part of the ceremony, the grandchildren handed her a bouquet of flowers, and all of her children and relatives lined up to bow before my mom. We lined up and bowed three times, kneeling with our head very close to the floor. Bowing is a sign of respect.

Afterwards, my family cut a cake with my mom. She held the knife, and the whole family surrounded and touched her while she cut it. My parents were given Korean rice wine to drink. After drinking everyone took part of the food on the buffet. Some people may give gifts, and often they will give money.

*It used to be rare for people to live up to seventy or eighty years old. Many Koreans had big parties for people who made it to sixty-one years old. Although people live much longer, many still have the traditional* hangap *for their sixty-one-year-old family member. My family and I (left) are celebrating my mother's (to my right)* hangap.

Now many people live longer than they used to, and the parties have been moved to when a person turns seventy or eighty years old. But many children will still have the *hangap* party for their parents, like we did for our mother.

◻ In August and September when there is a lot of sun, many Koreans buy fresh, hot red peppers at the market to dry. They lay out mats and spread the red peppers on the road, on the sidewalk in front of their houses, or on top of their houses.

When the peppers are dry and crispy, they are brought to a shop to be ground into powder; it is much cheaper to do this than to buy the red peppers already ground. Koreans use red pepper in a pickled cabbage called *kimchee*, hot pepper paste, sauces, or any dish to add spiciness.

## TAK JJIM
### Spicy Simmered Chicken

| | |
|---|---|
| 1 | whole chicken, cut into pieces |
| 1 | medium onion, chopped |
| 1 | green onion, chopped |
| 2-3 | garlic cloves, chopped |
| 2-3 | Tbsp. sugar |
| 2 | Tbsp. soy sauce |
| 1 | Tbsp. sesame oil |
| 1 | Tbsp. red pepper |
| 1 | tsp. salt |
| $1/2$ | tsp. black pepper |
| 2 | carrots, sliced |
| 2 | potatoes, cubed |

Combine all ingredients except carrots and potatoes; marinate in refrigerator for 2 to 3 hours. Cook over high heat until boiling; reduce heat to medium. Cook until chicken is tender, stirring occasionally. Add carrots and potatoes; cook until vegetables are done.
*6 to 8 servings*

◻ Koreans usually have a variety of *namuls*, or cooked salads, with their meals. Some may be lightly cooked like *shigumchi namul,* a spinach salad, and *sukju namul,* a bean sprout salad.

## SUKJU NAMUL
### Bean Sprout Salad

| | |
|---|---|
| $1^1/2$ | lbs. bean sprouts |
| 2 | green onions, chopped |
| 1 | garlic clove, chopped |
| 1 | tsp. sesame oil |
| $1/2$ | tsp. soy sauce |
| $1/4$ | tsp. red pepper |
| $1/4$ | tsp. salt |
| $1/8$ | tsp. black pepper |
| 1 | tsp. toasted sesame seeds |

Cook bean sprouts in boiling water for about 2 minutes. Sprouts should still be slightly crisp; drain. Add remaining ingredients; mix well.
*4 servings*

Every morning, every afternoon, and every evening, we ate rice. In Laos my family was big, eight including my mom and dad, so it was most important to plant and have rice as food for everybody. We planted the rice in the spring and harvested it in the fall.

First, my mom and dad plowed the land using a buffalo or machine, then we planted the rice seeds. We woke up early in the morning around six o'clock when the rooster crowed—he was a clock for us—to plant the rice. We had to work before we went to school at eight o'clock and before it got too hot. When it was time to harvest, the rice was cut with a knife and bundled together. The bundles were gathered in a big pile in the field then beaten until the rice fell out. The rice is green in the fields, but turns brown or yellow when ready to harvest. A machine removed the brown or yellow husks, then the fresh rice was ready to eat. Fresh rice is very soft, and it smells and tastes so good.

*We had beautiful land in Laos with rice fields, fruit trees, a pond, and many animals. I miss all the fresh fruit that came off our land. While we worked, we also played; we even swam in the rice fields when the water was deep.*

My parents put the rice in a large storage area almost the size of a two-car garage. The rice must last all year until the next harvest. Everyone around us farmed and produced their own rice except the city people, those who didn't have farms, and the poor people. The people who came from the city or didn't have farms came to buy rice from us. The poor people helped on the farm so they could also have some rice.

My family had a very big plot of land. We had everything: dogs, buffalos, pigs, chickens, ducks. We had a pond where we raised fish and lilies. Sometimes my mom and dad would plant rice in the pond. These plants grew very high because they had a lot of water.

The land around us was very green with so many coconut, banana, and mango trees. There were three nut trees called *mabuk* trees. There were three sisters in my family and three *mabuk* trees, so we each picked one tree to call our own. The biggest and tallest one was my older sister's; the middle-sized one was my middle sister's; and mine was the smallest. It was the prettiest one.

I was very young when we lived in Laos. I remember I liked having fun with my brothers and sisters in the rice fields. We enjoyed whatever work we had to do; it was part of our play. We'd pour water on each other when we had to carry water for the fields in the bamboo water baskets. We swam and rode the canoe in the pond. Sometimes my father would let the water into the field from the pond, and we would swim in the rice fields. I rode the buffalo only one time because I fell down and he almost stepped on me. The buffalo is really used just for plowing the fields, not playing. As a child I had a lot of fun in Laos.

My mom misses Laos so much. She asked my cousin to send her different seeds of rice so she could grow rice here. She tried very hard to grow the rice. She did everything she had done in Laos, but the rice wouldn't come up—only one seed came up. The temperature, the soil, and the seasons are so different here that the rice seeds just wouldn't grow. I guess she misses the land and rice. The land was beautiful. Even I wish I could go back and live there.

# Chansamone Thammavongsa

□ *Gang nor mi* is my mother's favorite food. Every time she eats this bamboo soup, it reminds her of Laos. *Gang nor mi* is very popular in Laos with the old folks.

Sometimes when the rice fields are flooded and the rice is destroyed, the people in Laos will eat bamboo shoots instead of rice.

### GANG NOR MI
### Bamboo Soup

| | |
|---|---|
| 3 | cups water |
| | fish, duck, or any meat to taste |
| 1 | large can bamboo shoots |
| 1 | 12.85 oz. can yanang leaves extract* |
| 1 | cup sliced mushrooms |
| 1 | tsp. salt |
| 1 | Tbsp. fish sauce |
| 1 | tsp. sugar (optional) |
| | green or red chili to taste |

Bring water to a boil. Add meat; cook over medium-high heat until almost done. Add remaining ingredients; cook for 10 to 15 minutes.
*3 to 5 servings*

□ *Kwa me* is a typical Laotian noodle dish. Every Laotian person knows how to make it. It's often brought to parties.

### KWA ME
### Fried Noodles

| | |
|---|---|
| 3 | garlic cloves, chopped |
| 1/4 | cup oil |
| 2 | Tbsp. sugar |
| 1 | large package rice or flour noodles, soaked |
| 1/4 | cup oyster sauce |
| 1 | Tbsp. fish sauce |
| 1 | cup raw bean sprouts (optional) |
| 1/4 | cup chopped onions (optional) |
| | any sliced meat (optional) |

Cook garlic in oil over medium-high heat. Add sugar; cook until sugar turns yellow. Add noodles. Stir in oyster sauce and fish sauce; cook until noodles are tender and sauce is mixed well. Add sprouts and onions, if desired, after cooking.

If using meat, add meat after sugar has turned yellow. Stir in oyster sauce and fish sauce with meat first, then add noodles.
*4 to 6 servings*

It is our custom in Laos to give *pa kwan* as a blessing party for many occasions. *Pa kwan* can be for a welcome home, going away, christening, New Year's, or wedding. All the neighbors, friends, and relatives help with the gathering. The women cook while the men set up the place either in the house or outside.

In the morning of the *pa kwan*, an elderly woman or women set up an ornament, also called a *pa kwan,* on a mat on the floor. The ornament is the centerpiece of the celebration. A silver tray serves as the bottom. A silver bowl, decorated with sticky rice inside, is placed on the tray. Then a cone and "arms" made from rolled banana leaves are put in the bowl. Three main arms are made for a good luck, like for going away; seven main arms are made for a wedding.

Many orange and yellow flowers or marigolds are slid into the banana leaves so the ornament looks like a large flower arrangement. Orange, yellow, pink, and white flowers are really good luck. Never use red flowers because they are bad luck.

Many strands of white yarn, used as part of the blessing, are cut and tied to sticks in the *pa kwan*. A candle is put in the middle on the top. Two platters are set next to the *pa kwan*: one with oranges, bananas, and rice cakes as an offering; the other with a boiled chicken and two brown eggs. The eggs are held by the host and hostess during the blessing. Sticky rice in a special bamboo holder called *thip kawe* is also placed next to the centerpiece.

Everyone comes in and takes a seat on the mat. The host family sits in front of the *pa kwan*, and the Buddha, who does the *taede,* or chanting, faces the host family. The rest of the people sit behind the host and hostess. Everyone holds one of the white yarns, still attached to the centerpiece, with their hands pressed together while the Buddha begins to chant. The chants are like a prayer, and there are different ones depending on the occasion.

*For me and my husband, Laos was like our own little world where we could go about our farming and raising chickens while living a simple and happy life.*

After the Buddha finishes the chants, the oldest to the youngest person takes a piece of yarn. The honored person holds one of the eggs and someone, like a grandmother, holds the person's arm up to show a connection. The grandmother ties her piece of yarn around the person's arm, then the next person ties another piece and says good luck—all the way to the youngest child. That person will have a whole lot of strings going up both arms.

The Buddha blesses the family again, then he eats. After the Buddha eats, the father, down to the youngest person, takes a bit of food. It is similar to communion. Afterwards, the rest of the food that everyone helped cook is eaten: *laup*, marinated beef; *nam miye*, bamboo soup; *kawe la song*, a rice and coconut dessert; and we must always have rice.

I had a *pa kwan* in Laos, given by my mother, and one in the Philippines, where my family lived for six months before coming to the States. Instead of giving gifts, some people put money on the yarns tied around our arms. My family and friends did the *pa kwan* for us because they were excited and happy for us. Laotian people are usually happy

*Family and friends gather around a* pa kwan *for my husband's welcome home party.*

all the time even if their family or friends are going away. They are especially happy if family or friends come back home or are getting married, so a *pa kwan* is always given.

# Vanthong Inthavongdy

❑ In Laos when a couple marries, the husband lives with the family of the wife. The houses there are really big. My custom is also that the younger sister cannot marry before the older one. If the younger one marries, the older one will have bad luck. If the younger one marries first *and* has children, the older one will never get married.

When the first grandchild is born, the grandparents give a buffalo and her calf to the parents as the baby's gift. The buffalo will have a baby every year, so the gift represents having more babies. Gold bracelets, anklets with a little bells for one to hear the baby walking, charms, and money may be part of the presents. A buffalo is also given to a family who moves into a new house.

Cows are expensive in Laos; buffalos are more common. Here cows are more common, so for this recipe, use beef.

### SEEN LAUT
#### Laotian Beef Jerky

| | |
|---|---|
| 5 | lbs. lean beef, thinly sliced |
| 1 | whole garlic head, crushed |
| 1 | 2-inch piece ginger, grated |
| 2 | Tbsp. salt |
| 3 | Tbsp. sugar |

Combine all ingredients; marinate meat overnight. Dehydrate in a dehydrator or in the very hot sun until almost dry, but not stiff. Cook dry meat in oil over medium-high heat or bake until crisp on the outside. Freeze uncooked meat.

❑ My parents go net fishing in the Rappahannock River. They'll leave after work and stay overnight. They fish all day, all night...forever and ever. One time my mom wouldn't even take me somewhere that I needed to go. She said, "No, I have to go fishing." It's like she's scared the fish will all be gone. She dries the fish to keep for a long time, but *lot na pah* is a recipe for fresh catfish.

—Lucky Inthavongdy

### LOT NA PAH
#### Catfish with Vegetables

| | |
|---|---|
| 1 | 3 to 4 lb. catfish, decapitated, skin on, and cut into 2 to 3 pieces |
| | salt and pepper to taste |
| 3 | garlic cloves, chopped |
| 1 | large onion, sliced |
| 1 | Tbsp. oil |
| 1/2 | head broccoli or cauliflower |
| 2 | Tbsp. sugar |
| | soy sauce |
| | fish sauce |
| 1 | Tbsp. water |
| 2 | green peppers, sliced |
| | jalapenos to taste, sliced |

Sprinkle salt and pepper over catfish; set aside for 30 minutes. Cook in oil over medium heat or bake at 325° until done.

Cook garlic and onions in 1 tablespoon oil over medium heat. Add broccoli. Sprinkle sugar, soy sauce, fish sauce, and water over broccoli; cook until almost done, stirring often. Add green peppers and jalapenos; cook for about 5 minutes. Place fish on a platter and spread vegetables on top. Serve with sticky rice.
*4 to 6 servings*

**My brothers and sisters** are very attached to me. They are like my children. My mother was sick all the time. She had children, but she couldn't raise them. I was only seven years old when my father pulled me out of school to help my mom. I stayed home and helped my mother with whatever she had to do.

I cooked for the family, cleaned the house, took care of company, and helped my mother wash clothes. When we did laundry, we washed by hand. She had one big basin to wash; I had one to rinse, then I would hang the clothes on the line. It was a lot of work.

Once I wanted to go with my grandmother into town to visit her family. Before my mom and I started washing clothes, my mom said, "You can leave me. Go now." So I left my mom to wash the clothes by herself, and I ran bare-foot after my grandmother, crying until she stopped. This was about forty years ago when people walked from town to town. My grandmother picked me up and carried me on her shoulders and we went to see her family. I knew I would have a good time with my grandmother.

When we returned after a week, I didn't recognize my mom; she was in bad shape. I didn't know that my mom was still not feeling well when I left, because I was so young. After that time, I stayed with her until her last breath.

In our Lebanese culture, we did not put our family in nursing homes. I didn't know what a nursing home was until I came to this country. I look at it that my mother raised us until she got sick; my father was working all day; and my grandmother was old, so it was up

*When my husband came to Lebanon, my father wanted me to get married. I was already thirty-two years old. He said, "Now is your time to relax. I want you to be married. Go and have a good time." So I married Mike and took a very long vacation.*

to me and my brother to help the family. My brother and I, because we were the oldest, took care of the problems of the family. My brother did not finish school because he had to work to help my father make money to support all of us. As the oldest sister, I took care of everything else, from my father to my brothers and sisters. I was the boss. I held everything in my hands.

I woke up every morning at five-thirty to make coffee for my father before he left for work. I would bring it to the balcony and wait for him to get up. Every morning I had coffee on the balcony with my father; I never skipped a day until I married. I packed his lunch, ironed his shirt, and took care of the kids so they could go to school and have their education.

I stuck with my mother until the day she died; I loved her. My brothers and sisters are very thankful and have a lot of respect for me because I raised them up. They ask me questions just like I am their mom. They are in Lebanon and I am here, but even if they want to break a toothpick, they'll call and ask! I am happy that I took care of my mom, and I know that my family appreciates what I did. They are all very special to me.

❑  My father did the grocery shopping in Beirut because he worked in the city.  Before he left for work, I would ask him what he wanted for dinner.  He would bring the groceries home.  He did this every day, even when my mother was not sick.

Stuffed cabbage, stuffed squash, *kebbi*, shish kebab, chicken with rice—we always had something different.  I learned how to cook from watching and helping my mom.  When I saw her cooking, I would stick my nose in it, "Let me do it.  Please let me do it."

*Kebbi* is a Lebanese meat pie.  Serve it with *tabouleh, fatoosh,* or pickled wild cucumbers which can be found in Middle Eastern or Mediterranean food stores.

## KEBBI
### Lebanese Meat Pie with Crushed Wheat

$3^1/_2$  lbs. lean ground beef
2   cups crushed wheat
2   large onions, chopped
1   tsp. salt
$^1/_4$  tsp. pepper
$^1/_4$  tsp. cinnamon
$^1/_2$  tsp. cumin
$^1/_4$  cup butter
$^1/_2$  cup pine nuts or walnuts, chopped
$^1/_2$  cup oil

Combine 3 pounds beef, wheat, 1 chopped onion, salt, pepper, cinnamon, and cumin.  Mix well in a food processor; set aside.

Cook remaining chopped onion in butter over medium heat.  Add remaining $^1/_2$ pound beef; season with salt, pepper, and cinnamon to taste.  Stir in nuts when ground beef is done.

Divide uncooked beef mixture into 2 parts.  Spread 1 part in a sprayed baking pan.  Spread cooked beef and nut mixture.  Top with remaining uncooked beef mixture.  Cut into 3-inch diamonds; drizzle oil on top.  Bake at 325° for 45 minutes or until brown.
*6 servings*

❑  My mother was placed in the hospital the night before my brother's wedding ceremony.  My father came to me and asked, "What are we going to do?"  So my father and I went to the hospital and asked my mother's doctor if she could come to her son's wedding.  The doctor said we could take her, but we had to bring her in the hospital bed.  We got a big van and brought my mother to the wedding in the bed.  She was right there at the wedding!

I have always been strong in my life.  Anything I want to do, I do it.  I took care of my siblings as if they were my own children.  I wanted my mother to be at her son's wedding and she was.  This is how much I loved her.

My mom taught me at a very young age how to cook for the family.  She taught me how to prepare *fatoosh*, a salad like *tabouleh*, but *fatoosh* has bread.

## FATOOSH
### Bread Salad

1   bunch parsley, chopped
3-4  tomatoes, chopped
3-4  cucumbers, quartered lengthwise and sliced
7   radishes, chopped
1   green pepper, chopped
    juice of 2 lemons
$^1/_2$  cup olive oil
2   pitas, toasted and crumbled
$^1/_2$  bunch mint leaves, chopped
2   spring onions, sliced
1   Tbsp. sumac*

In a large bowl, combine all ingredients; mix well.
*6 to 8 servings*

**When I lived in Lebanon**, never a day passed when I did not see my sister and my mother. We saw each other all the time. If I went out, I knew that when I came home, they would be there. My sister would come from school and would be sitting with my mother.

Most Lebanese women did not work outside of the home. They stayed home to take care of the children and the house. Children always knew that someone would be home waiting for them. There were a few women who worked, but not many. When we were children, my mother always had a meal prepared for us when we came home from school. We knew that once we arrived, we would find everything ready and on the table.

Back home, nobody left their parents' home until he or she were married; a daughter or a son, neither will leave. When we became adults we were not eager to separate and move away from our parents. I was eighteen when I married, so I moved to live with my husband. My sister

was twenty-three when she married, and she lived at my parents' home until then. Parents did not pressure their children to leave either. They loved their children and always wanted them near.

In Lebanon everyone knows everyone, and families are always very close. The Lebanese are very close because they spend their time together as a family and they communicate well.

*On the day of a marriage ceremony, the parents of the bride have a luncheon at their home. Just before my wedding, I was with my two sisters and brother-in-law. This was my last meal at my parents' home as Rogina Abdelkhalek. The next time I will be at my parents' home, I will be Rogina Abielmona.*

Almost every day some relatives come by the house to visit. I guess I just like having my family and relatives close to me, and I miss seeing them every day.

Before the bride meets the groom on the day of their wedding, her mother and father invite all the relatives, neighbors, and friends to their house for a big party with a buffet of typical Lebanese foods like *tabouleh, hummus,* and *maklube,* a rice dish with chicken, eggplant, and Arabic spices. This is the bride's last meal with her family as a single woman before she takes her husband's family name and becomes part of his family.

The luncheon lasts for one to two hours because there are lots of people—probably more than 100—are at the house. Afterwards, everyone goes to the reception area where her family will meet the groom's family. *Baklava*, a customary Middle East sweet, is given to all the people who come to congratulate the groom. The reception goes all out with a luxurious dinner, sweets, drinks, and live entertainment.

In general, all Arabic food is similar to each other: *falafels, shawarmas, tabouleh,* shish kebabs. Here is a Lebanese recipe for shish kebabs.

### KEBAB MISHWE
#### Shish Kebab

| | |
|---|---|
| 4 | lbs. boneless beef shoulder, cubed |
| 7 | small onions, quartered |
| 5 | tomatoes, quartered |
| $1/4$ | cup olive oil |
| $1/4$ | cup fresh lemon juice |
| 1 | tsp. salt |
| 1 | tsp. black pepper |
| 1 | tsp. ground cinnamon |

Combine all ingredients; marinate meat about 1 hour. Thread onto skewers, alternating with vegetables. Cook over grill to desired doneness.
*10 to 12 servings*

Wherever you go in Lebanon, you will feel right at home. The people are so kind and hospitable. You can't go into people's homes without being given food and drinks; you'll just be spoiled. They will bring everything to you from fruits and vegetables to even dinner or lunch.

Lots of people grow their own artichokes during the summertime, but if not, artichokes can be found in all the stores. *Salata artichoke* is served as a side dish.

### SALATA ARTICHOKE
#### Artichoke Salad

| | |
|---|---|
| 1 | garlic clove, crushed |
| $1/8$ | tsp. salt |
| $1/4$ | cup oil |
| | juice of 1 lemon |
| 1 | 8.5 oz. can artichokes or 2 fresh, cleaned and cooked |

Crush garlic and salt. In a small bowl, mix garlic, salt, and oil. Stir in lemon. Add artichokes; toss to mix.
*2 to 4 servings*

**Town was not too far**, maybe five miles. It was only a small town and we had no big roads leading there, only a small dirt one for us to follow when walking or riding the donkeys. We only went to town about once a week because we had almost everything else at our ranch in El Puerto de Catarin in Jalisco.

Where I grew up in Mexico, there were only twenty to twenty-five houses not very close together. They were more like small farms or ranches than houses. The houses, or *cabañas*, were made of stones and only had one door. The smaller ones had no windows.

Tomatillos, different beans like pinto, white and yellow, one or two fruit trees, and corn were some of the foods we grew on the ranch. Not much grew; the soil was poor and there were too many rocks. We needed the bulls, and sometimes horses, to till and work the rocky ground.

*I moved to America with my wife and children, but I miss my family and friends. My mother is still in the same place because she likes living in Mexico.*

Sugar, salt, potatoes, tomatoes, and flour were some of the products we bought in town. We made money by selling beans, corn, a donkey, or a cow. We had to go to town to sell. Sometimes we sold one hundred pounds of beans—a "whole donkey full," but this was only once a year because there was not much rain.

Because we didn't have much money, we never bought bread in the stores. We had corn at home to make corn bread, but we had to buy flour in town. My mother had an oven with two doors, one in the front and one in the back, and a hole in the top. We had to put a lot of wood inside of the oven for five or six hours to make it really hot inside. When the oven was hot enough, all the wood was taken out. After the corn bread and flour bread were put inside, the hole and doors were closed. In about thirty minutes the breads were ready. A lot of people didn't have money to put sugar in the bread, so they put salt. When my mother baked bread she made enough for one month. Sometimes the bread was hard and not fresh, but we still ate it.

For cooking the rest of our food, we had an *hornillo*, an outside stove made from clay and rocks—just like the house. We had to use wood to cook three times a day, every day. Once a week the whole family would go to the mountains, which was part of the ranch, to cut wood. We'd stay all day cutting the wood into small pieces and bundling them. We would cut enough for one or two weeks, probably three donkey loads, and carry the wood back home on the donkeys.

Everything in El Puerto de Catarin is still the same: same farms, same beans, same corn. Everybody cuts wood and makes the same food. Some people may have orange, peach, or lime trees, but life is the same for everybody.

□ Our ranch had horses, donkeys, cows, and chickens. We ate chicken but not a lot of meat; we had beef, which we bought in town, about once a month. If we killed a cow, we'd sell all the meat to make money.

These are a couple recipes that we would prepare on that rare day of having beef. *Birria* is my favorite. I like to have it for parties.

## BIRRIA
### Beef with Red Salsa

| | |
|---|---|
| 2 | lbs. beef |
| 6 | ancho chilies |
| 2 | cups water |
| 1-2 | bay leaf |
| | dash of cumin |
| | salt and pepper to taste |

Boil beef until tender; shred into small pieces. In a separate pan, boil chilies until tender. Reserve about $^1/_2$ cup water. Combine chilies, bay leaf, and cumin in a blender; add a small amount of water from chilies if needed. Place meat on a serving plate and pour sauce over. Add salt and pepper. Serve with tortillas.
*6 to 8 servings*

□ Besides beef, chicken or pork can also be used for *posole Mexican.*

## POSOLE MEXICAN
### Beef with Corn

| | |
|---|---|
| 2 | lbs. beef |
| 3 | garlic cloves |
| 1 | large onion, quartered |
| | salt and pepper to taste |
| 1 | large can white corn or hominy |
| 4 | ancho chilies |

Boil beef, garlic, onion, salt and pepper in enough water to cover meat. When meat is tender, add corn with its liquid.

In a separate pan, boil chilies until tender; combine chilies with a small amount of water in a blender. Add chili sauce to meat. Boil for 20 minutes.
*4 to 6 servings*

□ Mexicans have four different salsas: tomatillo salsa, burrito salsa, enchilada salsa, and chips salsa. Use the tomatillo salsa over eggs, with chips, or for *tacos de carne asada*, commonly called beef tacos.

## SALSA PARA DURITOS
### Chips Salsa

| | |
|---|---|
| 10 | tomatoes, peeled and chopped |
| 2-4 | jalapenos, chopped |
| 2-3 | garlic cloves, chopped |
| | salt to taste |

Combine all ingredients in a blender, but do not liquefy.

## SALSA DE TOMATES
### Tomatillo Salsa

| | |
|---|---|
| $1^1/_2$ | lbs. tomatillos, chopped |
| 5-7 | de arbol chilies, chopped |
| 2 | garlic cloves, chopped |
| | dash of cumin |
| | salt to taste |

Combine all ingredients in a blender, but do not liquefy. Slightly cook salsa over medium heat.

**When I think back** on my childhood in Mexico, one of my favorite, yet scary, times of the year was *El día de los muertos*, the Day of the Dead. I didn't always understand this celebration but I have since come to appreciate it. My specific memories have to do with eating candy shaped like *huesos,* bones; *calaveras,* skulls; and *esqueletos,* skeletons, made of chocolate, marzipan, or coconut.

In Guadalajara, Jalisco, you can find *dulce de melcocho*, blonde-colored candy shaped into skeletons holding tequila bottles, guitars, and so on. My father would buy me glow-in-the-dark skeleton key rings at the local *mercado*. Even some of the bakeries sold skeleton-shaped bread, or *pan de muerto*.

The part of the celebration that scared the daylights out of me was the *El panteón municipal*, the city cemetery. This cemetery was surrounded by a tall wall covered with broken glass to keep out intruders—ironically enough.

Andrea with her husband (left) and friend.

*A professor of mine once told me, and he said this in Spanish, "On the outside you are an American, but on the inside you have the soul of a Mexican."*

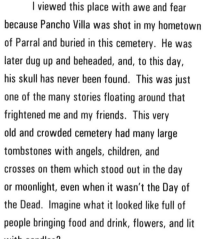

I viewed this place with awe and fear because Pancho Villa was shot in my hometown of Parral and buried in this cemetery. He was later dug up and beheaded, and, to this day, his skull has never been found. This was just one of the many stories floating around that frightened me and my friends. This very old and crowded cemetery had many large tombstones with angels, children, and crosses on them which stood out in the day or moonlight, even when it wasn't the Day of the Dead. Imagine what it looked like full of people bringing food and drink, flowers, and lit with candles?

Each locality may have different rituals, but for all, the preparation for *El día de los muertos* actually begins on October 31 on All Hallows' Eve. It is viewed as a time of the year to remember that we miss the dead and they us...so why not let them know? Plenty of food and drink is made to take to the cemetery for the dead, especially tortillas, chicken, tequila, hot chocolate, and a gruel called *atol* made of sweet corn. Families also bring candles, music, and flowers to adorn the tombstones of their dearly departed. The departed arrive at midnight to partake of the food and drink, which is actually the *alma*, or essence, of it. Toward the morning, the priest gives a mass and the spirits depart until the next year. The actual Day of the Dead on November 1 is spent resting from the festivities leading up to this day.

Looking back as an adult, I know that this Christian ritual is tied into the days of the Aztecs who used to practice human sacrifices and believed that death was a means of appeasing the gods and insuring health and continuity.

As Octavio Paz, the Nobel Laureate from Mexico, states in his book *The Labyrinth of Solitude*, "Life extended into death, and vice versa. Death was not the natural end of life but one phase of a natural cycle. Life, death, and resurrection were stages of a cosmic process which repeated itself continuously." Death wasn't an end. "Man fed the insatiable hunger of life with his death." With this in mind, *El día de los muertos* to me is viewed more with respect and admiration for these traditions that have been adapted for the present. Though I must admit, the old cemeteries can still make me shudder.

◻ The best chilies are from Poblano in Mexico or Anaheim in the U.S. Toast them over a gas burner or broil them in the oven. "Steam" or sweat the chilies in a plastic bag, then peel and remove seeds. If these chilies aren't available, use two cans of Old El Paso® green chilies.

Serve *chile con queso* with tortilla chips.

## CHILE CON QUESO
### Chilies with Cheese Dip

| | |
|---|---|
| 4 | green chilies, chopped |
| 1 | garlic clove, chopped |
| 1 | large onion, chopped |
| 1 | Tbsp. oil |
| 4 | oz. tomato sauce |
| 1/4 | tsp. baking soda |
| 16 | oz. Muenster or American cheese |
| 1 | 12 oz. can evaporated milk |
| | salt to taste |

Cook chilies, garlic, and onion in oil over medium-high heat until onion is transparent. Add tomato sauce; cook over low heat for 5 to 10 minutes. Add baking soda; mix well. Add cheese; cook until melted, stirring constantly. Add milk and salt; cook until warm throughout.

◻ A Mayan legend tells that when the gods first created man, he was made of clay, but when the rains came, he was washed away. They next attempted to create man from straw, but again when the rains came, he floated down the rivers. Finally, they made man from corn, and because he had roots in the earth, when the rains came, he didn't wash away.

Corn forms an integral part of Mexico's cuisine. It is the basis for many of the delicious Mexican meals, and it serves as a staple for breakfast, lunch, and dinner, much in the way people in the U.S. like to have bread with their meals.

This recipe using corn tortillas was given to me by my mother. It has been adapted for the U.S., but use original ingredients if they are available.

## ENCHILADAS VERDES DE POLLO
### Green Chicken Enchiladas

| | |
|---|---|
| 1 | whole chicken |
| 1 | large onion, quartered |
| 1 | garlic clove |
| | salt and black peppercorns to taste |
| 1 | large onion, chopped |
| 2 | Tbsp. oil |
| 8 | Anaheim or Poblano green chilies, peeled and chopped |
| 2 | tsp. salt |
| 1/2 | tsp. cumin (comino) |
| 1 | tsp. oregano |
| 4 | Tbsp. flour |
| 2 | cups sour cream |
| 16 | corn tortillas |
| 1 | lb. Monterey Jack or Muenster cheese, grated (Queso Chihuahua or Menonita is preferred) |

Boil chicken with quartered onion, garlic, salt and peppercorns. Strain; reserve 5 cups broth. Remove bones and chop chicken; set aside.

Cook chopped onion in oil over medium-high heat until transparent. Add chilies; cook for 5 to 10 minutes. Place in blender with 1 cup broth; blend well. Add salt, cumin, oregano, flour, and remaining 4 cups broth. Repeat blending.

In a large pot, cook sauce over medium heat for 45 minutes. Cool slightly; add sour cream. Lightly fry tortillas while sauce is cooling.

Dip each tortilla in sauce; fill with chicken and cheese. Roll each tortilla and place in a casserole. Leave some sauce to pour over enchiladas when finished rolling. Bake at 350° for 30 to 45 minutes or until sauce bubbles. Serve with refried beans and *sopa de arroz,* a dry Mexican rice. *¡Buen provecho!*
*8 servings*

**One of my warmest** memories of growing up was breaking the piñata. No birthday was complete without a colorful papier maché piñata loaded with candy. Mom used to make piñatas for each of her children. With six kids, Mom became an expert piñata designer.

Mom told my wife, Carla, that she wasn't sure where the concept of piñatas originated but she remembers them as a child some fifty years ago. She mentioned that they were also used every night of the *Posadas,* a Christmas reenactment of the holy family's search for shelter. After the prayers, people would gather for the breaking of the piñata.

Piñatas can be in any shape: moons, stars, animals. The best one Mom made for me was a large ship, like the Titanic. Piñatas are generally made out of papier maché. When Mom was a child, the piñatas had a clay pot in the center to hold the goodies, then the papier maché was wrapped around it into the design of choice. Today, piñatas tend to be made of newspaper with no clay pot.

*I have only been to the western and southern sides of Mexico. For our tenth anniversary, my wife, Carla, and I sailed around the Yucatan Peninsula on the eastern part.*

On our daughter's first birthday, Carla and I bought a piñata shaped like a "1" here in Virginia. I thought we needed a stick of dynamite to break it open! Turns out it was made of cardboard, not the most user-friendly material to crack open with a bat. Nevertheless, the thirteen-year-olds at the party had a good time slugging the piñata and grabbing all the candy and POGS.

As an adult, I'm having fun swinging the piñata just out of the reach of the little ones. We usually tie it to a string which we can pull up and down to tease the person underneath, while yelling, "There it is! There it is!" Then we'd yank it away. It's a bit cruel in a way.

Holding a piñata isn't for the faint of heart. Kids over six years old are blindfolded, so you must be able to move out of the way of a child wielding a bat, mop handle, broom, or any stick and whacking for all that he's worth.

I've seen a kid break a piñata, watch it fall to the ground, and keep beating the stuffing out of the defenseless bit of paper! Keep in mind, while all this whacking is going on, pieces of candy are flying out and children are scrambling underneath to grab the goodies. Adult supervision is required!

◻ *Mole* means a sauce made using several kinds of chiles as a base. The etymology is Náhuatl, the language of the Mexicans and Aztecs; *molli* or *muli* means chili sauce.

The recipe is from my mother, Adulfa Morales, who came to the U.S. from Parral, Mexico. My wife never liked chicken mole until she tasted my mother's. The thought of chocolate with chili doesn't sound particularly pleasing, but put together in this instance, it's a winner.

### MOLE POLLO
### Chicken Mole

| | |
|---|---|
| 2 | 3 lb. chickens, cut into pieces |
| 1/2 | tsp. salt |
| 2 | Tbsp. bacon grease |
| 2 | cups mole sauce (see below) |
| 1 1/2 | cups broth |
| 1 | rounded tsp. peanut butter |
| 1/8 | Mexican chocolate round* |
| 2 | tsp. sugar |
| | dash of *each*: coriander, cumin, garlic powder, cinnamon |

In a large pot, cover chicken with water; cook over medium-high heat until tender, adding salt to taste. Reserve broth and remove bones from chicken. Set aside.

Heat bacon grease over medium-high heat. Add mole sauce; cook for 3 to 5 minutes. Add remaining ingredients; cook for 30 minutes, adding broth for thinning if needed. Add chicken to sauce; heat thoroughly. Serve with buttered tortillas.
*8 to 10 servings*

◻ Chilies are indispensable for many Mexican dishes. It is no wonder since it is estimated that there are over twenty-seven varieties of chilies in Mexico alone.

### MOLE SAUCE

| | |
|---|---|
| 30 | chilies mulattos |
| 20 | chilies anchos |
| 10 | chilies pasillas |
| 1 | Tbsp. mixed seeds from chilies |
| 1/2 | cup almonds, not blanched |
| 1 | corn tortilla |
| 2 | French rolls, halved |
| 1 | onion, quartered |
| 2 | peppercorns |
| 1 | garlic clove |
| 1 | Tbsp. sesame seeds |
| | dash of anise seed |
| | dash of coriander |
| 1/4 | Mexican chocolate round* |
| 1/2 | cup oil |
| 1 | tsp. sugar |
| | dash of cumin |
| | salt to taste |
| | dash of ground cloves (optional) |
| 4-6 | cups hot chicken broth |

Wash and dry chilies. In dry, heavy skillet, lightly toast chilies. Remove seeds; set aside 1 tablespoon of combined seeds. Soak chilies in water.

In a dry skillet, toast seeds with almonds until brown. Cook tortilla in a small amount of oil over medium-high heat until crisp. Cook French rolls in a small amount of oil until brown.

Grind all ingredients to a paste, adding enough broth to ground chilies until thin enough to strain. Stir through sieve, adding more broth if needed. Sauce can be frozen in 2 cup amounts.
*8 cups*

At a very early age, I knew that some aspects of my culture, especially with women, were wrong. I cannot speak for the whole of Nigeria. I speak for my tribe, the Uruhobo tribe, in the midwestern part of Nigeria near the town Ughelli.

I grew up in a very chauvinistic society. For example, men could have many wives, and wives were often considered property. My favorite story is about my high school teacher. My friends and I were very close to him, and we went to his house all the time. When he went to his village and brought back his wife, we just stopped going to his house because it was part of our tradition to show respect for the marriage. He called us, asking why we stopped coming. We told him we wanted to give him more room with his wife.

He thought our answer was the most ridiculous thing he heard in his life. He said, "My wife is just a piece of furniture, a property. Don't let that stop you from coming to my house." Even though I was very young, I felt that it should not have been like that.

Steven and his daughter.

*In the culture that I grew up in, having all girls was a sign of weakness, so the men would continue to marry until they got a boy. I never believed this, and I love my children equally.*

If a marriage did not work out, the man kept the children and got rid of the wife. The wife usually went back to her town. Many times, she did not remarry. A woman, especially an uneducated woman, tended to marry at a very early age. If a couple separated later in life, the woman often ended up being a fifth or sixth wife in the next marriage.

If the man died, some of the wives, by tradition, were taken by the oldest son or an uncle. The whole idea was to keep the family together. If a man were to marry a woman who already had children from somebody else, he could not—probably because of pride—truly call those children his own because society did not recognize or accept stepchildren.

Such acts like a man opening a car door for a woman or cooking would be considered a disgrace to the family. They were unacceptable because they meant that the man was subservient to the woman. Men in my tribe were not allowed in the kitchen. Cooking was purely the women's job; men helped only by hunting or fishing. In my tribe, when the food was ready, it was brought out to the men. When I ventured on my own, I really had to struggle and learn how to cook.

It was understandable that many viewed women in this light because of tradition. Even my father had more than one wife. Most of my friends had a similar family situation. I never quite understood how the women communicated concerning which wife my father, or any man, had dinner or stayed with. It's a system that had been around for years, and the women understood it from their grandmothers, mothers, and other women.

If the system worked, raising all the children became a whole family affair. For example, if my mother did not have food, then my dad's second wife had food for everyone. All my father's children were considered my brothers and sisters, although my father's other wives were not considered my mothers. Once the children were part of the family, there was no division, no half-brother or half-sister.

Experiences like these in my life changed my view about the social treatment of women. Many people in modern society, like those who went to universities, want a different system. I assume—I have not been back to Nigeria for a while—that a society where the man always dominates has changed.

# Steven Buwe

When the men went hunting, about twenty to thirty men from the village would gather and map out a hunting area. Younger men who were not allowed to bear arms lined up on one side of the mapped area; older men, bearing guns, lined up on the other side.

The younger men beat the bush with sticks or machetes, driving the animals to the other side where the older men with guns were waiting. Some animals would escape. The idea was not to kill everything, just what was needed.

We hunted for antelopes, rabbits, and animals we called "grasscutters," which are similar to beavers. During my grandfather's time, lions were hunted also. If there were any near the villages, the people of the village went out and killed them, but lions are now extinct in that part of Nigeria.

Baboons were never eaten because of the mystical story behind them. Legend had it in my tribe that there once was a pregnant woman, about to give birth, who was stranded in the forest. No one was around to help so a baboon came out to help the woman give birth. Because of this, there was a lot of respect for that animal.

*Egusi,* a meal made with ground melon seeds, is common in West Africa. We used antelope, goat, or rabbit for this dish, but beef and fish can be substituted. *Egusi* powder can be found in African or Asian markets.

### EGUSI
### Ground Melon Seed Soup

| 1 | lb. beef or fish |
| 8 | cups water |
| 2 | cups ground egusi* |
| 1/2 | cup tomato paste |
| | salt to taste |
| | red pepper to taste |

Boil beef or fish for 5 minutes or until done.
In a separate pot, bring 8 cups water to a boil. Mix egusi with enough water to make a paste. Stir into boiling water; cook for about 10 minutes. Add meat and remaining ingredients; stir occasionally.
*4 servings*

For a young person who dies in Nigeria, a funeral is very sad and lasts for less than three days. But for an old person, the transition is very happy so everyone in the village celebrates for about three weeks. During this time, there is dancing, eating, everything.

For example, my father is the oldest man in the village. He is 102 years old. When he dies, by tradition the funeral will become a whole tribal affair. People from different tribes from as far as fifty miles will come to pay their respect.

The women of the village will cook and many will bring food with them, but the majority of the celebration will be the children's responsibility. Some will go up north where cattle are raised and buy one or two cows to feed everyone during the funeral.

It is not taboo to speak about my father's coming funeral because it is a celebration of a golden age. The idea is that if he achieved that age, he must have done right by the gods; he must have lived a very, very good life. People try to emulate his lifestyle because in that society, the life span is only around fifty years or so. People like my father are well-respected when they are at that age and die.

Coconut rice is a traditional dish that would definitely be at celebrations like funerals. I also prepared this often when I was single in Nigeria because it is simple. As I mentioned, men were never allowed in the kitchen when I was growing up; I knew where the kitchen was but never went into it. This recipe was really easy for me to learn.

### COCONUT RICE

| 1 | fresh coconut, grated |
| 2 | cups water |
| 1 | cup rice |
| | salt to taste |

Place coconut in cheesecloth; strain water over coconut. Reserve water; discard coconut.
Cook rice in coconut water according to package instructions or usual method. Add salt.
*2 to 3 servings*

Nigeria 137

In any culture in the world, good manners show how civilized people are and that they are well-taught and have a good upbringing. Their actions reflect their parents' hard work and the success or lack of it. If they don't follow the rules, the small things that are observed in a culture, someone may think, "Oh, their parents didn't teach them any manners."

In our Pakistani culture and religion, good manners are very important. The right hand is considered clean. When we pray or bear witness—like when taking the oath—the right hand is raised. We don't shake hands or initiate anything with the left hand. If we receive something, we receive it with the right hand. Using the right hand properly is considered good manners.

We also always eat with the right hand. It is considered bad manners to eat with the left hand because the left hand is used mostly for cleaning oneself. When we are eating, we start from the food that is right in front of us on the plate. We never start in the middle or the sides. We start in the front and progress back, bringing the food toward us. It's a clean way of eating. There's a haphazard way of doing things: sloppy. Then there's a way where motions and actions show a smooth performance. The smooth way looks nice and clean, and it shows rhythm and finesse. We are not barbarians. We just don't pick up some food and start chomping.

If the left hand is used, it is noticed, but nothing is said. The intention is not to embarrass that person. In our culture, we don't have caste systems or lower or upper class, even though money does make a difference. It is more about how a person is educated and civilized. These make the distinction between two individuals. They go back to how a person was brought up.

In our culture, it is very common to share with each other. Sometimes as kids, we would share food from the same plate. Our manner of eating is nice for everyone because, in a rough term, "We don't pollute the plate with our paws." Be considerate of others. For example, I used to share food with my brother from the same plate. If he started from the middle, I would think, "Eeww! Wait a minute! What is this?" Start from the front, share equally, and use common sense manners.

Rafaquat and his wife, Nosheen.

*Eating with the right hand goes back to Prophet Mohammed. He used to eat with his right hand, so now it is considered a good thing.*

Eating with the hands is a personal preference. Of course, utensils can be used. It depends on the food also. When eaten with the hands, food is not supposed to go beyond the middle knuckles. If the food can be kept lower than that, then that person really knows how to eat with the hands. Just the appearance of having food all over the fingers and palm is disgusting. Everyone will stop eating!

Licking the fingers is fine, but it is not good manners to talk with food in the mouth, mostly because of the possibility of choking. Burping is not such a bad thing as long as it's not very loud and barbaric; it's natural. In western cultures, people try to suppress the air, but it puts a strain on the body. It is considered *extremely* bad if a person notices it or says something about it. Just try to do it discreetly.

In all cultures, even in ours, there are sloppy ones who are just disgusting; then there are some who eat very nicely. Just by the way they are eating, food can look so delicious. They eat so beautifully and are well-mannered that, even though you're not hungry, you want to eat!

□ Besides *garam masala* and curry powder, my wife adds other spices independently according to how we like our food. You can use just these spices but increase the curry powder to two to three tablespoons. Goat or lamb can also be used for this recipe.

### ALOO GOSHT
### Beef and Potato Curry

| | |
|---|---|
| 1 | lb. beef, cubed |
| 2 | cups water |
| 1 | large onion, chopped |
| 4 | cloves garlic, chopped |
| 2 | Tbsp. coriander |
| 1 | Tbsp. red chili pepper |
| 1 | Tbsp. Indian curry powder |
| 1/2 | tsp. garam masala* |
| 1/4 | tsp. turmeric |
| 1/4 | tsp. ground ginger |
| 1/2 | cup crushed tomatoes |
| 1/2 | cup oil |
| 2 | large potatoes, cubed |

Cook all ingredients except tomatoes, oil, and potatoes over medium heat until meat is tender. When water is reduced, increase heat to medium-high; add tomatoes and oil. Stir constantly until mixed well. Add potatoes. Add enough water to cover. Reduce heat to medium. Cook, covered, until potatoes are just done. If too thin, remove cover and reduce to a gravy consistency.
*6 to 7 servings*

□ *Pakorahs* are perfect on rainy days when the sky is gray. We have them as a snack to lighten the mood. They can be made many ways—with cauliflower, eggplant, potatoes—but this is the most popular.

Gram flour is made from ground chick peas. It can be found in Indian and sometimes Asian stores.

### PAKORAHS

| | |
|---|---|
| 2 | cups gram flour* |
| 1 | medium onion, coarsely diced |
| 1 | green chili pepper, diced or sliced |
| 1/2 | tsp. red chili or cayenne pepper |
| 1/2 | tsp. salt |
| 1/2 | box chopped spinach (optional) |
| | water |
| 2 | cups oil |

Combine flour, onion, chili pepper, red pepper, salt, and spinach (optional). Add enough water until batter is a pancake consistency; set aside for 15 minutes.

Heat oil over medium heat. Drop by spoonfuls and rotate to cook evenly. Use this batter to dip different vegetables, but omit onions and spinach. Serve pakorahs with cilantro and mint chutney.
*6 to 8 servings*

### CILANTRO AND MINT CHUTNEY

| | |
|---|---|
| 1/2 | bunch cilantro |
| 1/2 | bunch mint |
| 2 | garlic cloves |
| | jalapeno to taste |
| | dash of salt |
| | dash of red chili pepper |
| | water |

Combine all ingredients in a blender, adding just enough water to help blend. Chutney should not be watery.

**Most marriages of Muslims** in the Indo-Pakistan subcontinent are arranged by the parents of the bride and groom. Muslims prefer to marry within the family, clan-cousins, or distant relatives, but this aspect is quickly changing.

The boy's parents start looking for a bride amongst relatives and friends when the boy finishes his education and/or starts a career. Once a match is located, the parents, either directly or through mutual friends, approach the girl's parents. If encouraged, marriage is pursued further; otherwise, the matter is dropped and other families are tapped.

Once a girl's parents agree, the families arrange the engagement ceremony. The groom's party goes to the bride's house, which is tastefully decorated with colored lights. The party brings a ring, several dresses for the bride, and sweets which may vary in number and quantity due to financial means. The groom's mother places the ring on the bride's finger. In modern days, the groom is also invited, and the girl's parents reciprocally place an engagement ring on the groom's finger. A priest may come to give a lecture on the sanctity of marriage. The evening is full of song, dance, and music, followed by dinner arranged by the girl's parents.

*My husband and I were married by arrangement. My husband was also instrumental in our daughters' marriages. We are all examples of very happy and successful marriages.*

Thereafter, the date for the *nikah*, or marriage ceremony, is fixed. A couple of days before the *nikah*, the groom's family carries several sets of clothes, jewelry, and more sweets to the bride. They also bring the *mehndi*, or henna, which is applied on the bride's hands and feet in beautiful floral designs. The groom, his family, and friends go to the bride's house, hotel, or hall for the ceremony, and the *nikah* is performed by a priest.

After the *nikah*, the groom is invited to the ladies section where the bride is shown to the groom through a mirror called *aarsi musaf*. The younger sisters of the bride steal the shoes of the groom and return them only after the groom pays a "ransom" in money or gifts. The *nikah* ends with a lavish dinner, music, and dancing. Then the bride leaves for the groom's house during the departure ceremony know as *rukhsati*.

At the groom's house, a room is decorated for the newlyweds. The ladies assembled there hold a ceremony to view the bride, who is laden with a beaded dress, jewelry, and other gifts of cash and jewelry. This ceremony wishes the bride and groom the best of luck, long life, and happiness. A couple days later, the groom's parents hold a big dinner reception, followed by music, for all the relatives and friends of the newlyweds. This dinner and music concludes the ceremony.

People of different cultures and customs around the world have developed different traditions for similar purposes. Marriage is the union of two human beings to continue the life cycle on this earth. Although few marriages of the Muslims in Pakistan begin with the consent of the bride and groom, it has generally been noted that 99% of such arranged marriages have been very successful, and the couples have lived happily.

❑ The food served at the wedding dinner varies according to the financial means of the family, just as the other items of jewelry, dresses, sweets, and other gifts may vary. The food is mainly comprised of *biryani*, a meat and rice dish, a variety of curries, chicken *tikka,* kebabs, vegetables, breads, and yoghurt followed by sweets such as rice pudding or *ras malai.* Here are a few recipes which may served.

## CHICKEN TIKKA
### Marinated Baked Chicken

| | |
|---|---|
| 1 | whole chicken, cut into 8 pieces |
| | yellow food coloring |
| 1 | Tbsp. ajwain powder* |
| 1 | cup plain yoghurt |
| 1 | tsp. red chili powder |
| 1$^1$/$_2$ | tsp. ground ginger |
| 1$^1$/$_2$ | tsp. garlic powder |
| | salt to taste |
| 4 | lemons, halved |
| 3 | Tbsp. oil |

Bring a pot of water to a boil. Add chicken; boil for 3 minutes and remove. In a bowl, combine all ingredients except lemons and oil. Rub yoghurt mixture onto chicken with pieces of lemon, squeezing the lemon juice into chicken. Marinate for 30 minutes. Grill chicken for 60 to 90 minutes; baste with oil while grilling. Bake at 350° until light brown on both sides.
*4 to 6 servings*

## RAS MALAI
### Creamy Cheese Sweet

| | |
|---|---|
| 32 | oz. Ricotta cheese |
| $^1$/$_2$ | cup dry milk |
| 2 | cups half and half |
| $^1$/$_2$ | cup sugar |
| $^1$/$_8$ | tsp. vanilla extract |

Combine Ricotta and dry milk. Spread into 9 x 12 baking dish; bake at 350° for 30 minutes. Boil half and half, sugar, and vanilla extract over medium heat. Cool both mixtures; pour half and half over Ricotta. Cool in refrigerator. Cut into squares before serving.
*8 to 10 servings*

❑ *Shami kebab* is a minced meat patty which can be served for breakfast with toast, tea parties as snacks, or any occasion.

## SHAMI KEBAB
### Ground Beef Kebab

| | |
|---|---|
| 2 | lbs. ground beef |
| 1 | medium onion, chopped |
| 4 | garlic cloves |
| 2 | bay leaves |
| 6 | whole cloves |
| 1 | stick cinnamon |
| $^1$/$_2$ | tsp. black pepper |
| $^1$/$_4$ | tsp. red chili pepper |
| 1 | tsp. salt |
| $^1$/$_4$ | cup gram lentil (daal channa)* |
| 4 | cups water |
| 1 | egg |

In a large pot, combine all ingredients except egg; cook over medium heat for 30 to 40 minutes or until water evaporates. Cool; grind in food processor. Add egg; mix well. Make into round patties. Cook in a small amount of oil over medium-high heat until light brown. Serve with bread or rice.
*4 servings*

**Not knowing** what to expect from the political turmoil, I was nervous about bringing my two daughters, aged four and seven at the time, to Palestine. I was not nervous as far as what they would learn. I wanted them to learn about their culture and language. After three months, they spoke the language better than I did. They were also able to meet their father's side of the family.

My father-in-law lives in a very small village named Jayous. His two-level house is enclosed by pomegranate and fig trees in the back. There is a hen house in the backyard, and the neighbors have goats and sheep. It's very scenic.

All of this was new to my children. They had never picked fruit from trees or seen animals raised for food. They loved being able to go to the back yard and pick a pomegranate or a fig. They also fed the chickens. In the beginning, my eldest daughter wouldn't get near the chickens, but in the end after my mother-in-law slaughtered a chicken, she was actually holding and removing the feathers with my mother-in-law. She assimilated very well. Even I couldn't do it.

Abbey with her husband
and children.

*My family shares a tight bond
in Palestine.*

Every morning the *bayah*, a seller of vegetables, came by with his little pushcart. He would go through the streets, yelling out what he was selling. The village is so small that everyone can hear him. He sold whatever was in season: parsley, cauliflower, squash, string beans. If anyone needed vegetables, they would come out and buy from him. Sometimes my daughters would run out when they heard his yelling and call the *bayah* to come to the house.

There are many little stores called *dukanas* all over the village. The *dukanas* are owned by one person and are usually attached to the bottom of a house. Because they are so tiny, they sell only candy, canned foods, and other necessities.

My daughters had the freedom to go to these stores in the village and buy whatever they wanted. I just gave them money and sent them on their way. The stores are not that far because the village is not big. I didn't have to worry about them.

Everyone in Jayous knows and trusts each other, but it's not like this everywhere in Palestine. In Jayous the people have a bond—a freedom. It was very different for the girls when I told them to go by themselves to the *dukanas* or in the yard. Otherwise, I would never let them go out alone, even on the front porch.

As far as security goes, I would love for my children to grow up in a place like Jayous. But I would not want the turmoil and uncertainty of the future. I prefer if they lived in a safe environment on a continuous basis. They wouldn't have to worry that an act by anyone could change the environment. I don't want my kids to think that tomorrow they may be under curfew; or school is open today but it may not be tomorrow.

When there is war in Palestine, even Jayous is tainted. We were extremely fortunate that everything was quiet when we were visiting. There was no war at that time. I would love to live in Palestine with my family and with the peace and security of the village itself, but without political turmoil.

❑ It is so hard to prepare food homemade after coming home from work. When I make *fatayar*, or spinach pie, I use frozen, ready-made dough for convenience sake. It's very close to the dough that you have to measure, knead, and let it rise; this way is much easier.

I'll serve this with vegetable soup or as a snack. If serving as an hors d'oeuvre, cut each dough into three parts. *Sumac* is a red, lemony spice found in Middle Eastern stores.

### FATAYAR
### Spinach Pie

| | |
|---|---|
| 1 | medium onion, chopped |
| 2 | Tbsp. olive oil |
| 2 | 10 oz. boxes frozen spinach, thawed and squeezed |
| 1 | small bunch green onions, chopped |
| 2 | tsp. sumac* |
| | juice of 1 lemon |
| | salt to taste |
| 1 | package Riches® frozen roll dough |

Cook onions in oil over medium-high heat. Add spinach, green onions, sumac, lemon, and salt; mix well.

Flatten dough into circles. Place about 1 tablespoon of spinach mixture onto dough, leaving a 1-inch edge. Fold into triangular shapes, flattening edges to seal. Bake on cookie sheet in a 350° preheated oven for 10 to 15 minutes or until golden brown.
*24 pies*

❑ *Tabouleh* is a typical Mediterranean salad found throughout the Middle East. Serve *tabouleh* on a bed of lettuce.

### TABOULEH
### Mediterranean Salad

| | |
|---|---|
| 1/2 | cup bulgur wheat* |
| 4 | medium tomatoes, chopped |
| 1 | bunch green onions, chopped |
| 1 | bunch parsley, chopped |
| 1 | cucumber, chopped |
| 1 | sprig mint leaves, chopped |
| 1 | tsp. salt |
| 1 | Tbsp. lemon juice |
| 1 | Tbsp. olive oil |

Soak wheat in warm water for 2 hours; drain. Combine vegetables and wheat. Add salt, lemon juice, and olive oil; mix well.
*6 servings*

❑ *Kanafa* is an easy dessert to prepare. The shredded pastry dough can be found in Middle Eastern stores.

### KANAFA
### Shredded Pastry with Cheese

| | |
|---|---|
| 1 | package shredded pastry dough, thawed* |
| 1/2 | cup butter, melted |
| 1 | 16 oz. Ricotta cheese |
| 1 | 8 oz. package mozzarella cheese |

| | |
|---|---|
| | **syrup:** |
| 2 | cups water |
| 2 | cups sugar |

Prepare syrup. Combine water and sugar; cook over medium heat until slightly thick. Set aside to cool.

Pull dough apart into fine pieces. Mix with butter and continue to pull apart. Spread a thin layer in baking dish. Spread layers of Ricotta and mozzarella. Add remaining dough. Bake at 350° for 10 minutes or until golden brown. Remove from oven. Pour syrup over pastry.
*8 to 10 servings*

**There are really** only two holidays in Palestine: *Eid al Fetar*, the Holiday of Feast, and *Eid Adha*, the Holiday of Sacrifice. *Eid al Fetar* is after the fast of Ramadan. The fast lasts for twenty-nine to thirty days. Moslems do not eat or drink from sunrise to sunset during Ramadan. The fast teaches patience and empathy for the needy. *Eid Adha* celebrates when Abraham was about to sacrifice his son, but his son was saved when God told Abraham to sacrifice a lamb instead. It is also a holiday for the pilgrims who are in Mecca.

For three days before the holidays, the mosques have Islamic chants after each of the five calls for prayer. The chants are very peaceful, and we can hear them from more than one mosque at a time because loudspeakers are placed throughout the city. The chants may say, "God is great. God is great. There is no god but Allah, the same god that Christians, Jews, and Moslems believe in. Mohammed is his prophet and messenger of Allah." The chants are repeated twice during the call for prayer.

*My grandmother owns olive groves about fifteen miles outside of Jerusalem. As a kid, I drank water at a natural spring on her property. A long time ago, the shepherds used this spring for their livestock.*

On the holidays, as well as other days, all Moslems are called to the first prayer at six-thirty in the morning. Afterwards, we go to the cemetery to visit grandfathers, uncles and others who had passed away. There is no fear of cemeteries there. Before entering the cemetery, we read a verse from the Koran, then stop by the martyrs' graves—the people who died for Palestine. Again, someone reads a verse from the Koran at the martyrs' graves.

After the cemetery, the rest of the day is spent visiting relatives. In the evening, I return home to be the man of the house and play host to people who visit. The kids love the holidays because they are usually given money, so the small local stores set up for their little customers. You know it is a holiday because of all the toys outside of the stores.

On the second holiday, *Eid Adha,* I help my mother distribute meat and whatever else we can give to the needy. In this region, it is hard for a man to work and even harder for a woman to work, so what little money people have, they help take care of those who are less fortunate. The less fortunate may be people who are homeless or children who are fatherless because of the war.

We always love the holidays because they are a time of peace and a time to be together with our families and friends. However, our holidays in Palestine are not commercialized. We look forward to the visits, not to going out shopping and receiving expensive gifts. *Eid al Fetar* and *Eid Adha* are holidays based on our Moslem religion. This is one of the beauties of Palestine.

▫ During the holidays, special food is always prepared. Lunch, the main meal of the day, may be a leg of lamb or whole lamb stuffed with pine nuts, rice, and almonds. Every house will have fruit drinks, *baklava,* and many other foods for the guests while they are visiting.

In Palestine and throughout the Middle East, *baklava* is served especially on occasions such as anniversaries, weddings, graduations, after the fast of Ramadan on *Eid al Fetar*, and during the holiday for the pilgrims called *Eid Adha.*

## BAKLAVA
### Walnut and Phyllo Sweet

| | |
|---|---|
| 1 | lb. walnuts, crushed into pieces |
| $^1/_2$ | tsp. nutmeg |
| 2 | tsp. cinnamon |
| 1 | box large-sized phyllo |
| 1 | 16 oz. can shortening, melted |

**syrup:**

| | |
|---|---|
| 2 | cups sugar |
| 2 | cups water |

Combine walnuts, nutmeg, and cinnamon; mix well. Spread $^1/_2$ of phyllo in a baking pan. Spread walnut mixture over phyllo; spread remaining phyllo over walnut mixture. Cut into blocks or triangles. Cover with shortening. Bake at 350° for 40 to 50 minutes or until brown. Set aside for 3 to 5 minutes; carefully drain shortening.

Prepare syrup. Cook sugar and water over low-medium heat until sugar dissolves. Drizzle syrup between cut pieces.

*24 servings*

▫ Palestinians are very hospitable, so when you visit a friend or relative, you may want to bring a small gift as a friendly gesture. The gift can be just a box of wrapped chocolates.

It's a hard habit to break. I find myself bringing a gift even if I am invited to a barbecue here in the States. I always make the effort to bring something, whether it is a pineapple or a bunch of grapes.

*Hummus* is a typical food of Palestine. If you were to have a meal at someone's home, *hummus* is usually served as a dip with pitas.

## HUMMUS
### Chick Pea Dip

| | |
|---|---|
| 1 | 20 oz. can chick peas, drained |
| 2-3 | Tbsp. tahini* |
| | juice of $^1/_2$ lemon |
| 1 | garlic clove |
| | salt to taste |
| | chopped fresh parsley |

Combine $^1/_2$ of chick peas, tahini, lemon juice, garlic, and salt in a blender. Gradually add remaining chick peas, adding water if needed. Garnish with parsley.

*2$^1/_2$ cups*

**There are so many things** I love about Panama: the beaches, the weather, the food, my family, and especially the traditions. In Panama, the most important part of a person's life is the family. The best time for the family to gather is at the evening meal, which typically lasts two to three hours.

As children, my sisters and I suffered through countless hours of boring conversations, from which there was no escape. As tradition went in my family, my uncle always sat at the head of the table, and nobody left until he was ready. We tried everything to get away from the dinner table. I would begin to stand and my uncle would say with his heavy Spanish accent, "Ah, ah, ah. Where are you going?"

"I'm taking my plate to..." and before I could finish, he would tell me to sit down.

We even tried the bathroom excuse. Only in extreme cases did it work, but we had to return to the table immediately. We had to stay because of the tradition. It was a tradition I have come to respect and have tried to emulate.

Another example of the Panamanian tradition and importance of the family was when we visited Panama in the summer of 1995. My uncle took the whole family to stay at a resort in the mountains called *Cerro Viejo,* or the old man's mountain. We were the only people at the barren resort in the middle of Panama, but we had a great time. We ate, danced, sang, and played dominoes all night.

On the evenings of our stay, all thirteen of us sat at a huge round table and ate and talked for hours. Fortunately, we were the only people at the resort. We were very loud, which is a typical trait of Panamanians. My cousin, Frederico, began a series of toasts each night, and everyone followed with their own. After each person said their toast, the family pounded on the table while yelling *"Cien! Cien!"* meaning "give it your all."

*On this afternoon, my uncle Freddy and I enjoyed salsa dancing under the* bohio *at his beach house. The* bohio—my *favorite place to relax—is a palm-leaf covered hut with hammocks hanging under it. The family likes to come here for conversations, meals, dancing, and napping.*

□  I was eight years old the first time my mother found plantains in a local grocery store in the United States, and I will never forget what my friend said when he saw the plantains in our kitchen. "That's the biggest banana I've ever seen!" he yelled. We laughed while my mother explained that it wasn't a banana.

When I visit Panama, I look forward to eating all the fried foods and exotic fruits that can't be found in the U.S. Though plantains can be found locally, they are always in season in Panama and available at any market and restaurant.

Plantains are served before the main course of a meal. They can be cooked two ways: sweet and green.

### PLÁTANOS MADUROS or TAJADAS
#### Sweet Plantains

| | |
|---|---|
| 2-3 | plantains, soft and black |
| 1 | Tbsp. butter |
| 1/2 | cup sugar |
| 2 | tsp. cinnamon |

Cut plantains lengthwise. Cook plantains in butter over medium heat until brown. With a fork, make holes in plantains. Add sugar and cinnamon; bring to a boil. Reduce heat to low; cook for 15 to 20 minutes or until soft.
*4 servings*

### PLÁTANOS VERDES or PATACÓNS
#### Green Plantains

| | |
|---|---|
| 2-3 | plantains, green and unripe |
| | oil for frying |

Cut plantains into 1-inch slices. Flatten each piece in a wood presser or with bottom of an unbreakable mug or cup. Cook in oil over medium-high heat until lightly golden; drain on paper towel. Sprinkle with salt or top with ham and cheese.
*4 servings*

□  *Hojaldres*, which are cooked at local bakeries, look similar to Mexican sopapillas. They are bland-tasting like bread and served for breakfast. My grandfather goes to the bakery every morning around seven o'clock to buy breakfast. He buys baked bread called *machitas*, fried corn tortillas, *hojaldres,* and *plátanos*.

My sister likes to eat *hojaldres* with honey; she can eat them at any time. I, however, like them with cheese for breakfast.

### HOJALDRES
#### Puff-Pastries

| | |
|---|---|
| 1/3 | cup oil |
| 2 | tsp. salt |
| 2 3/4 | cups flour |
| 2/3 | cup milk |
| 2-3 | cups oil for frying |

In a large bowl, combine $1/3$ cup oil and salt. Add small amounts of flour and milk, stirring constantly with a fork. Form balls using $1/4$ cup mixture for each ball.

Heat remaining oil over medium-high heat. Cook balls until lightly brown. Drain on absorbent paper. Serve with honey, butter, or ham and cheese.
*4 to 6 servings*

**Tennis shoes and America.** Only kids wear tennis shoes in Panama. I don't remember wearing tennis shoes after seventh grade unless I was in gym in high school. I wore high-heels to try to look a little taller or sandals. I always wore nice shoes. Whenever I see tennis shoes here, I think of how beautifully we dressed for the parties in Panama and how much fun we had dancing.

No matter where I went in Panama—to a party, to the store, or to the bank—I, as well as other Panamanians, always dressed well. If I tried to go into a bank with shorts on, they would not let me in. Jeans were okay, but not shorts. When I went to parties, I would spend the whole day getting ready, beginning in the morning with rolling my hair and painting my nails. I either bought a new dress or wore the best one I had. The men dressed nicely also; they would never wear jeans to a party. Even the children wore their best clothes.

When there was a party for Christmas, birthdays, New Year's, or any occasion, the whole family was invited. No one would ever say, "Don't bring the kids." Children were welcome all the time. When we arrived at the party one hour late—a typical Panamanian trait—the family room would already be cleared for a dancing area. Everyone loved to dance. I danced with my mom, my kids, even alone. We danced salsa, merengue, and cumbia. The music, probably combined with a little drink, made everyone excited. We talked loudly, danced, and laughed. We had a really good time. The kids jumped all around and danced, too.

We would stay up all night and dance. If this were a Christmas party, we would start at midnight and keep going until six o'clock in the morning. I remember in college, my friends and I could dance for two hours straight. We were all sweaty, but we didn't care. When it was good music, we just didn't want to stop.

Besides dancing, there was always food at the party. The hostess prepared all the food from scratch and served everyone. It was not a buffet and no one brought a dish. *Tamales*; *pollo guisado,* chicken with salsa; *arroz con pollo,* rice with chicken; fruit drinks, maybe a cake, pie, or *arroz con leche,* a rice pudding—all were typical foods which were served. At one point, the hostess would say that it was time to eat and she would begin to serve. Afterwards, it was back to dancing.

Now I have gotten used to dressing casually and bringing food to parties. I still dress up for special occasions, but sometimes my husband will ask, "Why don't you dress like you used to?"

*When my sister and I (left) were in Panama, we always dressed up together to make sure we looked perfect. We had a good time getting ready and looking forward to the party.*

There was a small store on the corner where my family lived in Chiriqui. It sold a little bit of everything. The store bought a cow for each week. The owner then would cut and separate the meat into bags. If all the meat didn't sell that day, it was frozen. When the meat was gone, it was gone. Sometimes, we went to the store and they didn't have any more meat. We'd say, "Okay," then go home and eat beans or whatever we had in the house.

The store also sold chickens, but most people had their own chickens at the house or they bought them from neighbors. When we bought chickens, we couldn't select only breasts or legs, we got the *whole* chicken—uncut.

Strangely enough, we used soy sauce and Worcestershire sauce in our cooking. I think they came from the influences of the people passing through the Panama Canal.

### POLLO GUISADO
#### Chicken with Salsa

| | |
|---|---|
| 1 | whole chicken, cut into pieces |
| 1/4 | bunch cilantro, chopped |
| 1 | medium onion, chopped |
| 3 | garlic cloves, chopped |
| | garlic powder to taste |
| 1 | tomato, chopped |
| 1/2 | tsp. oregano |
| | salt to taste |
| 1/4 | cup tomato paste |
| 1/4 | tsp. black pepper |
| 1/2 | tsp. soy sauce |
| 1/2 | tsp. Worcestershire sauce |

In a large pot, combine all ingredients. Cook, covered, over medium heat for 1 hour or until chicken is done.
*6 to 8 servings*

We never had money to buy many groceries ahead because my parents were paid each day. We'd just walk to the store to pick up a few items at a time. We would buy two or three eggs, a fresh whole loaf of bread, and ten cents worth of butter. We did this almost every day.

### PLÁTANOS EN TENTACIÓN
#### Spiced Sweet Plantains

| | |
|---|---|
| 2 | yellow plantains |
| | water |
| 1/3 | cup brown sugar |
| 1 1/2 | Tbsp. butter |
| 1/2 | tsp. cinnamon |

Cut plantains into 1-inch slices. Add enough water to cover; cook over medium heat for 15 minutes. Add brown sugar, cinnamon, and butter. Mix well and cook for 5 minutes. Serve hot.
*4 servings*

I came from a town called Lagonoy in Camarines Sur, a province of the Bicol region of the Philippines. Coconuts are plentiful here, so the people of the area have learned to use the coconut in many of their dishes. Most of the time, Filipinos' diet consists of boiled rice and a vegetable dish flavored with dried fish like *toyo* or some other type of meat. Mind you, the fish or meat is just for flavoring. They are included in dishes to break the everyday vegetable flavor.

Preparation of food is not a one person's affair in my family. If the whole family is included, labor can be divided. The taste and flavoring of the dish is always done by the "Master Chef," who is Mom. Until we are ready to do this ourselves, we don't dare put salt or anything in the cooking. Mommy does it. The only critic we have is Dad—"Aah! That's too salty! It's too sweet!"—but he never goes into the kitchen to help.

The only people in the kitchen are my mom, my aunt, and the children. We are all given a task such as grating the coconuts, chopping the shrimp or oregano, or stirring the pot so the milk doesn't curdle. Procedures rotate. Maybe one day, I am grating coconuts; tomorrow, I may be chopping shrimp. This way we learn every procedure.

When we start serving the dish, Dad is already at the table ready to start complaining about the things he doesn't like. The good part about having everyone help is that you will never hear anyone who had helped say anything bad about the dish. We were proud that we contributed to the meal. Other hidden benefits of everyone helping are the passing down of the recipe and the methods of its preparation. This is how I learned how to cook.

Back then, we didn't have a regular cooking stove. We cooked outside under a lean-to, but we also had a smaller stove in the house if it rained. We would put three stones together in a triangle and place the pot on top of the rocks leaving enough space in the bottom to put a fire. We had to learn how to maintain the fire at the correct temperature by either adding or removing wood. If Mom said that she needed to simmer after the pot was boiling, I would have to remove the wood, leaving only the embers and maintain it that way. So, you think that these cooks out here are the best? No, I give credit to the people who know how to put in and take out wood to change temperatures without regulators!

We cooked like this four times a day. Besides the usual breakfast, lunch, and dinner, we had *merienda,* a snack time around three o'clock. We never thought that cooking like this was a hassle. The pleasure was that we had our family with us and that we were learning something that someone before us had to learn also.

*The taste of my native food never leaves me. This is why I love going back to the Philippines.*

□ *Adobado* and *tinoktok* are Filipino dishes which are from the Bicol region where coconut dishes are common. These recipes are reserved for special occasions such as when a dear friend or kin come to visit.

## ADOBADO
### Stewed Chicken

| | |
|---|---|
| 1¹/₂ | cups warm water |
| 1 | medium coconut, grated |
| 1 | tsp. coarse salt |
| 6 | peppercorns, crushed |
| 2 | garlic cloves, crushed |
| 1 | whole chicken, cut into pieces |
| 2 | lemon grass stalks, crushed |
| 4 | fresh banana peppers |

Add water to coconut and squeeze repeatedly to extract milk. Strain liquid into pot; discard coconut. Add salt, peppercorns, and garlic. Cook over medium heat, stirring constantly to prevent curdling. When simmering, add chicken and lemon grass. Stir until milk stabilizes. Cook, covered, until milk reduces to ¹/₂ the volume; stir often. Add banana peppers.

Adobado is best when reduced to almost a caramel consistency. Serve with rice and ripe bananas or other fruit.
*5 servings*

□ Wrapping the *tinoktok* is an art. For an amateur, a tie to keep the leaf from loosening is a must; for the expert, the correct folding and placement of each wrapped mixture in the pot are sufficient.

The first step of this dish may be offensive to some, but strangely enough, the desired taste cannot be achieved by omitting this step. I have tried and it is not the same. In a fly-free space, store the shrimp at room temperature for twenty-four hours. Afterwards, follow the rest of the instructions for this odorous shrimp.

## TINOKTOK
### Braised Chopped Shrimp

| | |
|---|---|
| 1 | lb. shrimp, shelled and deveined |
| 2 | large young coconuts, minced* |
| 1 | cup fresh oregano, chopped |
| 1 | cup fresh mint, chopped |
| 1 | cup coconut palm heart, minced* |
| 1 | medium coconut, grated |
| | gabi leaves, elephant ears, or oriental yellow squash leaves* |

Mince shrimp with young coconuts, oregano, and mint. Add coconut palm heart; stir to a paste-like consistency.

Spoon 1 to 2 tablespoons onto stem side of each leaf. Fold in sides and roll to the tip. Tie if necessary. Place wrapped mixture carefully in pot, seam side down.

Extract coconut milk from grated coconut as described in the adobado recipe. Pour milk in pot; add salt. Cook, covered, over medium heat for 30 minutes. Reduce heat to low; cook 1¹/₂ hours.

The dish should have small morsels of coconut milk that are almost solidified, and the leaves should be very tender to the touch. Serve with rice.
*4 to 6 servings*

**I was sitting** on the stairs, enjoying the fragrant smell coming from the long, yellow blossoms of the *ilang-ilang* tree. It was our neighbor's tree, but the wind carried the smell to our house. This was one of the days in the Philippines when I was very young; time seemed forever and I could have sat there smelling the scent from the hanging petals for that long.

My family was really poor. I knew we were poor because we always ate dried fish; that was the cheapest food. We managed to survive day by day by selling *bibingka,* or rice cakes, and corn. We always had food, and we never had to borrow money to put it on the table. We helped each other, and more or less we were content with our way of life.

I was about eight when my eldest brother, *Totoy* Ray, and I began helping our mom, "Inda," earn money. We would go to Barrio Carangian in the countryside to purchase sweet corn straight from the fields. The seller would pack the ears of corn in a rented buffalo-drawn cart, then the three of us, sitting on top of the corn, would ride down the bumpy road back to the marketplace in town.

With seven children in the family, we all shared in selling the corn. Sometimes we boiled or cooked the corn over hot charcoal at home, then sold them along the street, to the vendors inside of the market, and from house-to-house. I used to carry about twenty-five ears at a time in a metal foot-tub on top of my head. When I ran out, I would return home to get more; we lived just behind the market.

Natividad (right) with her brother, Emmanuel, and nephew.

*Whenever I eat mangoes, I think of the Philippines. Mangoes were a luxury for my family. Only one or two mangoes were cut for all nine of us. We used to fight over the seed because it had the most meat!*

Inda also earned money by praying for the dead. It was the custom of the Catholics to mourn for nine days. When someone died in a family, Inda was hired to mourn and pray for the soul. We children would kneel and, like a chorus, pray with her. My grandma also prayed for hire. With all the money she made, she always bought a chicken to put in the coop.

Although we had to work as children to help our family, I still have good memories of being carefree. Children there didn't have much recreation. There was no basketball; there was no football. On full moon nights, the kids of my neighborhood would go out and play hide-and-go-seek under the light of the moon. Every month all of us looked forward to this because it was the only time we were allowed to stay up late.

On the days when the rain came pouring down suddenly, typical of tropical countries like the Philippines, my brothers, sisters, and I would run out into rain, laughing, singing, and just having a good time. The rain showers felt so good on those hot summer days! And in my province, Tarlac, I recall swimming with other boys and girls, naked, in the river.

My father would always take me to the movies—American cowboy movies. Of course, the actors spoke a language different from ours. We could never fully understand what they were saying, but we could see the picture! Though we were a poor family, we didn't have problems as far as relationships. We loved and helped each other, and we were able to enjoy and appreciate the simple things in our lives.

When I came to America I wanted to become "rich" because I grew up being poor. My parents never owned a piece of property, not even a twelve-inch square. Even though I am in America and I own this and I own that, I can never forget where I grew up. Until this day, I still feel poor. Inside of me, I never changed. I still feel humble. I never did get rich.

◻ My mom raised hogs to put one of my brothers through medical school. She loved and tamed the hogs; she even scratched their black tummies. When it was time to sell them, she would cry because she had grown attached to them.

Reminiscent of my mom, I raised four pigs when my children were younger. I would call the pigs like my mom did. Once I entered a hog calling contest at the Fredericksburg fair, and I won first prize!

My children never touched the meat of the animals I raised because they considered the pigs as pets, but *adobo*, marinated chicken and pork, is still one of my children's favorite, especially the eldest, Larry. *Adobo* can be made with just chicken or pork, but the dish tastes better with the two combined.

## ADOBO
### Marinated Chicken and Pork

| | |
|---|---|
| 2 | lbs. pork, cubed |
| 1 | chicken, cut into pieces and remove skin |
| 1 | tomato, diced |
| 1 | large onion, sliced |
| 5 | garlic cloves, crushed |
| 3/4 | cup soy sauce |
| 3/4 | cup vinegar |
| 3/4 | cup water |
| 2 | bay leaves |
| 1/8 | tsp. black pepper |
| | dash of oregano |

Rinse pork and chicken. Place pork on bottom of cool pot; place chicken on top. Add remaining ingredients. Bring to a boil over high heat for 5 minutes. Reduce heat to medium; cook, covered, for 45 minutes or until pork is done. Do not stir while cooking. Remove cover; cook for 15 minutes to reduce liquid. Serve with rice.
*8 to 10 servings*

◻ When I was younger, I was a midwife assigned to the rural areas in the Philippines. I stayed with the women in their houses while they were in labor. Sometimes I even had to spend the night. The families appreciated my work and were always very nice to me. One family gave me a set of geese as a gift; another gave me a baby cow which was quite valuable because beef was expensive.

I think back to those days fondly because the people were so generous. Beef is inexpensive here, but it was and still is a luxury in the Philippines.

## BEPSTIK
### Lemon Beef with Onions

| | |
|---|---|
| 3 | lbs. boneless beef, thinly sliced |
| | juice of 3 lemons |
| 5 | garlic cloves |
| 1 | cup soy sauce |
| 2 | bay leaves |
| | dash of black pepper |
| | dash of oregano (optional) |
| 3-4 | large onions, sliced into ringlets |
| 6 | Tbsp. oil |

Slice beef; remove ligaments and fat. Pound meat with back of knife to tenderize. Combine beef, lemon juice, garlic, soy sauce, bay leaves, pepper, and oregano (optional); mix well. Marinate for at least 30 minutes, stirring occasionally.

Cook onions in 2 tablespoons oil over medium-high heat for 3 minutes. Remove and set aside.

Heat remaining oil over medium heat. Squeeze marinade from meat; reserve marinade. Cook meat until liquid is almost gone. Add marinade. Bring to a boil over high heat; cook until liquid is reduced to a small amount of thin sauce. Stir in onions. Cover and remove from heat; let sit for 10 minutes. Serve with rice.
*8 to 10 servings*

The *barrios* in the Philippines are boring places, so every now and then, the mayor and governor of these villages will do something fun. They collect money and plan for a festival or carnival for the people. Some *barrios* have an annual festival, but many *barrios* cannot afford it every year and may not have it as often. When it happens, everyone, from the youngest to the oldest person, is looking forward to this event.

The *palasebo*, or the pole climb, is the most fun event to join in the festival because it is very challenging. A bamboo pole, the length of a telephone pole but only six to seven inches in diameter, is made very smooth by removing the notches. It is so slick to the touch. On top of that, the pole is greased and polished for the contest and a bag of money with about 1,000 pesos, or about fifty dollars, is tied to the top. It is not easy to climb.

It's a man-thing, so many men plan to climb the pole. They think they are so macho with their egos showing. They all think they can do it, and they tease each other. Kids challenge the older men, "Oh, we're younger. You old men, you're not going to make it!" The older men think they can do better than the kids because of the kids' lack of experience. Still everyone is talking about what they are going to do with the money when he wins it.

Anita with her son (left) and Romel.

*When we visit the Philippines, just being there means a great deal to us. The Philippines is the land where we grew up, and it's still our country.*

On the day of the festival, the mayor announces the start of the contest. Everyone, with his own idea of how he is going to climb the pole, lines up. Most men have only shorts on and they cover themselves with dirt and sand for friction. Some even put honey on themselves first so the dirt will stick on them more!

The first one who tries to climb the pole gets a lot of applause; everyone is excited. He may only get three feet off the ground and he already falls. The crowd boos, and it's off to the next person. Some almost reach the bag, but they slide down before they grab it, and the crowd sighs, "Awww!" Somehow there is one person—lucky him—who will go up there and get the money.

Besides the *palasebo*, the festival has singing and dancing, lots of food, and contests with prizes. My brother, Romel, always joins the eating contests. Whoever eats all the food first wins a prize, and Romel always wins. For some reason, he can eat the hard-to-chew foods like rice cakes and the ones that stick in the throat like *bibingka*, a sticky rice cake, and other powdery sweets. As soon as he gets his prize money, probably only ten pesos, or about fifty cents, he runs home, "Mommy, Mommy! I won! I won!" and my mom would say, "Okay, let me have it so I can buy soap to wash the clothes," or something like that. Then she gives him back one peso!

We all love the festivals. I love being there with my cousins, laughing and walking around the town. We like to see the guys challenge each other and make fools of themselves at the *palasebo*. Some of our friends, cousins, and even our dad have tried to climb the pole, but they have never gotten the money. At night the roads are blocked for a disco and we dance all night. The festivals are fun, and we always look forward to the next one.

◻ Many Filipinos go to the village festivals just for the food. Just mention food and everyone will be there—like bees. Even the prizes for different games may be groceries.

Vendors at the festival sell many kinds of food and drinks. Filipinos hardly drink soda; they like the typical Filipino drinks such as *gulamen*, cubed gelatin in coconut juice, and *buko*, young coconut juice mixed with water, shredded coconut, sugar, and a bit of vanilla. The vendors also sell barbecue, boiled peanuts; *lugo*, a rice soup; and *pancit*, noodles with vegetables.

## PANCIT
### Noodles with Vegetables and Meat

| | |
|---|---|
| 1 | large package Canton noodles or rice noodles* |
| 3 | garlic cloves, crushed |
| 1 | medium onion, sliced |
| 3 | Tbsp. oil |
| 1/2 | lb. shrimp, pork, and/or chicken, cooked and shredded |
| 3 | medium carrots, sliced |
| 1/2 | lb. snow peas |
| 1/4 | lb. green beans |
| 1 | small cabbage, chopped |
| | soy sauce |
| | salt and pepper to taste |

If using rice noodles, soak rice noodles in water for a few minutes; drain and set aside.

Cook garlic and onion in oil over medium-high heat until lightly golden. Add meat; cook for 2 to 3 minutes. Stir in vegetables, crunchier ones first. Sprinkle with soy sauce, salt and pepper. Add noodles and ¹/2 cup water; add more water if needed. Cook, covered, until noodles are tender; stir occasionally.
*6 to 8 servings*

◻ The Filipinos started to cook *lugo* during World War II because food was very hard to find. Rice could not be bought in the market anymore; people were hiding and reserving it for themselves. They boiled a little bit of rice—maybe just one cup—and it kept multiplying until that one cup became one big pot of rice. That's the magic of *lugo*. Rice can be boiled and boiled until it feeds five people or it can be boiled even longer until it feeds ten people. This kind of recipe helped many Filipinos survive during the war.

To this day, even though there is plenty to eat, *lugo* has become part of the meals in the Philippines. *Lugo* has been revised since World War II. *Goto* is *lugo* with pig intestines, and *arroz caldo* is *lugo* with chicken and ginger. Plain *lugo* is also used to soothe upset stomachs.

## LUGO
### Rice Soup

| | |
|---|---|
| 3 | garlic cloves, crushed |
| 2 | Tbsp. oil |
| 2 | cups rice |
| 8 | cups water |
| 2 | tsp. salt |
| 1/4 | tsp. pepper |

Cook garlic in oil over medium-high heat until golden. Add rice and water. Bring to a boil over high heat. Reduce heat to medium; cook until rice is tender. Add salt and pepper.

Garnish with diced fried garlic, chopped green onion, lemon, or *patis*, Filipino fish sauce.

Variations: for goto, add intestines cut into 2-inch pieces. For arroz caldo, sauté ginger and chicken with the garlic. Add 1 cup of water and cook until chicken is almost done. Then follow the rest of the instructions for lugo.
*6 to 8 servings*

Among a variety of Polish traditions, there are two I am particularly fond of: customs concerning bread and Christmas Eve.

Polish people have always had a great deal of respect for bread. Bread is not just basic food; it is treated with reverence and has symbolic meaning.

I remember that when my mother dropped a piece of bread, she would often kiss it after picking it up—as if she apologized. And it was not just her. I know that it was a custom of older people in the part of Poland where I lived, and I remember reading about it in literature. My mother never threw any bread out, and I wouldn't do it either. Even now, in America, I cannot bring myself to throw bread in the garbage can.

Bread is also a part of marriage ceremonies. When newlyweds come home from church, they are offered bread and salt. The bread symbolizes a wish that they will never be without food in their lives; the salt reminds the couple that life holds tears and hard work.

Krystyna with her son, Micheal.

*Today in our American home, we keep this beautiful tradition [of Christmas Eve] not because we should but because it has always been a part of our lives.*

In Poland, Christmas Eve is especially treasured, and everyone, religious or not, celebrates it. The Christmas season is not as spectacular as in the U.S., but it is very emotional. It is a part of our culture everybody identifies with.

The Christmas Eve celebration begins when the first star appears in the evening sky. It is always the kids' job to look for the star. With the star shining, the family gathers at the table which is covered with a white cloth. Some hay may be put under the cloth as a reminder that Christ was born in a stable. Dishes are set for everyone present with an extra one for someone who is not there, like a family member who has died or lives far away, or a stranger who may happen to knock at the door.

The electric light is turned off and a candle is lit. Mother says a blessing and breaks *oplatek,* a white bread wafer. Everyone takes a piece and goes around to offer and take bits of *oplatek* while exchanging good wishes and kisses with the others.

After that, Christmas dinner can begin. There are supposed to be twelve dishes because there were twelve disciples, but in my family we never had that many. We wouldn't be able to eat that much. The food always tasted so good, perhaps because we fasted all day long before dinner.

Presents are exchanged after dinner. When I was a child, Poland wasn't very rich, so the gifts may have been chocolates, oranges, or a book, but everyone was happy to receive them. After enjoying the presents, we would sing Polish carols. I remember my brother playing the accordion while the rest of us sang.

People stay awake late that night because there is a custom to go to church at midnight for a special mass called *Pasterka*. Animals are said to talk in human voices on Christmas Eve. It may not be a very good idea to eavesdrop on their conversations and find out what the animals have to say about their owners!

Christmas Eve is always very special to me. When I was a little child, I often got sick on Christmas Eve and no one knew why. Now I know it was all the pressure and excitement caused by waiting for something magical and special to happen.

At that time I was not aware that we kept tradition. It was so natural to us. We celebrated a special day—a day to be open, to forgive everyone, and to give to someone. This is why I love it so much. Today in our American home, we keep this beautiful tradition not because we should, but because it has always been a part of our lives.

◻ There is a town in Poland called Torun which is famous for two reasons: it is the birthplace of Copernicus, and it boasts the best *piernik*, or Polish gingerbread. There are many recipes for *piernik*, but all of them list honey as the main ingredient. This recipe, challenging but rewarding when followed properly, requires that the dough be prepared two to four weeks before baking and placed in the refrigerator to mature.

## PIERNIK
### Layered Gingerbread

| | |
|---|---|
| 18 | oz. honey |
| 2 | cups sugar |
| 1 | cup butter |
| 8 | cups flour |
| 3 | eggs |
| 3 | tsp. baking soda |
| 1/2 | cup cold milk |
| 1/2 | tsp. salt |
| 1 1/2 | tsp. cinnamon |
| 1/4 | tsp. ground cloves |
| | dash of allspice |
| | chopped walnuts (optional) |

Cook honey, sugar, and butter over medium heat until almost boiling; remove from stove. When lukewarm, gradually add flour. Add eggs; mix well by hand. Dissolve baking soda in milk and add to mixture. Add salt. Combine cinnamon, cloves, and allspice; add to mixture. Dough will be sticky. Mix until smooth and shape into a ball. Add walnuts, if desired, before shaping.

Place in a ceramic or enamel-coated container. Cover with cloth to allow breathing and keep in the bottom of refrigerator for at least two but not over four weeks. After two weeks dough will be very stiff. Divide dough into 3 to 4 cake pans; bake at 325° for $^1/_2$ hour or until dark brown.

When cool, layer with lukewarm prune butter or blackberry preserves. Cover with paper and press evenly—for example, with books—for 2 to 3 days until softened (the bread will be hard after baking). Piernik will have the texture of bread. It will stay fresh for a long time if kept in a cool place.
*1 gingerbread*

◻ You cannot imagine a Polish kitchen without potatoes. They can be fried, baked, or used to make potato pancakes and many other dishes. In America, people may have only one potato with their dinner; in Poland, you have lots of potatoes because they're supposed to stuff you.

## PLACKI ZIEMNIACZANE
### Potato Pancakes

| | |
|---|---|
| 6 | medium potatoes, grated |
| 3 | Tbsp. flour |
| | salt and pepper to taste |
| 1 | onion, grated (optional) |
| | oil for frying |

Drain excess juice from grated potatoes.

Combine all ingredients; mix well. If needed, add a small amount of flour until consistency is like yoghurt.

Heat oil over medium heat. Drop mixture by 3 tablespoons, flattening into a patty. Cook both sides until golden brown and crispy. Serve plain or with sour cream, apple sauce, or goulash on top.
*6 servings*

**We celebrate namedays** in Poland instead of birthdays because most Polish people are named after saints. Each day of our calendar has a few saints' names on it. When a person's name, being the same as a saint, appears on a particular day, that is his or her *imieniny*, or nameday.

For example, my mother and father chose Margaret, or *Małgorzata* in Polish, as my name. I was born on December 26, but the following nameday is not until January 18. January 18 is when I celebrate my nameday. There is another nameday for Margaret in August, but I only celebrate the one closest to my birthday. I didn't celebrate my birth date at all.

My family made a big deal about namedays. Mom would invite family and friends, and everyone would come nicely dressed—like on Sundays—and bring gifts. Mom would do the cooking; I would do the decorating. Everything was the best.

*Standing on Polish ground while holding the baby of my best friend was truly a happy moment in my life.*

When the guests arrived, all the food was already set up on the table. First, we'd have cold cuts: ham, salami, pastrami; pickled mushrooms and pickled cucumbers. Another dish was *nozki*, pigs feet in its own jelly cooked with vegetables. I know people will laugh, but *nozki* is delicious and it's my favorite food!

We always had wine and Polish vodka, more vodka than wine because Polish people definitely drink a lot of vodka—straight up. The vodka stayed on the table throughout the entire meal.

All the food mentioned is just the beginning. Then we'd have the main course. The main entrée was normally *flaczki. Flaczki,* pig intestines cooked in a spicy thick stew, is very Polish and most delicious! *Chleb razowy*, Polish rye bread with a thick amount of butter, was also a must on every table for any occasion.

Next would come *sledz w oleju*, herring in oil with sliced onions. We'd put herring on the rye bread with a little onion and a sprinkle of lemon in one hand; vodka in the other. Then we'd take a bite, drink vodka right afterwards, and it was heaven on earth!

Then would come desserts. The table dented from the weight of the desserts. There were at least three to five Polish cakes. We don't have a nameday cake like a birthday cake, just lots of food. Mom did everything from scratch. It took her three days to prepare for this occasion.

We loved to talk about family matters at occasions like namedays. We could sit for five to seven hours straight. We couldn't get out because we were stuck at a huge table in a little room. We'd just keep eating and drinking.

Now I celebrate my birthday on December 26, just after Christmas, and who remembers that? But the really sad part is being deprived of my nameday after twenty-eight years of celebrations. I had always looked forward to my nameday. In Poland there was no question if anyone would remember my nameday because it was such a special day.

❑ My mother didn't want me to learn how to cook at an early age. She used to tell me, "Your future is ahead of you. You're very young, so enjoy life while you can. Cooking isn't that much fun, especially when you do it for twenty years. It is very hard on women with children. We all have to cook." She said when I get married, then I could learn. She went through a hard life, so she meant this in a loving way.

*Zupa jarzynowa* is a typical Polish soup. When I make it, it reminds me of my mother and Poland.

### ZUPA JARZYNOWA
#### Vegetable Soup

| | |
|---|---|
| 1 | whole chicken |
| 2 | leeks, chopped |
| 5 | carrots, sliced |
| 2 | parsnips, cubed |
| 1 | small cabbage, cubed |
| 1 | large bunch fresh dill; chop leaves and tie stems |
| 1 | bunch fresh parsley; chop leaves and tie stems |
| 1/4 | tsp. thyme |
| 1/4 | tsp. rosemary |
| 3-5 | tsp. Vegeta * or soup base salt and pepper to taste |
| 4 | medium potatoes, diced |
| 2-3 | Tbsp. sour cream |

In a large pot of water, boil chicken until done; skim fat. Add remaining ingredients except potatoes and sour cream; cook until vegetables are half-done. Add potatoes; cook until potatoes are done. Discard tied stems of dill and parsley. Stir in sour cream.
*8 to 10 servings*

❑ We always looked forward to family gatherings at Aunt Zosia's house. All of her cooking was so delicious, but she was definitely famous for her *szarlotka* and cheesecake. Although our stomachs were stuffed to the maximum, we would still eagerly await dessert. It was almost a sin, but we enjoyed ourselves so much.

I truly enjoyed sharing the happiness of being together as a family at the table. I wish you all were with me to experience these wonderful moments.

### SZARLOTKA
#### Polish Cinnamon Apple Cake

| | |
|---|---|
| 2.2 | lbs. soft sweet apples, peeled and cored |
| 1/4 | cup sugar |
| 1 | tsp. cinnamon |
| 1 | tsp. vanilla extract |
| 1/2 | cup bread crumbs |

| | **dough:** |
|---|---|
| 2 | cups flour |
| 2/3 | cup powdered sugar |
| 1 | cup butter |
| 2 | egg yolks |
| 1/4 | cup sour cream |

Cook apples in a small amount of water over medium heat until soft; drain. Add sugar, cinnamon, and vanilla; mix well. Set aside.

Prepare dough. Combine flour, sugar, butter, yolks, and sour cream; mix into a dough. Knead until smooth. Divide dough in half. For a crispier crust, place other half in freezer until ready to use.

Grease baking pan with butter; sprinkle with 3/8 cup of bread crumbs. Roll out dough and spread gently over crumbs. Bake at 325° to 350° until lightly brown. Sprinkle remaining crumbs. Spread apple mixture. Roll out other half of dough and place on top. Sprinkle with powdered sugar; cut into 2-inch squares. Bake until golden brown.
*6 to 8 servings*

**I remember the summer** vacations spent at my aunt's house in the country, the smell of eucalyptus, the beautiful waterfalls and how I quenched my thirst on hot summer days. This is the Portugal that I miss most.

I can never forget the long walks in the woods where I would spend most of my afternoons exploring their beauty. At night, I would leave my bedroom window open to wake in the morning and smell the mix of the wildflowers from the fields. My aunt would say to me, "Open your arms wide and breathe the air that is so fresh and clean. It's great for your lungs."

My aunt, who is now ninety years old, is so wonderful to me. She is my best friend and my second mother because my parents passed away very young. My aunt taught me so much. She made me become aware of things that I never knew. She was my inspiration and was always full of good advice. Oh, how I miss being with her!

*I took my son, Charles, to Portugal on my first return visit after I came to America. He was two and a half years old then.*

The custom of Portuguese people is to go out after dinner to the sidewalk cafés for a cup of coffee or a soft drink. There, they can chat for a while with their friends and family. Growing up in Lisbon, you feel free to walk everywhere, especially on all the sidewalks made of cobblestone. As a young girl, I remember having fun with my friends as we pointed to the American tourist women walking on the cobblestone sidewalks and getting their high-heeled shoes caught between the stones. They would try to get the shoe out of the hole afterward, but they never could.

I miss the bakery man who stopped at our door every morning to deliver the hot bread that was ordered the night before, the sounds of the boy who yelled from the street to sell the paper, and the woman who made a living selling flowers from a large basket carried on her head. I remember the beautiful park of my youth and the cathedral just across from it. There, all the teenagers would play. We would jump rope for hours! My aunt would remind me that when the cathedral bells rang at five o'clock, it was time to go home for tea.

As I grew older, I had a great desire for travelling. Many years ago, when I was in my twenties, I came to the U.S. to visit my sister, Lisa, and her husband, Ren Shores. I arrived in America and decided to stay, get married, and have a family. Now, here I am today as a citizen of this enormous country, leading a busy life as a mother and a worker—each day of the year. However, I will never forget my memories as a young person in my old county of Portugal.

In Nazare, everyone makes his living from the ocean. On the days when the ocean is scary and the waves are big, the wives of the fishermen dress in black and sit on the beach, praying until the men return for the day. When the men are fishing for cod, they may leave their families for six to seven months to fish near Newfoundland and Canada. The women never know if anything will happen so they wear a black scarf in their hair until the men come back.

It is said that any Portuguese chef knows about 135 ways to cook cod. I have tried so many ways but not all 135. *Caldeirada de peixe*, a seafood stew made with cod, is just one of the recipes I know.

## CALDEIRADA DE PEIXE
### Seafood Stew

| | |
|---|---|
| 1 | red pepper, thickly sliced |
| 1 | onion, thickly sliced |
| 1/2 | cup chopped celery and leaves |
| 1 | cup sliced carrots |
| 2 | Tbsp. chopped fresh parsley |
| 2 | bay leaves |
| 5 | Tbsp. olive oil |
| 5 | cups water |
| 5 | potatoes, peeled and diced |
| 1 | lb. fresh codfish, cut into chunks |
| 2 | Tbsp. paprika |
| | salt and pepper to taste |

Cook red pepper, onion, celery, carrots, parsley, and bay leaves in oil over medium-high heat for 5 minutes. Add water; bring to a boil. Add potatoes. Reduce to medium heat; cook for 15 minutes. Add codfish, paprika, salt and pepper; cook for 15 minutes. Let stand, covered, for 10 minutes and serve.
*5 to 7 servings*

The head of the fish is part of the beauty when serving *pargo assado*, or baked red snapper. I passed this recipe to one of my bosses, but he was a bit scared of the eyes so he put black olives on them!

## PARGO ASSADO
### Baked Red Snapper

| | |
|---|---|
| 1 | whole red snapper |
| 1 1/2 | tsp. salt |
| 1 | tsp. black pepper |
| 6 | bacon slices |
| 1 | cup tomato sauce |
| 1/2 | cup water |
| 1 | medium onion, sliced |
| 3 | Tbsp. margarine, melted |
| 1 | tsp. paprika |
| 3-5 | potatoes |
| 1 1/2 | cups white wine |
| 3 | bay leaves |
| | fresh parsley |

Make 3 vertical slits in fish. Sprinkle salt and pepper on both sides. Roll each slice of bacon and place in slits.

Mix tomato sauce, water, onion, and margarine; pour over fish and sprinkle with paprika. Arrange potatoes around fish; cover with wine. Add bay leaves and parsley. Bake at 350° for 60 minutes or until potatoes are done.
*4 to 6 servings*

**Although I am** Portuguese, I come from the beautiful islands of the Azores in the Atlantic Ocean. Beginning in March and all the way to October, the Azores become a big tourist attraction because of the feasts of the spirits, or *festa do espiritosnto*. I, along with the rest of the locals, looked forward to the feasts every year because there was not much happening on those small islands otherwise.

Every village has a feast named after the village or the patron saint. The first feast may begin on March 15, go for seven days, then another village will have its feast for seven days, and so on. It's a tradition that the people from one village must travel around to the feasts of other villages. Something is always going on every night of the seven days of the feasts. Each village has its own band for folk and big band music. At least one night in the week has *fado*—a good translation being the Portuguese blues—which originated from the mainland. All the time people are dancing, eating, and drinking the traditional red wine made in the Azores.

During this time the streets are covered with Christmas-like lights. Pine trees, stripped of their bark, are made into posts to hang lights from one pole to another along the streets. At night the lights are turned on, and the streets are just glowing. Branches from an *alcasa*, a fragrant tree in the bay leaf family, are placed on each light post. The streets smell really good, and the smell lasts the duration of each feast.

On Sunday, the big day of the feast, the villagers cut flowers to make a carpet of different designs in the middle of the main street. Usually it's in front of the church. On this day, the festivities start early with mass. Around eleven o'clock, statues of the saints and Jesus Christ are taken from the church on a platform. Eight men, dressed in black suits with red capes, carry the platform on their shoulders and walk down the main street and through the village. These villages, each only about a mile long, have only one main street and small streets on the side. The *whole* island has only one main street.

Al (front) with friends.

*I didn't lose my love of Portuguese music. I continue playing the music in the U.S. with a band. Sometimes when I am in the Azores, my friends from a band I had will ask me to sing a couple of songs. It's very special for me to be asked.*

The rest of the people who leave mass also walk through the street singing joyous hymns. Everyone parades around the village, then returns to the church. The saints are put back except for the main statue of the village and Jesus Christ; they stay out until the evening.

After the parade, everyone eats and has a good time. Food—corn bread, sweet breads, *al catra*, and *sopa espirito santo*—is set up on long wooden tables. *Al catra*, marinated beef, and *sopa espirito santo,* soup of the spirits, are typical for the feasts. *Sopa espirito santo* is a beef broth with lots of peppermint poured over big slices of bread in clay bowls.

My village, Santa Rita, was just like the others with the same feasts. When the feasts were going on, they were the best times I ever had as a child. Every village also had bullfights in the streets right before the nighttime programs. I used to play with the bulls in the streets, showing off to the girls. It was every kid's dream.

When I lived there, I got used to what was going on and didn't pay attention to the beauty of the islands. I love going back to the Azores, especially during the summer. Every time I'm there, I think about my childhood and the feasts, and they bring back really nice memories.

◻ *Al catra*, a traditional marinated beef dish originating from the Azores, is always served during the village feast. It comes from the farmers who, a long time ago, did not have that much to cook with. *Al catra* was kept in special, handmade clay pots. The dish was then baked outside in clay ovens heated by wood. Some people still use these ovens, but not the new age because people are not too interested in burning wood to cook food.

## AL CATRA
### Beef Marinated in Wine

| | |
|---|---|
| 4-5 | lbs. beef roast, cut into chunks |
| 1/2 | lb. bacon |
| 2 | medium onions, quartered |
| 2 | garlic cloves, crushed |
| 2 | Tbsp. butter, melted |
| 2 | bay leaves |
| 3-4 | whole cloves |
| 1 | tsp. red pepper |
| | salt to taste |
| | red wine |

Combine all ingredients, using enough wine to cover meat. Marinate 48 hours. Bake in a 325° preheated oven for 8 hours or until meat is tender. Serve with garden rice.
*8 to 10 servings*

## GARDEN RICE

Cook rice according to package instructions. Mix rice with chopped parsley, green pepper, onion, green beans, carrots, and olive oil. The amounts of the vegetables and oil are to taste.

◻ Fishing and farming are the occupations of most people on the Azores. When the boats come in, auctioneers sell the fish for the fishermen by weight. Whoever buys will then go door-to-door to sell the fish. Some use small trucks to sell the fish; some use horse and buggy; and some walk, carrying a stick across the shoulders with two hanging baskets. The ones with the stick and baskets are the most unfortunate because it takes them all day to sell their fish.

Believe it or not, the fishermen like to eat what they catch. *Peixe a pescador* is best translated as "fishermen-style fish."

## PEIXE A PESCADOR
### Fisherman-Style Fish

| | |
|---|---|
| 3-4 | garlic cloves, crushed |
| 1/8 | cup chopped fresh parsley |
| | salt and pepper to taste |
| 2 | Tbsp. butter |
| 2 | 1 1/2 lb. fish |

Cook garlic, parsley, salt and pepper in butter over medium-high heat. Remove from heat. Marinate fish in sauce, turning every 10 minutes, for 1 hour. Grill fish. Serve with boiled potatoes or white rice and Azorean salad.
*4 servings*

## AZOREAN SALAD

| | |
|---|---|
| 1 | head of leaf lettuce, finely chopped |
| 1 | medium onion, finely chopped |
| | salt to taste |
| | olive oil to taste |
| | vinegar to taste |

Combine all ingredients; toss to mix. Cover; set aside 1 hour before serving.
*4 servings*

In Puerto Rico we celebrate Three Kings Day, the day when the three kings brought presents to Jesus. In America, some people are already throwing out their tree on New Year's Day; in Puerto Rico, the final day of the Christmas season is Three Kings Day on January 6.

As children we believed that the three kings were coming to our houses with their camels, so we had to feed the kings' camels because they would be hungry after their long trip. We filled shoe boxes with grass for the camels. We also picked little wild flowers in the forest and placed them in the boxes for decoration. It was more exciting when we saw other kids in the neighborhood—all grabbing grass and flowers for the camels—with their shoe boxes, too.

Afterwards, we put the shoe boxes under the bed when we went to sleep. And the next morning on Three Kings Day, the boxes were empty because the camels came to eat the grass. We also received presents from the three kings; the kings are like Santa Claus here. When we woke up, presents were under the bed or in the living room, and the shoe boxes were always empty.

*I have always wanted to share the Puerto Rican traditions of my childhood with my children.*

I modernized my childhood for my daughter last year. I asked her, "Do you think that Santa's reindeer will be hungry?"

She said, "Yes, Mama. Why don't we put carrots out for them?" So I put out a tray with carrots for the reindeer and cocoa milk and three cookies for Santa.

I typed a letter from Santa, "Ho! Ho! Ho! The cookies were delicious, and the reindeer enjoyed the carrots. Keep up the good work." My daughter said that Santa wrote her!

These days it's not like when I was growing up. The children are only six or seven years old and they know that there is no Santa Claus. I was twelve years old when I found out that the three kings weren't the ones who brought me presents and the camels didn't eat the grass. I guess I wanted to believe in the kings and camels. All the other kids in the neighborhood believed in them; they were also picking grass and flowers to fill their shoe boxes.

Now Puerto Rico is Americanized. Puerto Ricans celebrate the birthday of Jesus and Three Kings Day. For example, my sister buys clothes as gifts from Santa and toys as gifts from the three kings. They also have a big meal with each celebration. In Puerto Rico they're very lucky!

My mother has never told me what she did with all the grass that her six children picked. Maybe my father took the pile away in the car. I have asked her; she says she doesn't remember. I know she remembers, but I don't force her because she smiles when she says that. I guess she wants to keep the mysteriousness of the time. I'm pretty sure she enjoyed it as much as we did.

□ On Three Kings Day, my mother always cooked a feast just like people here would cook a big meal for Christmas. Instead of a ham or turkey, she prepared what the family enjoys. Usually the meal had roast pork, rice and beans, and desserts.

We enjoyed the whole day eating, playing with the toys, and going to other people's houses. We would also go to my grandparents, aunts, and other relatives who lived close by to see what the kings had left for us at their houses.

## PASTELILLOS DE GUAYAVA
### Guava Paste Pastry

| 1 | package puff pastry |
| 1/2 | cup guava paste, melted* |
| | powdered sugar |

Cut puff pastry into 2-inch squares; bake according to package instructions.

Cook guava paste in microwave for 1 minute until softened. When puff pastry squares are done, split with fork. Spread 1 tablespoon guava paste in between pastry. Sprinkle with powdered sugar.
*24 servings*

□ *Sazon con culantro y achiote* is a packaged seasoning with coriander and annato. It is used in many Puerto Rican dishes.

## PERNIL ASADO
### Baked Picnic Pork

| 1 | 10 lb. picnic pork |
| 4 | garlic cloves |
| 4 | tsp. salt |
| 1 | tsp. pepper |
| 1 | tsp. oregano |
| 1 | envelope sazon con culantro y achiote* |

Wash picnic pork. With a knife, slice several openings; set aside.

In a mortar, pound garlic and salt. Add pepper, oregano, and sazon; mix well. Fill openings with mixture and spread remaining mixture on pork. Cover and place in refrigerator for at least 4 hours. Bake at 350° for 3 hours or until tender.
*20 servings*

## HABICHUELAS ROSADAS
### Pink Beans

| 2 | Tbsp. sofrito [see page 169] |
| 1 | envelope sazon con culantro y achiote* |
| 3 | Tbsp. tomato sauce |
| 1/2 | cup chopped ham |
| 1 | Tbsp. vegetable oil |
| 1 | 15 oz. can pink beans or any preferred variety |
| 1 | cup water |
| 1/2 | cup chopped potatoes or squash |
| | salt to taste |

Cook sofrito, sazon, tomato sauce, and ham in oil over medium heat for 5 to 10 minutes, stirring constantly. Add beans, water, potatoes or squash, and salt; cook for 20 minutes or until sauce thickens. Serve with your favorite recipes or white rice.
*6 servings*

**Thirty-eight years ago** I left Puerto Rico, and I still can't get the island out of me—at least, not out of my taste-buds. I still remember the Twelve Days of Christmas celebrations with lots of parties and specialty foods; the carnival season when the streets were closed off in the old part of the city and steel bands came from all over the Caribbean to play while the people celebrated; and the Feast of San Juan, Puerto Rico's patron saint, when it was de rigueur for everyone to go to the beach at night to party and go into the water at midnight.

Though I have made my life in the "ole USA," I still haven't gotten used to doing without Puerto Rican food and drink. That's not to say I haven't enjoyed food and drink since leaving the island, because I definitely have, especially my wife's Italian cooking as well as the ubiquitous hamburgers, hot dogs, and pizzas that my kids love. However, I have never gotten used to peanut butter and American coffee.

My four sons' favorite snack was peanut butter on toast. They could *really* put away a *whole lot* of it every day. They ate so much peanut butter on toast, between and after meals

*You can take the boy out of the island, but you can't take the island out of the boy.*

and at any other time, that we had a problem keeping enough bread around the house.

On one memorable occasion, Mimi, my wife, got tired of never finding bread for breakfast and the boys' complaint that we never bought enough. Exasperated, Mimi stormed out and bought a whole rack—100 loaves of sandwich bread—from the grocery store! After cramming the freezer and refrigerator, we still had about thirty loaves left, so my second son loaded the bread onto my fourth son's Radio Flyer wagon and sold them around the neighborhood, much to my wife's embarrassment.

Once my kids noticed that I would never partake of peanut butter on toast. They asked me, all full of curiosity, how come I never ate peanut butter. I explained to them that in Puerto Rico, as in most other Spanish households, kids didn't eat peanut butter often. I was eighteen years old when I came to the States and too old to acquire a taste for it by then. All four of them stared at me in awed silence, and my third son could barely hold back the tears when he exclaimed in sympathy, "What a terrible childhood you must have had!"

❑ When my father and mother used to visit us every year, they would bring whatever they needed to prepare coffee and a few goodies. After my father retired, they moved in with us to allow my wife to work on her doctoral studies, and my mother took over the cooking. Meals at home have since alternated between our Italian and Hispanic favorites.

My father had a gift for making coffee, and while my mother's cooking was legendary, she had a genius for preparing desserts. These are a few of her dessert recipes.

## PUDIN DE ARROZ CON COCO
### Coconut Rice Pudding

| | |
|---|---|
| 1 | cup rice |
| 6 | cups coconut milk or 2 cans Coco Lopez® |
| 1 | tsp. cinnamon |
| 1-2 | pinches of ground ginger |
| 1 | tsp. salt |
| 1 | cup sugar |
| | raisins |
| | cinnamon |

Soak rice in water for 1 hour; drain.

In a large pot, combine rice, 5 cups coconut milk, cinnamon, ginger, and salt. Cook over low heat for 30 minutes without stirring. Add sugar, raisins, and remaining cup of coconut milk; cook another 40 minutes, stirring constantly to prevent sticking. Pour into a serving dish or individual cups and sprinkle cinnamon on top. Serve chilled.
*6 to 8 servings*

❑ *Pudin tembleque* must be stirred constantly. My mother made us kids take turns stirring.

## PUDIN TEMBLEQUE
### Trembling Pudding

| | |
|---|---|
| 6 | cups coconut milk or 2 cans Coco Lopez® |
| 1/2 | cup cornstarch |
| 2/3 | cup sugar |
| 1/2 | tsp. salt |
| 1 | Tbsp. orange blossom water* or 1/2 tsp. vanilla extract |
| 3 1/2 | cups water |

In a large pot, combine all ingredients; mix well. Cook over low heat for 40 minutes, stirring constantly. Pour immediately into a glass pie plate mold that has been rinsed in cold water. Chill thoroughly. Place a serving platter over pie mold and turn over, transferring pudding to platter. Serve chilled.
*6 to 8 servings*

## FLAN DE HUEVOS
### Puerto Rican Egg Custard

| | |
|---|---|
| 1 3/4 | cups sugar |
| 10 | eggs |
| 2 | 12 oz. cans evaporated milk |
| 1 | tsp. salt |
| 1 | tsp. vanilla extract |

Prepare syrup. Cook 3/4 cup sugar in a Pyrex®-type mold over low heat until sugar begins to liquefy. Increase heat to medium; cook until liquid turns light brown, stirring constantly with a wooden spoon. Coat sides of mold; set aside.

Beat eggs with mixer, then gradually add remaining sugar. Add milk, salt, and vanilla. Beat for 3 minutes. Pour mixture into mold coated with caramelized syrup. Place mold into a larger pan containing enough water to cover half of the pan (a bath). Bake at 350° for 1 hour or until firm. Cool thoroughly; gently turn mold onto a platter. Serve chilled.
*8 to 10 servings*

**They would come** around eleven o'clock. I remember a lot of noise. I could hear the pots going like crazy and Mamá, my grandmother, arguing with the ladies because they were not coming to the house at the same time. She wanted to fry all the chicken at the same time. They were complaining that the chicken was cold—we didn't have a microwave at that time—or that they had the smallest piece of meat. Mamá would just say, "Well, you should have gotten here earlier!"

That's the way it was almost every day at Mamá's house. The women worked at a clothing factory just walking distance from the house. They liked her food, and instead of going home or to the restaurant, they came to Mamá's. Mamá was very poor. She raised three children by herself and had never worked outside of the house. Cooking was the way she made her money.

*You don't have to settle for being average when you can be the best. This is what I believe, and this is what I teach my children.*

As a child, I used to sit quietly at the table as the women talked about their lives and the factory. When adults were around, kids weren't supposed to say anything. It was very strict. Parents would hit kids in the head if the kids contradicted them. Like if my dad, Papi, said he caught a fish that was thirty pounds and I said, "No, it wasn't Papi. It was only twenty pounds," he would hit me on the head. The fish probably was only twenty pounds, but it was none of my business. It didn't matter what he said, he was right all the time.

I got upset with some of the ladies. One of them was my own aunt. She would inspect the food with her fork and it made Mamá very mad. "Why are you looking at the food like that? Are you trying to find bugs?" Mamá would yell. My aunt also smelled the food. Every time she put it in her mouth, she'd smell it. After they were gone, Mamá would say, "Ha! Look at the way she is," and she complained and complained about the ladies. A couple of other ladies ate at the house just to look at Papi. They thought he was the greatest and so good-looking; he was always the center of attention. Those women were drooling while they were eating. It used to make me mad, but now it's funny.

Mamá also brought home income from selling desserts during Thanksgiving. She made pumpkin pies; *pudin de pan*, bread pudding; and flans. She made the greatest desserts. We'd go to town and get the best pumpkins, judging by their hollow sound and their color, for the pies. Pumpkins in Puerto Rico are dark green with yellow stripes, not orange. Just going to buy the pumpkins was a trip in itself.

All the grandkids were involved in making the pies. She gave us each a spoon. We asked her how much money she'd give us, but we only got to lick the spoons and bowls afterwards—all that work, just to lick the spoon! She would leave one pie for us, but we couldn't eat it until the end of the holiday just in case someone needed a pie at the last minute. Now I wish I had paid more attention to how she made her pies so I can make them like her. She never had a recipe and ingredients were put together just right.

Mamá loved to cook and she enjoyed the people—when they weren't complaining. Even after all these years, people who were in my school will tell me, "Yeah! I remember your grandmother made the best *pudin* in town. I have never eaten one like that." She did it for a long time. If her food was good every time, it meant that she really loved what she did.

◻ Puerto Ricans celebrate Thanksgiving Day. We have the turkey, baked sweet potatoes, and macaroni salad, but we stuff the turkey with *mofongo*, mashed green plantains. We also have rice with pigeon beans and potato salad.

When it comes time for Thanksgiving dinner here in America, my children and I are very involved. It's not just another dinner or another day. I want my children to love and be involved with the family, and I want to pass on traditions, like this recipe.

## BUDIN DE CALABAZA
### Pumpkin Custard

| | |
|---|---|
| 6 | eggs |
| 2 | Tbsp. cornstarch |
| 3 | Tbsp. butter, softened |
| 1 | tsp. vanilla extract |
| 1 | tsp. salt |
| $1/2$ | cup evaporated milk |
| $1^1/2$ | cups sugar |
| 3 | cups pumpkin, mashed |

**glaze:**

| | |
|---|---|
| 1 | cup sugar |

Prepare glaze. Cook sugar over medium heat until sugar becomes a light brown syrup; stir constantly. Spread evenly in pan including edges; set aside.

Combine eggs, cornstarch, butter, vanilla, salt, milk, and sugar; mix well. Add pumpkin; mix well. Strain mixture through colander. Pour into glazed pan. Place pan in a larger one filled with $1/2$ inch water. Cook over high heat for about 1 hour; replenish water as needed.

*4 to 6 servings*

◻ *Sofrito* is the first ingredient in any Puerto Rican dish. The meal just wouldn't be complete without it. Use *sofrito* in beans and rice. I make a large amount at once and store it.

## SOFRITO

| | |
|---|---|
| 1 | green or red pepper |
| 4 | garlic cloves |
| 1 | small onion |
| 8-10 | cilantro stalks, chopped |
| | salt and pepper to taste |

In a blender, mix all ingredients to a paste; refrigerate.

When using sofrito, first sauté 1 to 2 tablespoons in oil.

◻ This very simple soup is a common remedy for hangovers. Mamá says that after four or five beers in a restaurant, people order this so they can drink more. Try it sometime.

## CALDO DE PESCADO
### Fish Head Soup

| | |
|---|---|
| 1 | fish head |
| 2 | cups water |
| 1-2 | garlic cloves, crushed |
| | salt and pepper to taste |

Cook all ingredients over medium-high heat for 15 to 20 minutes; strain.

*2 servings*

**When December begins**, the parties kick in. You will hear people screaming and music all around. It doesn't matter how loud they are; people don't call the police over there in Puerto Rico. It's definitely the Christmas season.

As December progresses, there are more and more moving parties called *parrandas*. *Parrandas* begin when someone invites his family and friends to his home. Everyone—religious and not—is in a festive mood, so when they hear the music of the *parrandas,* they just come and join the parties.

Usually a couple of people will get together and ask where *parrandas* are happening. When they find out, they will gather people who play the guitar; the *cuatro,* a guitar but smaller and with a higher pitch; the *güiro,* a hollow wooden instrument with a raspy sound used to create the tempo; and maracas. The *cuatro* gives the music flavor, but all that is really needed is a group of happy people and a guitar.

Once a group is gathered, they will go to any house and start a party. Usually the people know the family of the house, but sometimes not. Houses in Puerto Rico have porches in the front, so most of the time the *parrandas* start outside. The people of the house will open the door to a bunch of people singing, clapping, and dancing, then the party begins. That is why this uninvited party is sometimes called an *asaltos,* or a happy surprise.

The party moves into the living room, then into the kitchen. Everyone is grabbing things to help start the cooking. No one knows if the party will be at that house for ten minutes or ten hours. The whole time people are eating, drinking, and singing Christmas songs, like carols, but these songs are much happier. The singer builds up a song at that moment. The music is a traditional sound and the singer just fits in. He sings about Christmas, the island, the women, just anything. The chorus picks up and repeats the verses until the song is finished.

Many songs are the same traditional ones, but if the *trovadores* are singing, they will create beautiful lyrics that have so much meaning. Because the *trovadores* are typically country people, they are so connected to the natural part of Puerto Rico

*I am very proud to be Puerto Rican because my traditions bring people closer together. I want my daughter to experience the warmth that I did.*

and its environment that they see life with a much higher beauty. They see the country, the flowers, and all the different aspects of Puerto Rico, and they compose the lyrics to tie all these together. You have to listen to the lyrics to really understand them.

The objective of the *parrandas* is to bring everyone from house to house and have a party at each place. A few *parrandas* in the area can be going on at the same time. Everyone is expecting them. People prep up with food and rum because they don't know when the parties will come. The *parrandas* build up bigger and bigger, and everyone is having so much fun. The next thing they know, it's five o'clock in the morning.

*Parrandas* are a traditional part of Puerto Rico. A lot of people who are growing up learn the tradition from the older folks, then they pass the tradition on. I guess some people would say that Puerto Rico has lost some of its traditions or has gone to the American styles, but the *parrandas* are still one tradition that is typical of my country. You have to live it and see it. It's really unbelievable!

# Johnny Serrano

□ During the Christmas season, everyone is expected to help out with the cooking. For example, I remember collecting a bunch of banana leaves for *pasteles*, mashed green bananas wrapped in banana leaves. After collecting these long leaves, I would pass them over a fire until the leaves were flexible, peel the leaves off the stem, then cut off portions for the *pasteles.*

For the ties, we found a particular plant that was all over Puerto Rico. We would cut and strip these thin leaves and use the stem as string. Banana leaves and stems—we used whatever was natural.

I was learning Puerto Rican traditions without even realizing it. *Pasteles* are difficult to make, so here is another recipe typically made during the Christmas season.

### PONCHE DE LA REINA
#### Queen's Eggnog

| | |
|---|---|
| 1 | cinnamon stick |
| | peel of 1 lemon |
| 2 | cups milk |
| 4 | egg yolks |
| 1/4 | cup sugar |
| 1/4 | tsp. salt |

Combine cinnamon, lemon peel, and milk; bring to a boil. Beat yolks with sugar and salt. Gradually add milk, stirring constantly. Serve hot.
*6 servings*

□ In December cool breezes chill the air in Puerto Rico and the temperature drops. It's not cold like here, but Puerto Ricans are accustomed to hot weather. *Te de jengibre* is served to warm up the body.

### TE DE JENGIBRE
#### Ginger Tea

| | |
|---|---|
| 1 | 2-inch piece ginger root, crushed |
| 4 | cups water |
| 8 | tsp. sugar |

Bring ginger and water to a boil; remove from heat. Strain; add sugar. Serve hot.
*4 servings*

□ Imagine being full of beans and rice on a hot day—you just want to take a siesta. Many houses in Puerto Rico are made of concrete; some people will just grab a pillow and take their siesta right on the cool, concrete floor. When you wake up, you can have pineapple custard and coffee.

### PINEAPPLE CUSTARD

| | |
|---|---|
| 2 | cups pineapple juice |
| 1 | cup sugar |
| 8 | eggs, slightly beaten |

Cook pineapple juice and sugar over medium heat to a syrup consistency; cool. Add syrup to eggs, stirring constantly. Pour into a mold. Place mold into a larger mold containing enough water to cover half of the inside mold (a bath). Bake at 350° for 1 hour or until firm.
*8 servings*

I was brought up to be a housewife and I loved it. By the age of ten, I knew how to iron and cook. By the age of fifteen, I was helping Mami, my mom, serve dinner when we had company. I didn't have hobbies like sports or anything like that. In Puerto Rico I was brought up to serve the man.

I come from a middle-class family in San Juan, so I know it is not a low-class or male-dominated attitude. It's just the way it is. The man is responsible for taking care of the family financially, even if he must take two jobs. The woman stays at home and takes care of the household.

When there is company for dinner, the woman stays in the kitchen preparing the food while the man plays the host. After everyone is seated at the table, the woman serves the children first. All the male company is next, then the female company, the man of the house, and finally the woman. If a person needs anything during the meal or if something is missing, the woman is the one who interrupts her meal, gets up, and goes to the kitchen to serve.

*In Puerto Rico receiving Holy Communion calls for a big family celebration. My family is gathered here for my daughter's first Holy Communion.*

I was raised to believe that taking care of my husband is a satisfaction, a way of showing him I love him. I should serve him by washing and ironing his clothes and having meals ready when he comes home. In turn, he would give financial support and the man-labor part to me and the family. It would all equal out. I should do it with great pleasure, just as being the man of the house should give him great pleasure. My husband and kids would enjoy the meal I prepared for them. I had worked hard, but the smiles on their faces in the end is great and worth it.

Life in America is a bit different. My parents have a hard time because I have to work now. They can't get used to the idea. Working and raising children have been very hard on me because I was brought up to stay at home. I'm married to an American, so I had to learn his ways. It is easier for him to cope with my ways because I'm serving him, but now I have become more Americanized. Every now and then I may say, "Go get it yourself."

Serving my family is still almost automatic. It doesn't bother me, and I don't even think about it. I still like the American style where everyone serves themselves. At first I thought I was a horrible wife and a horrible mother, but I'm just getting used to the nineties and the American way.

❑ *Mofongo* can be a classy meal. In Puerto Rico there are actually expensive restaurants that specialize in the dish. I remember when my family went to a *mofongo* restaurant, it was a big deal even though the meal could be made at home quite inexpensively.

### MOFONGO CON CHICHARON
### Ground Plantains with Pork Skin

| | |
|---|---|
| 3 | large green plantains, peeled and cut into 1-inch slices |
| 3 | cups water |
| 1 | tsp. salt |
| | oil for frying |
| 1/4 | lb. fried pork skin, crushed |
| 1/2 | cup beef or chicken broth |
| 3 | garlic cloves, crushed |

Soak plantains in water with salt for 15 minutes; drain. Cook in oil over medium-high heat until tender.

Grind small amounts of plantains and pork skin alternately in a blender, adding broth to mix. Add garlic and 1 tablespoon warm oil. Remove from blender; shape into balls. Serve in a deep plate with chicken or beef soup.

*5 to 7 servings*

❑ *El dia de San Juan*, the Day of Saint John, is a Puerto Rican holiday on June 23 when masses of people go to the beach and at midnight walk backwards to the ocean. They throw themselves into the ocean—still backwards—three times to release bad luck and receive good luck. If a person has bad luck throughout the year, people say he or she had picked up someone else's bad luck on *el dia de San Juan* at the beach.

My family didn't celebrate like this. We just went to church then returned home to have a huge, quiet meal. *Arroz con gandules y costillas* was often served on this holiday.

### ARROZ CON GANDULES Y COSTILLAS
### Rice with Pigeon Peas and Pork Ribs

| | |
|---|---|
| 1/4 | cup chopped ham |
| 2 | Tbsp. oil |
| 1/2 | cup sofrito, [see page 169] |
| 1/4 | cup tomato sauce |
| 1/8 | tsp. oregano |
| 1 | bay leaf |
| 1 | Tbsp. vinegar |
| 1 | beef bouillon cube |
| 1 | envelope sazon con culantro y achiote* |
| 1 1/2 | cups water |
| | salt to taste |
| 1/2 | lb. pork ribs or any cut, cubed |
| 1 | 16 oz. can pigeon peas |
| 2 | cups rice |

In a covered pan, cook ham in oil for 3 minutes. Add sofrito, tomato sauce, oregano, bay leaf, vinegar, bouillon, sazon, water, and salt; mix well. Add ribs; cook, covered, over medium heat for 20 minutes. Add pigeon peas with liquid; cook for 10 minutes. Add rice; cook until tender, stirring occasionally.

*5 to 7 servings*

*Tapas* are a very special part of Spanish culture. They are little plates of individual foods. The dishes may have two or three shrimp cooked in garlic, croquettes with béchamel, clams with marinara, or very small fried sardines called *boquerones*. *Tapas* can also be cold like potato salad with shrimp or octopus. There are many kinds of *tapas*.

Having *tapas* is a way for friends to get together and have a good time enjoying food, drink, and conversation. I love it! We always go in groups, maybe four or five couples, from one *tasca*, or *tapas* bar, to another. The enjoyment is walking around and trying the different dishes.

In my home town, Jerez de la Frontera, there were about fifteen to twenty places for *tapas*, each having a specialty. We would go to one *tasca*, try their specialty, and when we finished, someone would say, "Let's go to this one; they have wonderful shrimp." Then we'd leave to try the shrimp. We only stayed at each place for maybe fifteen minutes; *tascas* are for *tapas*, not meals. Sometimes we just stood up at the bar because the place didn't have tables. But most places had tables outside and people were walking around, going in and out. People were in the streets and they were happy.

*My friend, Almudena, and my husband, John, and I (center) are in the Plaza Mayor in Spain, waiting for tapas.*

We always ended up at *Juanito's*. *Juanito's* was a small place where out-of-town people from all over came just to have the specialty: *goriones*. Only the beaks and feathers of these sparrows were taken off, then the birds were put in a big pan with garlic, wine, and oil and fried until crispy. As soon as the tray came—with all the sparrows' legs sticking up—everyone got up at once. *Goriones* must be eaten when they're hot, or they're no good. We would pick them up, holding them by the feet, and we eat everything except for the feet. Ah, they were delicious! I remember that was a lot of fun.

Our favorite time to have *tapas* was during Holy Week when the processions come down the main street from the churches. Every night during Holy Week, five or six churches come out with their floats. Men, dressed in long robes and head covers, walk from the churches to the cathedral, then back to the church around one or two o'clock in the morning. The floats, with their bases and canopies made of gold and silver, are magnificent. Hundreds of fresh flowers and lit candles, singly and in ornate candelabra, cover the floats. Usually the first float has a statue of Christ and the last one has the Virgin. The statues are all dressed up. The Virgin has a big, big trail embroidered with gold. When some people die, they leave their jewelry to the Virgin and she wears all the jewelry—gold, diamonds, emeralds—in the procession. It is fascinating!

The way to see the procession was to sit in a *tasca*, eating *tapas* and drinking wine all night. The *tascas* would have all their tables and chairs out in the streets. One may think that watching the procession like this is really not religious, but the people are *really* religious. Some are just fanatic about the procession.

When I go to Spain, my friends, my family and I still go out for *tapas*. Now the town is getting bigger; people are moving out so sometimes we have to drive from one place to another. My brother knows all the best places—of course!—and if we can walk, we walk. But if it is too far, we'll take the car. We're getting modernized. There is always a place that is the best, so as a tradition, we must try it.

◻ *Paella*, originating in Valencia, is the most traditional Spanish dish. There are many ways to prepare this Spanish rice and different ingredients may be used. *Paella* used to be made over a fire outside. When I was little, my parents had a friend from Valencia, and when he came to the country during the summer, he would make a big fire to cook the *paella*.

## PAELLA
### Spanish Rice

| | |
|---|---|
| 1 | medium onion, chopped |
| 1 | garlic clove, chopped |
| ²/₃ | cup olive oil |
| 5 | tomatoes, peeled |
| 3 | chicken breasts, cut into small pieces |
| ¹/₂ | lb. pork tenderloin, cut into pieces |
| 12 | small or medium clams in shells |
| ³/₄ | lb. shrimp, with shells |
| ¹/₂ | lb. squids, cut into ringlets |
| 2 | cups rice |
| 4¹/₄ | cups water |
| ¹/₂ | tsp. saffron |
| 1 | tsp. Spanish paprika |
| 2 | chicken bouillon cubes |
| | salt and pepper to taste |
| ¹/₂ | cup artichoke hearts |
| ¹/₂ | cup peas |
| | pimentos |

Cook onion and garlic in oil over medium-high heat until onions are soft. Add tomatoes; cook for 3 to 5 minutes, stirring with a wooden spoon. Add chicken and pork; cook for 8 to 10 minutes. Add clams, shrimp, and squid; cook for 5 minutes or until clams open. Add rice, stirring constantly to prevent burning.

In a separate pan, boil water with saffron, paprika, bouillon, salt and pepper; add four cups of this liquid to the pan with rice. Add artichokes, peas, and pimentos; bring to a boil. Reduce heat to medium; cook, uncovered, for 20 minutes or until rice is done, adding more water if needed.

When cooked, remove from heat; set aside for at least 10 minutes before serving. Garnish with pimentos, clams, and shrimp.
*8 to 10 servings*

◻ *Tortilla española* is a Spanish omelette. We always take the omelettes, cut into wedges, on picnics or to the beach during the summer. They are delicious cold.

The first time I had a Spanish omelette in the States—I couldn't believe it—it had tomatoes and all kinds of other stuff in it. I thought, "This is not a real Spanish omelette." Here is an authentic recipe from my mother for *tortilla española*.

## TORTILLA ESPAÑOLA
### Spanish Omelette

| | |
|---|---|
| 6 | large potatoes, peeled and finely chopped |
| 1¹/₂ | cups olive oil |
| 1 | medium onion, chopped |
| | salt and pepper to taste |
| 6 | eggs, beaten |

In a 10-inch pan, cook potatoes and onions in oil over low heat until soft; stir often while pressing with fork. Remove potatoes and onions from oil and add to eggs; mix well, adding salt and pepper.

Drain oil except 1 tablespoon. Increase heat to medium; pour mixture into pan and cook until brown. Flip omelette using a plate which is larger than the pan. Heat another 1 tablespoon oil in pan; slide omelette back into pan to brown other side.
*4 to 6 servings*

**At the courthouse,** a firecracker is thrown and the holiday of San Fermín begins. Every city in Spain has a patron saint celebration which is usually held in the summertime. San Fermín is the patron saint of Pamplona. Beginning on July 7, the city celebrates for seven days.

Because I was born in Pamplona, I know about its traditions, but I think that almost everyone knows that Pamplona is a very famous city known for the running of the bulls. We Spanish do not say "the running of the bulls"; we say "encierro," or the enclosing of the bulls.

The running of the bulls from the corral to the bullring is well-known, but only the people from Pamplona know about the small *encierro*. On the night before the bulls run, the bulls are first collected from the pastures and brought to the corrals. This small running only takes about five minutes and people don't run with the animals. Around midnight we go near the pastures and stay *very* quietly on the road behind bushes and watch the bulls go by. We see the bulls walking in the street. They are so huge and very heavy! I don't know if people are allowed to watch anymore because there aren't fences for protection in case the bulls run after the people.

In the morning around eight o'clock, the doors of the corrals are opened and the bulls run through the narrow streets of the old part of town. Only the people running stay in the streets.

Sagrario (fourth from right) with her family.

*My mother owns this house in a little village about ten miles from Pamplona. The house has been in the family for six generations. It is a place where the family unites for a few days during the summertime.*

Some places have fences where spectators can get close, but those areas are usually for the runners who need to jump from the bulls. Most people watch the event on television; or if they have friends who live in one of the houses along the way, they can watch from the balcony. The crowds are cheering and yelling as the bulls are run every morning for the *corrida de toros*, the bullfight with the matador, which is held later around six o'clock.

I remember some of my friends who ran told me that the people of Pamplona really know how to run. They said that runners should always carry a newspaper in their hands, in case they have to distract the bulls. They never run the whole length from the corral to the arena; each has just one small section. If they fall, they should never stand up—always stay on the ground. When they stand up, that is when the bull can kill.

For seven days it is a holiday. Music is heard all day long in the streets. There is dancing and singing, and people drinking lots of wine and champagne. After the bulls, we usually have breakfast at one of the many sidewalk cafes. A typical breakfast after the running of the bulls is hot chocolate with *churros*, light donut-like pastries sprinkled with sugar. If we can stay awake, we keep going; if not, we go home and take a nap. In the evenings, everybody goes out to eat, or people will go to friends' houses for big meals, then go to the clubs and dance to live orchestras until almost morning.

Once I had friends who invited me to watch the bulls from their balcony. It was very impressive! The bulls looked humongous as they ran down the narrow streets of Pamplona. And everyone was having a party just for the bulls' running.

❑ Spanish recipes use so much garlic, the smell on the fingers never goes away. I thank my sister, Juana, for showing me how to remove the smell of garlic from my hands. After chopping garlic, simply run cold water over your hands, fingers downward, for a few seconds. Do not rub or use soap. It is hard to believe, but this really works. Try it!

❑ In Spain families also get together on Christmas Eve. Christmas Eve is spent with one side of the family, Christmas Day with the other.

*Zarzuela de pescado* is a popular fish stew especially on Christmas Eve. Dinner on Christmas will usually have a lot of meat, so a lighter seafood or shellfish dish is preferred the day before.

### POLLO A LA CAZADORA
#### Hunter-Style Chicken

| | |
|---|---|
| 2 | lbs. dark meat chicken |
| 1/4 | cup olive oil |
| 1/2 | tsp. flour |
| 1 | large onion, sliced |
| 3 | garlic cloves, chopped |
| 1 | cup beer |
| 1 | bay leaf |
| 1-2 | bouillon cubes |

Cook chicken in oil over medium heat until brown. Stir in flour. Add onion, garlic, beer, bay leaf, and bouillon. Cook for 45 minutes or until chicken is tender and sauce thickens.
*4 to 6 servings*

### ZARZUELA DE PESCADO
#### Fish Stew

| | |
|---|---|
| 1/2 | onion, chopped |
| 2 | garlic cloves, chopped |
| 4 | Tbsp. olive oil |
| 2 | Tbsp. chopped parsley |
| 1 | Tbsp. flour |
| 2 | lbs. any white fish fillets or scallops |
| 1/2 | lb. shrimp, clams, and/or mussels |
| 1 | 8.5 oz. can peas |
| 1 | 8.5 oz. can asparagus spears |
| | dash of saffron |
| | salt to taste |

Cook onion and garlic in oil over medium heat until slightly golden. Stir in parsley and flour. Add seafood, peas and asparagus with liquid, saffron, and salt. Cook, covered, for 5 to 10 minutes for scallops or 10 to 12 minutes for fish. Serve with Spanish or French bread.
*6 to 8 servings*

**In the mid-1920's,** my mother and her younger brother left their home and roots in Switzerland and immigrated to America. They were just eighteen and sixteen years old, without any knowledge of the English language. Aboard ship they both became very seasick. The men and women were kept separate, so the two siblings could not be of any comfort to each other.

Once they reached New York, they took a train to California where they would meet their older brother. On the train they were given bananas to eat. They had never seen bananas, let alone know how to eat them. They were about to eat the fruit, skin and all, but some kind gentleman took pity on them and showed them how to peel and eat the bananas.

In those days in Switzerland, fruit was scarce because the terrain and short growing seasons were not conducive to growing many fruits. My mother's family lived high in the mountains, off the beaten path. Horses and wagons were the delivery vehicles then; refrigerated trucks were unknown. I remember my mother saying that each of the children in the family received a single orange on Christmas day, and that was a special treat.

*My husband, Joe, and I took a trip to Switzerland to renew my Swiss roots and visit my cousins. We are on Lake Lucern.*

While employed by a wealthy family in California, my mother learned to cook well by observing how the good meats and vegetables were prepared and served. I remember that she always used several spices in the preparation of her meals to enhance the flavor of the food.

There was a large Swiss colony in California working in the dairy and winery industries. From southern California to Washington, the culture and traditions of the various cantons were kept alive by the families in these groups. They were proud of their Swiss heritage and also their adopted country. I have great admiration for my mother and her family for their courage to face so many unknowns and to have faith in America. They make me proud to be of Swiss descent.

*This photo was taken on the Sunday before my mother (back row, center) and uncle (back row, left) left Switzerland to begin new lives in America.*

◻ Because we were Catholics, my family did not eat meat on Fridays. Here are some of the recipes that my mother served as our evening meals on these days.

## TATSCHMANEDEL
### Broken Raisin Pancakes

| | |
|---|---|
| 1 | cup flour |
| 1 | egg |
| 1/2 | cup water |
| 1 | tsp. sugar |
| 1/2 | cup raisins |
| 1-2 | Tbsp. oil |

Combine all ingredients except oil; mix well. Heat oil over medium heat. Pour batter; cook until golden brown. Turn over and chop with spatula.
*3 to 5 servings*

## MALUNS
### Fried Potatoes

| | |
|---|---|
| 1-2 | potatoes |
| 1/2 | cup flour |
| 1 | tsp. salt |
| | butter or bacon fat for frying |

Boil potatoes. Grate when cooled.
Combine 1 cup grated potatoes, flour, and salt; mix well. Cook potatoes in butter or bacon fat over medium heat until golden on both sides. Serve with apple sauce on top.
*2 to 3 servings*

◻ My mother and her two sisters made carnival cakes for dessert when the families got together. It was always a treat for us as kids.

The dough is rolled out as thinly as possible. Like a turnover, *dustgets* are very thin and flaky, and they crumble when bitten into.

## DUSTGETS
### Carnival Cakes

| | |
|---|---|
| 8 | eggs |
| 1/2 | cup cream |
| 3 | Tbsp. sugar |
| 2 | Tbsp. butter, melted |
| | dash of salt |
| | flour |
| | butter for frying |

Combine eggs, cream, sugar, butter, and salt. Mix well; gradually add enough flour to make a dough. Set aside for 15 minutes.
Cut out 2-inch pieces of dough; roll out as thinly as possible into rectangular shape. Carefully stretch dough by hand until dough is as thin as tissue paper. Cook in butter over medium heat. Remove from pan and sprinkle with sugar. Cakes will keep for weeks.

There was only one income for my family as I was growing up—my mom's. She sold food to the government workers in the camp where we lived. It was a government compound that moved from place to place building Thailand's highways. Thailand usually has lots of food stands but they were far away from where the men worked. Many of the guys were single and didn't want to cook after working all day. Some were raised as middle class and were well-educated and didn't know how to cook. Mom's name just got around so they asked her to cook for them in the evenings.

Mom prepared dinner for about ten guys every day. They sat down, relaxed, and ate. They sat together in a circle, and I served the food. I was the only helper. My older sister had married; the other was working out of town; and my brother was too young.

Two girlfriends and I were so happy to see the king of Thailand pass by us in Bangkok on his way to the temple. Many people in Bangkok do not show respect for the king, but we, being country girls, have great love and respect for him. Placing our palms together, we raised our hands to him as a sign of respect. He saw us and gave a big grin—three little monkeys with their hands up!

Sometimes one of them would bring a guitar, and they would sing and have a little to drink. "Gim, you've got to sing for us!" they'd say. At that time, I loved English music—you know, being a teenager—but I didn't even know what the music was saying! They played the guitar and I sang a couple of words in English, then they would sing. They even played the home instruments like spoons or banging glass. It was a good time.

I miss it: seeing those guys so happy, singing songs, laughing, eating all the food, and my singing American songs which no one understood—even myself. Mom would say, "Gim, you sing better in English than in Thai."

During the daytime, Mom also had a dessert food stand, set up just on the side of the street in the compound. Thais like sweets, but not like cake and ice cream. She made Thai desserts like sticky rice with mango, bananas with coconut milk, and beans with coconut. We Thais love coconuts! She had about six or seven varieties. Sometimes people didn't want to eat lunch so they had dessert instead. After twelve o'clock, I would take over because Mom had to go to the market to get ready for dinner. When she came back around two o'clock, I would have everything cleaned up. Mom was the only one in the compound who made the best food and desserts.

I am proud of Mom and am happy to have been a part of her work. Mom trusted me enough to run the food stand while she was shopping. That's kind of nice. I am not as great of a cook as Mom; my sister is the one who followed Mom's footsteps. She has two big food stands in the market. Her husband runs a stand on one side and she has one in the middle—in case someone misses him. At least, one of us is carrying the tradition.

One time a neighbor said that I married the wrong guy because he doesn't eat Thai food, "Here you are married to an American, and you will leave being Thai behind and learn to cook American food." But I still cook Thai food for myself and my friends. I didn't forget.

◻ We Thais eat spicy food because we like rich tastes. If we didn't eat spicy food, we would feel like we didn't eat anything at all. Strong and salty, strong and sweet, strong and spicy—these are the three combinations. If you don't have any of these, the food is just plain.

### MOO PAD PRIK BAI HORAPA
**Stir-Fried Pork with Chili and Basil**

| | |
|---|---|
| 1¹/₂ | Tbsp. chili paste (see below) |
| 1 | cup thinly sliced pork loin |
| 1 | Tbsp. fish sauce |
| 1 | cup celery, julienned |
| 3 | hot chilies, julienned |
| 15 | sweet basil or mint leaves |
| 2 | Tbsp. oil |

Cook chili paste in oil over medium-high heat until fragrant. Add pork and fish sauce. Cook until pork is done. Stir in celery and chili. Stir in sweet basil or mint. Remove from pan once cooked. Serve with steamed rice.
*2 servings*

◻ Besides coconuts, Thai people love to eat rice. If I don't eat rice, at least one tablespoon, I think my heart will stop!

### NUA PAD PRIK
**Stir-Fried Beef with Chili**

| | |
|---|---|
| 1¹/₂ | Tbsp. chili paste (see below) |
| 1 | lb. beef tenderloin, cut into pieces |
| 1 | Tbsp. oyster sauce |
| ¹/₂ | Tbsp. fish sauce |
| 1 | cup carrots, julienned |
| 5-7 | red hot chili or jalapeno, cut into strips |
| 2 | celery stalks, julienned |
| 2 | Tbsp. oil |

Cook chili paste in oil over medium-high heat until fragrant. Add beef and oyster sauce. Cook until beef is done, stirring constantly. Add fish sauce, carrots, chili, and celery; cook until carrots are half done. Remove from pan. Serve with steamed rice.
*4 servings*

### THAI CHILI PASTE

| | |
|---|---|
| 25 | red chilies, cut into small pieces |
| 15 | shallots, finely chopped |
| 10 | garlic cloves, finely chopped |
| 1 | tsp. salt |

In a mortar, pound all ingredients to a smooth paste. Place in a tightly closed jar and keep in refrigerator.

**Bangkok was once known** as the "Venice of the East." Thai people always say "Wherever you see water, you see fish. Wherever you see fields, you see rice." That's how I grew up. There was fish everywhere.

I grew up with my grandparents who lived next to the Maekrong River in Photaram Ratchaburi. Before we ever saw the fish for dinner, Grandma would go ahead and start cooking. She had the pot of water on, and she was working on the vegetables. In one hand, she had a bamboo fishing pole. She could catch a fish, usually catfish, in five minutes, probably less, from right there on her porch. If the fish were too small, she threw them back. She cooked on the porch on a clay stove using wood or coal underneath.

Sometimes she kept the small fish to make *nampla*, or fish sauce. First she collected many small fish, then she mixed them with lots of salt. She packed this into a giant container and let it ferment for a few months. The fish was removed, and the liquid was strained and boiled. This was the fish sauce. She used the fish she removed as bait when she fished off the porch.

*Most males in Thailand become monks for about a month when they are teenagers. During this time, they live at the* wat, *or temple, and must go out every morning to collect their food from the nearby homes. The monk I am giving rice to is my younger brother. Females must be barefoot to show respect to the monks.*

We caught fish also by digging holes between the rice fields and the canal. There was a small area, like a bank about three feet wide, separating the rice fields from the canal. During the monsoon season, which lasts about three to four months, fish were swept away with the flooding water. Some fish ended up in the rice fields. As the fish tried to work themselves from the rice fields back to the canal, they would "fall" into the holes. In the morning, we would come by to collect all the fish from the holes. I guess most made it to the canal, unless they fell into the holes.

As a kid, I don't remember ever going to the market. Vendors came up to the house by boat. The houses were built on sticks because of the flooding during the monsoon season. Water stayed under the house for a few months during this time of year, so everyone in this area owned a little boat.

We knew when the vendors were coming because they yelled out to the customers, advertising what they were selling. They knew their customers by name. If the vendor had shrimp he'd yell, "*Krung sod sod mae ouy!*" or "Very, very fresh shrimp!" The vendors sold everything, even meat. If we wanted what they were selling, we would run out before the boat passed and pay right there.

Photaram Ratchaburi was a beautiful, natural place, not like the city of Bangkok. It was very green with the rice fields and the trees along the canal. There was lots of water. Our neighbors were like our family. Everyone knew each other in the neighborhood—even the vendors who came by boat.

□ When I went to college in Bangkok, I was introduced to food from the different regions of Thailand. I was from the middle part of Thailand; northern and southern cooking were very different.

Many street vendors in Bangkok were selling barbecue, chicken rice, sticky rice, and *som tom*, a green papaya salad. All the food was made right there on the vendors' carts.

## SOM TOM
### Green Papaya Salad

| | |
|---|---|
| 1½ | lbs. green papaya or 2 medium, peeled |
| 4 | garlic cloves |
| 4 | small Thai chilies (priek kheen nu) |
| ½ | cup green beans, sliced |
| 1 | medium tomato, quartered |
| 3 | Tbsp. fish sauce |
| 1½ | Tbsp. coconut palm or brown sugar |
| 6 | Tbsp. fresh lime juice |
| ½ | cup roasted and unsalted peanuts, crushed |

Cut papayas lengthwise; remove seeds. Shred and set aside.

In a mortar, pound garlic and chilies. Gradually add shredded papaya and green beans to garlic and chilies. Pound gently. Add tomatoes; repeat light pounding. Add remaining ingredients; mix well.
*4 servings*

□ *Goy tod* can be bought almost anywhere in Thailand from street vendors, even in the country. Thais eat the banana fritters as a snack.

## GOY TOD
### Banana Fritters with Coconut and Sesame Seed

| | |
|---|---|
| 1 | cup rice flour |
| ⅓ | cup flour |
| 1⅓ | cups coconut, dried and shredded |
| 3 | Tbsp. sesame seed |
| 1 | tsp. baking powder |
| 1 | cup water |
| | oil for frying |
| 6 | medium bananas, ripe but firm |

Combine flours, coconut, sesame seed, and baking powder. Add water; mix well. Let batter stand for 5 minutes.

Heat 1¾ inch oil to 375° over medium heat. Peel bananas and slice into quarters lengthwise. Dip each piece into batter, coating evenly. Cook a few pieces at a time for 2 for 3 minutes or until golden brown; turn occasionally. Drain on absorbent paper.
*2 dozen*

**Once a year**, usually in September, the Thai people where I am from in Surathanee go to the temple for a festival. Our temples, called *wats*, are like the churches here. On this day everyone brings an ingredient to the *wat* to make *kwa kow tip*, which translates as "amazing or incredible rice."

Thai people know that they have to cook this kind of food once a year for good luck. Some people bring rice; some bring bananas. Everyone brings at least one item, but some may bring more, like potatoes, sugar, salt, most anything. They know what to bring.

*Kwa kow tip* is cooked in a pot that looks like a giant wok. The pot is at least six to eight feet in diameter and about four feet high. It is only used for this occasion. After the festival is finished, the pot is cleaned and hung up in the *wat* until the next year.

The pot is placed on three stones so a fire can be made underneath. Water is poured in first, then the people begin putting in their food until no one has anything else to put in the pot.

No one measures. One year *kwa kow tip* may be too sweet; the next year it may not be sweet. Every year it tastes different, but it tastes good. The food is brought to a boil, like lava. By twelve o'clock everyone is at the temple and no one has anything else to put in the pot.

People must keep cooking and stirring the food until six o'clock in the morning. The stirrer looks like a boat oar. It's huge with a long handle because the pot and fire are very hot. There is only one pot, but five or six people are stirring at one time. When the people get tired of stirring, they will sit down and others will start stirring. By morning the food is really thick.

Everyone stays at the temple all night. There may be up to 100 people. Most of them are young, around twenty to thirty years old. They don't go to sleep, maybe just a nap. They see a lot of their friends at the *wat* and they have fun all night.

*The different areas of Thailand have different foods, but Thais are common in that they always use fresh ingredients. If you go to the markets in Thailand, you will never see a frozen chicken.*
*I had opened a few restaurants in Fredericksburg, but Thai food has not caught on here yet. People should give it a try because it is delicious.*

The monks of the *wat,* dressed in their *geevong*, or yellow robes, also sit with the people throughout the night. In the morning when the *kwa kow tip* looks like a thick caramel, the monks pass some to the people on pieces of banana leaf. If there is any leftover, the monks will give it to the people who come to the temple. This is the time that the monks give back to the people because the people who belong to the temple bring food for the monks daily.

Many people, but not everyone, believe that eating *kwa kow tip* makes them strong so they will not get sick for the whole year. That is why it is called "amazing or incredible rice."

# Piyapong Jatuporn

In January and February after the rice is harvested with a sickle and beaten out, the leftover is like straw. We use this straw to cook chicken outside. While the chicken is cooking, we sit around the fire, talk, have a little to drink, and just enjoy ourselves in the cool weather.

The chicken is hung on a short stick and covered with a *pipe*, a square metal container previously used for sugar or oil. We push dirt around the container so air won't get inside; then we put straw around the outside and light the fire. In about thirty minutes, the chicken is done, and it tastes really good with the straw flavor. For convenience, the chicken can be baked in the oven, but it will not have the delicious straw flavor.

### MUK KAI
### Marinated Chicken

| | |
|---|---|
| 3 | cilantro roots, chopped |
| 1 | Tbsp. whole peppercorns |
| 2 | tsp. sugar |
| 3-4 | garlic cloves |
| 3/4 | cup soy sauce |
| 1 | whole chicken |

In a mortar, pound cilantro, peppercorns, sugar, and garlic. Add soy sauce; mix well. Marinate chicken for at least 2 hours or overnight. Slightly dry chicken before baking. Bake in a 350° preheated oven for 1 hour or until chicken is done. Serve with namjim.
*4 to 6 servings*

### NAMJIM
### Dip for Marinated Chicken

| | |
|---|---|
| 3 | garlic cloves |
| 2-4 | red chilies |
| 1/2 | tsp. sugar |
| 6 | whole peppercorns |
| 1/4 | cup fish sauce |
| | juice of 2 limes |
| 3-5 | Tbsp. chicken drippings |
| 3 | cilantro leaves, chopped |

In a mortar, pound garlic, chilies, sugar, and peppercorns. Add fish sauce, lime juice, and drippings; mix well. Sprinkle cilantro on top. Serve as a dip with chicken.

When I was young, I would go net fishing with my father, uncles, and cousins. We would spend all day catching fish. We placed the caught fish in a *kong*, a small bamboo basket, and set it in the water so the fish wouldn't die before we returned home. Net fishing was not always easy; there was a way of throwing the net from the elbow so, as it swung out, it stayed flat as it fell over the fish.

When we bought fishing nets, we had to make the nets stiffer so they would sink faster. We soaked the nets in cow's blood, bought from the butcher, for about five days. Then we boiled the nets in the blood. After removing the nets from the blood, we hung them to dry. We only needed to do this once, and the nets would stay stiff from then on.

I always had a lot of fun fishing and laughing all day with the men. After coming home, the women would make *tom som pla* with the fish we had just caught.

### TOM SOM PLA
### Hot and Sour Fish Soup

| | |
|---|---|
| 5 | lbs. whole bass, cleaned |
| | fresh tamarind leaves* or 1 instant package |
| 5 | red chilies, crushed |
| 1 | tsp. whole peppercorn |
| 2-3 | lemon grass stalks, crushed |
| 1 | 1-inch ginger root, sliced |
| 2 | Tbsp. fish sauce |
| 1 | tsp. sugar |

Fill pot with enough water to cover fish. Add tamarind, chilies, peppercorn, lemon grass, and ginger; bring to a boil over high heat. Add fish, fish sauce, and sugar. Reduce heat to medium; cook for 20 minutes or until fish is done.
*3 to 5 servings*

**My mom knows** that the monks will come by around six o'clock every morning. She gets up early to cook food for the ones who will stop at our house in Ayulthaya. In Thailand the monks leave the *wat*, or temple, every day to give blessings to the people who cannot go to the temple and to the animals. While they are out, they also collect their meals for the day. The monks eat breakfast and lunch but no dinner, their last meal being between half past eleven and noon.

The monks collect food from the houses near their *wat*. Sometimes the food is a lot; sometimes not. All people are not able to cook for them every day; others may not cook at all. Mostly the older people are the ones who cook for the monks. My mom does it about three or four times a week. She cooks different foods each day. It can even be just a boiled egg, but she always gives rice because Thai people eat rice with every meal.

Carrying their large clay bowls, the monks come by walking or by boat, but never by car. It depends on the season. If it is the rainy season, they will come in small boats. They wear the yellow robes of the monks in Thailand. Their heads are shaven, and they are always barefoot.

Many monks pass the house. Before they come, my mother and I are prepared and outside to meet them with the food. Usually we have a table, but sometimes we have to run quickly. If we don't have the food out, they will just walk past. But if one passes by, there will be another.

Because we are women, Mom and I must be barefoot and must not touch the monks. We pray first, bowing very low, and the monks will give us a blessing when they take the food. Afterwards, we pray again.

*One hundred days after a death, monks are invited to pray with the deceased member's family. I (center) invited these monks to my home after my mother's 100 days. I am with my daughter (left) and "second mom."*

Mom and I also cannot give the monks their food hand to hand; only men can do that. The monks will lay part of their robe on the table, then my mother or I will place the food on their robes, without ever touching them. We cannot touch their bowls either. We put the food in separate containers or bags and very gently place the food in the bowls.

When the monks return to the *wat*, they eat then they pray. The extra food is left at the temple for people who pass by or work at the *wat*, especially the boys who help the monks. Some families will send a boy to the temple to help out, or on occasion a few boys whose homes are far from school will live at the temple for a short time while they go to school. These boys may also help at the temple.

Thai people give food to the monks as blessings for the people who have already died. They also believe that whatever they give to the monks, they will get that back when they die. For example, I like *Pad Thai,* so I would make the noodle dish for the monks to bless, and I can have it later, after I die.

Usually people give the monks their favorite food or the favorite food of someone who has passed away. The monks take the food and bless it, then those people who died can get it or those who haven't died yet will get it. It's like life after death. That's what we believe in the Buddhist religion.

◻ There's a saying that there are two seasons in Thailand: hot and hotter. For many Thais, one way to cool down the body is to eat a hot and spicy dish. Take a bite of green curry, and it bites back! The intensity of many curries comes from Thai peppers called *priek kheen nu.*

I enjoy cooking for my friends and family. Now I'm cooking for a bigger family—the city of Fredericksburg; I'm the owner and chef of the *Bangkok Café.* These dishes are among my favorites, and I'm delighted to share them.

### GAENG KEOW WAN GAI
### Chicken with Green Curry

| | |
|---|---|
| 2 | cups thick coconut milk |
| 3 | Tbsp. green curry paste (see below) |
| 3 | lb. chicken, cut into chunks |
| 2 | cups thin coconut milk or milk |
| 2 | Tbsp. fish sauce |
| 6-8 | young citrus leaves (ma grood)* |
| 1/2 | cup fresh sweet basil leaves |

**green curry paste:**

| | |
|---|---|
| 3 | pieces Laos (ka), chopped or 1 tsp. powder* |
| 1 | tsp. dried ginger |
| 1 | tsp. coriander, ground or seeds |
| 1 | tsp. caraway seeds |
| 12 | black peppercorns |
| 4 | whole cloves |
| 1 | whole nutmeg |
| 2 | lemon grass stalks, minced |
| 2 | Tbsp. chopped coriander roots |
| 2 | Tbsp. chopped garlic |
| 2 | Tbsp. chopped shallots |
| 1 | tsp. lime juice |
| 8 | whole green chilies |
| 1 | tsp. shrimp paste |
| 1 | tsp. salt |
| 3 | tsp. vegetable oil |

Prepare paste. In a mortar, pound all whole dried spices. Add remaining green curry ingredients; pound or grind to a paste. Set aside.

Cook thick coconut milk over low heat until it thickens and oil appears around edges; stir constantly.

Increase heat to medium-high. Add paste; cook for 5 minutes. Color and smell will noticeably change. Add chicken, thin coconut milk, fish sauce, and citrus leaves. Bring to a boil. Reduce heat to medium; cook until meat is tender. Pour into serving dish and sprinkle with basil leaves.
*10 to 12 servings*

◻ One of Thailand's best known noodle dish is *Pad Thai.* It is eaten as a light meal and is especially popular at the night markets.

### PAD THAI
### Thai Noodles

| | |
|---|---|
| 8 | garlic cloves, finely chopped |
| 1/2 | cup oil |
| 1 | cup small shrimps, cooked |
| 1 | Tbsp. sugar |
| 3 | Tbsp. fish sauce |
| 1 1/2 | Tbsp. tomato catsup |
| 2 | eggs, beaten (optional) |
| 3/4 | lb. rice noodles, soaked |
| 1 | cup bean sprouts |

**garnish:**

| | |
|---|---|
| 1 | Tbsp. shrimp powder (optional) |
| 2 | Tbsp. peanuts, coarsely ground |
| 1/2 | tsp. dried red chilies, ground |
| 2 | green onions, finely chopped |
| 2 | limes, sliced into 1/8-inch circles |

Cook garlic in oil over high heat until golden. Add shrimp; cook until done. Stir in sugar, fish sauce, and catsup; cook until sugar dissolves. Add eggs; cook for 2 to 3 minutes, then scramble. Add noodles; toss and cook for 2 minutes. Add bean sprouts, reserving 4 tablespoons; cook until barely done. Pour into platter. Place reserved bean sprouts on one side. Sprinkle with garnishing ingredients.
*4 to 6 servings*

**The Turkish lifestyle** is at a much slower pace than in the U.S. We don't have to drive the distance between home and work. Our jobs and homes are right there in the city. We go home and eat, then take a walk and come back. If we decide to have dinner or a coffee, it's nice to have a restaurant close by.

One of the best times I had growing up was going to the seashore on the European side of Turkey. After having a meal at home, we would go out as a family for a walk, or we'd stop by the tea and coffee houses called *cayhane*. Besides tea and coffee, these sidewalk cafes had different pastries or ice cream. Many people stopped at the cafes just for desserts, while some guys played backgammon or other games provided by the restaurant. Others enjoyed smoking tobacco from the water pipes which gurgled softly as the smokers inhaled.

The most well-known seafood restaurants were in the same row as the coffee houses. The seafood was caught daily, and the waiters would come and show the seafood—sometimes

*Reaching out to the hungry is part of my Moslem faith. My friend, Claude, and I are at the Second Harvest Network meeting for the Food Banks.*

still alive—to the customers so the seafood could be personally selected. Portable vendors, set up across the coffee houses and restaurants, sold steamed corn-on-the-cob, shish kebabs, and shish kofte served with fresh pita bread brushed with olive oil. We'd just stand on the side of the road and eat.

It was so beautiful with the moonlight hitting the water right in front of us. We could see the lights and boats of the people fishing for fire fish. They fish only at night because the fire fish are attracted to the lights on the boat. A few families would come down the water slowly in their boats, playing Turkish music while having a meal on the boat. We could hear them coming from the sounds of the ut, violin, or flute playing, and then we'd see the other little boats following.

If we were sitting by the bank and wanted tea, we had only to beckon a waiter from the restaurant. He'd run across the street, bringing the tea on the Turkish brass trays which are held at the top. I don't know how they ran across the street, carrying that tray with all the tea, without dropping anything!

Tea is such a part of our culture and hospitality. If a person goes into a barber shop, the shop owners will serve tea right away. Even in a store, the customers will be asked if they want tea or coffee while they are shopping.

Oh, yeah, I miss it! Sometimes my friend, Essa, who is from Bosnia, and I will talk about all the food we miss from our countries: *pastirma*, cured meat covered thickly with red pepper; the hot bread just out of the old-fashioned ovens; *sucuk*, beef and black pepper similar to pepperoni. It drives me crazy! I miss it a lot. I still go back occasionally, but I left Turkey thirty-six years ago. I lived away for a long time in Europe and here in the States. Still the way I feel—that's home. That's *my* home. I guess that's something I'll never get out of me.

◻ My dad learned how to cook from an elderly man from a village in middle Turkey. The man was my grandmother's cook, and although he was a country person, he was the world's best cook. My dad had an interest in cooking and he liked to eat, but when he cooked, he made such a mess. He managed to dirty everything: the floor, the sink, every inch of counter, you name it.

This is my father's recipe for *yaprak dolmasi.* I have never had stuffed grape leaves that taste as good as his!

## YAPRAK DOLMASI
### Stuffed Grape Leaves

| | |
|---|---|
| 3 | lbs. ground lamb or beef |
| 5 | onions, chopped |
| 3 | garlic cloves, chopped |
| 2 | cups rice, uncooked |
| | salt and pepper to taste |
| 1 | bunch fresh mint or 6 Tbsp. dried |
| 2 | 16 oz. jar grape leaves or 100 steamed fresh leaves |
| 5-6 | beef bouillon cubes |
| 2 | cups water |
| 2-3 | Tbsp. olive oil |
| | lemon wedges |

Combine meat, onions, garlic, rice, salt, pepper, and $1/2$ of mint; mix well.

Drain grape leaves; rinse well. If using fresh leaves, remove stems. Place 1 tablespoon of mixture in center of each leaf, close to stem. Fold sides to the center and roll from the base to the tip of the leaf.

Grease a large pot with olive oil. Add remaining mint to pot. Place stuffed leaves, seams down, in pot closely together.

Dissolve bouillon cubes in water. Pour water and oil over leaves, adding more water until leaves are covered. Cook, covered, over low heat for 1 to $1^{1}/2$ hours. Garnish with lemon wedges.
*6 servings*

◻ *Pirincli lahana*, or cabbage with rice, can be cooked with olive oil and onions or with any meat such as cubed lamb, beef, or veal. This is the vegetarian one which may be served with meat on the side.

## PIRINCLI LAHANA
### Cabbage with Rice

| | |
|---|---|
| 2 | medium onions, chopped |
| $1/4$ | cup olive oil |
| 1 | cup tomato sauce or blended fresh tomatoes |
| $2^{1}/2$ | cups water |
| 1 | small cabbage, chopped |
| | fresh oregano |
| | salt and pepper to taste |
| $3/4$ | cup rice |

Cook onions in oil over medium heat until brown. Add tomato sauce or tomatoes, water, cabbage, oregano, salt and pepper. Bring to a boil over high heat. Reduce heat to medium; cook for 10 minutes. Add rice. Cook, covered, over low heat for $1/2$ hour or until done.
*4 servings*

**I was raised** in a "traditional American" family. My mother's family was ridiculed for being Polish-Lithuanian. Her father spoke in an accented, broken English. Because of this, she became as "American" as possible. None of her family's ethnic traditions were passed down to me. I was thrilled to marry into a Ukrainian family, with almost identical Eastern European traditions, who still proudly upheld all the customs of their heritage.

The most celebrated holiday for Ukrainians is Easter. Each family prepares for Easter by filling an Easter basket lined with white linen with certain foods which have special meanings.

*Pascha*, meaning "Christ Risen" or passover, and *Babka*, meaning "Blessed Mother," are the Easter breads added to the basket. Since Christ was the "living bread," they are a rich symbolism for Ukrainian Catholics. The breads are baked in tall, round loaves and decorated to symbolize the joy of Mary at the news of Christ's resurrection. *Pysanky*, the traditional Ukrainian decorated Easter eggs, represent new life.

Cynthia with her
mother-in-law.

*I think it's really important
to know my ethnic heritage
and keep the common
thread in my family.*

Horseradish, shaved from the stalk and put in beet juice and vinegar, represents both the stain of sin and the suffering caused it. Cream cheese, served with *pascha*, symbolizes purity and goodness. Butter, also served with *pascha*, represents the burial ointment taken to the empty tomb of Christ. Salt is put into the basket, representing God's grace in our lives. Meat, usually ham and *kielbasa*, Polish sausage, is finally put into the basket. They represent the richness of God's mercy, a true reason to celebrate.

This very full basket is taken to church and blessed by the priest right before or right after Easter Sunday mass. Each family places their Easter basket, often decorated with fresh flowers or Ukrainian embroidered linen, on tables arranged in a horseshoe to enable the priest to walk among them. Each family stands behind their basket. The linen covering the food is folded back, and the wrapped food is opened. A white candle, placed between the food and the edge of the basket, is lit. The priest says a prayer over the food then walks from basket to basket, sprinkling each with holy water. Each member of the family is blessed at the same time. This has always been a time of trepidation for me, since I am not Ukrainian-born. Not only is the priest checking worthiness by the quality of workmanship, but all the Ukrainian-born women are checking, too!

My fondest recollection of Easter was about ten years ago when my mother-in-law, Mary Wuyek, was still alive. Our whole family met outside the church after the basket blessing and couldn't wait to get home. We had been fasting during Lent. We shared the contents of our Easter baskets with each other in the church parking lot!

Now it is difficult for our entire family to be together on Easter, but those who are together convene after church to carry on this ritual. I wonder if, generations from now, the families will know where this custom originated. This is a wonderful, rich tradition that our family carries out through the sharing of food.

My mother-in-law, Mary Wuyek, gave this recipe for *pascha* to me when I married into the Wuyek family. It has great sentimental value to me because it was an "Old World" recipe brought over from the Ukraine two generations ago.

In order to pass her recipes to me, my mother-in-law went to her mother-in-law's house to measure what she was putting into her bowls. She knew the recipes by heart using only "a handful of this" and "a cup of that," the cup being a tea cup that belonged to her ancestors. My mother-in-law had to keep stopping to measure the ingredients.

*Pascha* is sometimes decorated with braided dough in the shape of crosses. This recipe is used also to make the traditional Ukrainian wedding cake.

## PASCHA
### Ukrainian Easter Bread

**starter batter:**

| | |
|---|---|
| 5 | envelopes dry yeast |
| 4 | cups milk, scalded and cooled to warm temperature |
| 1 | tsp. salt |
| 1/2 | cup sugar |
| 5 | cups flour |

**dough:**

| | |
|---|---|
| 1 1/2 | cups sugar |
| 1/2 | cup unsalted butter, melted |
| 1 | shot glass or 1 1/2 oz. vegetable oil |
| 7 | eggs, beaten (set aside 1 egg white) |
| 9 | cups flour (approximately) |
| 2 | cups yellow raisins |
| 1/2 | cup flour |

Combine starter batter ingredients; mix well. Cover with damp cloth; let rise until doubled and bubbles appear.

Add sugar, butter, oil, eggs, and 9 cups flour; mix with electric mixer or knead by hand for 5 minutes.

In a small bowl, combine raisins with 1/2 cup flour. Add to dough; mix well.

Place in a large greased pan. Cover and let rise for 3 to 4 hours or until doubled. Punch down dough; let stand for 10 minutes.

Divide into 5 well-greased pans. Pans can be Pyrex® bowls, metal mixing bowls, or coffee cans. Add braided decoration, if desired. Let rise for 1 hour or until doubled. Brush tops with egg white. Bake at 350° for 35 to 40 minutes or until deep brown. Cool for 15 minutes; remove from pan and cool thoroughly on wire rack.

*5 loaves*

*Pyrohy* is a traditional dough and potato dumpling dish from Eastern Europe. This recipe was also given to me by my mother-in-law; it was handed down to her from generations past. Traditionally, she makes *pyrohy* for Christmas.

## PYROHY (PIEROGIE)
### Potato Dumplings

| | |
|---|---|
| 3-4 | lbs. potatoes, peeled and cubed |
| 1 | cup onions sautéed in butter |
| 2 | 12 oz. packages farmer's cheese |
| | salt and pepper to taste |
| 7 1/2 | cups flour |
| 3 | eggs |
| 1 | tsp. salt |
| 2 | cups cold water |
| 2 | shot glasses or 3 oz. vegetable oil |

Boil potatoes until tender; drain and mash. When lukewarm, add sautéed onions, cheese, salt and pepper. Mix well; set aside.

In a large bowl, add flour, making a well. Add remaining ingredients; mix by hand or in food processor. Add flour if dough is sticky or a few drops of water if stiff. Dough should be firm, not sticky. Cover dough.

Roll out a handful of dough 1/4 inch thick on a well-floured counter. Cut out circles, about 4 inches in diameter. Place 1 tablespoon potato filling in center. Fold over, pinching edges to seal. If needed, place a drop of water on edge. Seal securely to prevent filling from leaking when boiled. Place filled pyrohy on well-floured cheesecloth.

Add 1/2 cup oil to a pot filled 2/3 with water; bring to a boil. Boil about 12 at a time for 8 minutes or until they float. Remove with slotted spoon; rinse under cool tap water for a few seconds. Place in serving dish; cover with a few teaspoons of sautéed onions and butter to prevent sticking. Serve hot with a dollop of sour cream.

*10 to 12 servings*

Christmas is a very exciting time of the year for us, just as it is for any nationality that celebrates this holy day. Mom and Pop are busy preparing for the great holy day with shopping for the Christmas tree and presents for family and friends. The big event takes place on Christmas Eve, and we always celebrate it in a Ukranian fashion.

While Mom does her cooking and baking, the children are also preparing for the event. The children prepare special treats for the animals and make sure there is clean bedding in the barn, because that is where the Christ-child was to be born.

The table is set with the finest table cloth and the best china and silver. A lighted candle is placed in the center of the table; another is placed in the window. The lighted candle in the window welcomes any strangers to come and share our Christmas Eve dinner. The four legs of the table are tied with bailing twine, crossed in the middle, to signify the four corners of the world coming together for the greatest event in the history of the world: the birth of the Savior, Jesus Christ.

*St. Nicholas, here with my children, is the patron saint of the Eastern Church. He is equivalent to the modern day Santa Claus.*

Dinner consists of wine and twelve meatless dishes which may vary by the different nationalities. We, as probably many Slavs, have narrowed the dishes into a few such as mushroom and sauerkraut soup, fish, *pyrohy,* which are potato dumplings, fruit salad, nut and poppy seed rolls and bread. Dinner begins with Mom passing out little pieces of garlic and pieces of bread dipped in honey—our version of the Christmas wafer—to signify the bitter and sweets of the earth. While each person eats the garlic and bread, Mom dips her finger into the honey and makes the sign of the cross on each forehead, saying, *"Christos Razdajetsja,"* meaning "Christ is born." Each person replies, *"Slavite Jeho,"* meaning "Glorify Him."

Next, we prepare for midnight Mass, or liturgy, as it is referred to in the Byzantine Rite. Children are taken to an earlier liturgy because it is difficult for them to stay awake. The church is beautifully decorated, and a manger is set up in front of the church to receive the Christ child. The Byzantine liturgy is very beautiful and mystical; it leaves one in awe. After the liturgy, we go home to Mom and Pop's and begin our Christmas Day festivities, like opening presents and eating the meat foods such as ham and Polish sausage called *kolbasi*, and sweet breads, horseradish, and candies. Caroling rounds out the Christmas season.

# George Kuzma

❑ Eastern European cooking applies to all the Slavic countries such as the Czech Republic, Slovakia, Poland, Ukraine, and Russia, to name a few. Many of the foods are similar in nature. The same dish or food may also have a different name according to the country. For example, Polish sausage is called *kolbasi* in Slavic and *kielbasa* in Polish.

Daily Slavic cooking consists of many of the same dishes we all enjoy here in the United States. The main difference is that during the two holidays, the holy days of Christmas and Easter, the Slavic people cook their very special foods and baked goods. Many of these foods are available during the year, but on these occasions they taste extra delicious.

Mushroom soup is served as one of the meatless dishes for Christmas Eve dinner.

### CHRISTMAS EVE MUSHROOM SOUP

| 1 | lb. fresh mushrooms |
| 4 | cups water |
| | sauerkraut and juice to taste |
| | salt and pepper to taste |
| 1 | onion, chopped |
| $^1/_2$ | Tbsp. butter |
| $^1/_2$ | Tbsp. flour |

Cook mushrooms in water; drain, reserving water. Chop mushrooms and set aside. Add sauerkraut and juice to mushroom broth; cook until tender. Add salt and pepper.

In a separate pan, cook onions in butter over medium-high heat. Stir in flour and cook until brown. Add $^1/_4$ cup water; bring to a boil, stirring often. Pour into broth. Add mushrooms; cook over medium heat for 5 to 10 minutes.
*5 servings*

❑ A twelve fruit compote is typical of the Christmas season and can be served instead of a fresh fruit salad.

### TWELVE FRUIT COMPOTE

| 3 | cups water |
| 1 | lb. mixed dried fruits |
| 1 | cup pitted prunes |
| $^1/_2$ | cup raisins |
| 1 | cup pitted sweet cherries |
| 2 | apples, peeled and sliced |
| $^1/_2$ | cup cranberries |
| 1 | cup sugar |
| 1 | lemon, sliced |
| 6 | whole cloves |
| 2 | cinnamon sticks |
| 1 | whole orange |
| $^1/_2$ | cup grapes or pomegranate seeds |
| $^1/_2$ | cup fruit-flavored brandy |

Combine water, mixed dried fruits, prunes, and raisins; bring to a boil over high heat. Reduce heat to medium; cook, covered, for 20 minutes or until fruits are tender. Add cherries, apples, and cranberries. Stir in sugar, lemon, cloves, and cinnamon. Cook, covered, for 5 minutes.

Grate orange peel; set aside peel.

Section orange, removing all skin and membrane. Add to fruits. Stir in grapes and brandy. Bring to a boil; remove from heat. Stir in orange peel. Cover; let stand for 15 minutes.
*12 servings*

*Pysanky* is the Ukrainian art of egg dyeing that has been passed down from mother to daughter for centuries. The custom dates from when Christianity was introduced into Ukraine in 988 A.D. It has survived to this day as part of the Ukrainian Easter celebration in which eggs are exchanged with special friends to show affection and caring.

This particular art uses a dye method similar to batik. Melted beeswax is applied to a fresh, uncooked egg with a *kistka,* or stylus. The *kistka* is a tool with a metal funnel attached to a stick wrapped with copper wire. The wire keeps the tool hot and holds the metal tip steady.

Then the egg is dipped into a succession of chemical dyes which eventually produces intricate, multi-colored designs with unlimited color combinations. The wax is melted off over a candle flame, revealing the jewel-like creations. The finished egg is varnished to preserve the colors.

The eggs are not blown or cooked. Traditionally, it is considered bad luck to work on an empty *pysanka*. The yolk will eventually become a dry lump, and the white will turn to dust. The approximate age of an egg can be determined by its weight.

*Becoming aware of my cultural heritage came from dance. During my student days at Madison College (now known as James Madison University), I was active in a folk-dance troupe. My mother, having the patience to let me grasp our heritage on my own, took the time to pass on what she knew. She would help me with the choreography, adding traditional steps that she had learned years ago.*

My grandmother was not able to perfect the delicate art as a young girl, due to the outbreak of war a little after the turn of the century. My mother, Olga Pakush, yearned to learn the traditional process and her wish came true years later in southwestern Virginia, where a Catholic nun was offering *pysanky* classes at the church convent. My mother and I took the class together and have kept the art of *pysanky* alive by conducting classes for the young and old alike.

Another Ukrainian art passed down to me by my mother is the love of music, most notably expressed in Ukrainian dance. Since my early teen years, I have participated in some type of folk dance troupe. My greatest joy as a young adult was receiving the custom-made red Ukrainian dance boots that were given to my mother by her parents when she was a young girl growing up in New York City. Mom and I have spent many wonderful hours collaborating on dance routines to share in workshops with children and adult groups.

Mom's great enthusiasm has always been the main energy behind the work, in both the art of *pysanky* and Ukrainian dance. Her labor of love always produced smiles of joy on the faces of her "students" as she helped them create the perfect *pysanky*. I will always cherish the memories of my mother's dedication to teaching the technique and her great pride in her culture.

# Christine Pakush Vaughan

To the Ukrainians, Christmas is not Christmas without *kutya*. Custom dictates that everyone must partake of *kutya* on Christmas Eve. The origin of this dish goes back to when the early Ukrainian ancestors first cultivated wheat, 3,000 years before the birth of Christ.

I have fond memories of the *kutya* being served as part of the Holy Night Supper on January 6. My grandmother, affectionately called "Baba," adhered to the custom of waiting until the first star was visible in the evening sky. This was the sign to light the candle and serve the *kutya* as the first course at the Holy Night Supper. The important task of "reporting" the first star was my job.

## KUTYA

| | |
|---|---|
| 2 | cups whole grain wheat |
| 3/4 | cup poppy seed |
| 2 | cups honey |

Remove foreign material from wheat and wash thoroughly. Place in a saucepan; cover with cold water. Cook over medium heat for 2 hours or until tender, stirring occasionally. Cool.

Cover poppy seeds with boiling water; let stand for 15 minutes. Drain. Slightly grind poppy seed; add to wheat. Add honey to taste. Refrigerate until served.

*6 to 8 servings*

In Ukraine, as in many other countries, the hard-working tillers of the soil seldom serve desserts, except on holidays. This is especially true of feast days when a variety of fancy desserts is featured. *Pampushky* is a light and fluffy pastry served at the culmination of the Holy Night Supper.

The *pampushky* was one of the early Ukrainian dishes my grandmother showed me how to prepare. Hers always turned out in perfect form. She never measured out a single ingredient; all were combined according to taste and texture. I worked out these proportions. The wonderful fragrance of the *pampushky* still brings back memories of working alongside my favorite Baba.

## PAMPUSHKY
### Pastry Puff

| | |
|---|---|
| 1 | package dry yeast |
| 3/4 | cup milk |
| 8 | egg yolks |
| 2 | tsp. sugar |
| 1/2 | tsp. salt |
| 1/2 | cup butter, melted |
| 4 | cups flour |
| 4 | egg whites, beaten well |
| 1 | tsp. vanilla extract |
| | peel of 1 lemon |
| 4 | cups oil |

Dissolve yeast in $1/4$ cup of milk. Set aside.

In a separate bowl, beat yolks with sugar and salt until light in color. Add butter; mix well. Add milk and yeast mixture, mixing alternately with flour. Add egg whites, vanilla, and peel; knead in bowl for 10 minutes or until soft. Cover; let rise in a warm place until dough doubles in size.

Roll out dough $1/2$ inch thick. Cut out with small glass or cookie cutter. Place on floured board and let rise again for 2 hours. Do not cover.

Heat oil to 375°. Place the side of the pampushok that was on the board into oil first. Cook, covered, for 3 minutes or until brown. Cook other side, but do not replace cover. Drain on absorbent paper. Sprinkle with sugar.

*8 to 10 servings*

**I am an Alaskan** Indian from the Koyukon Athabascan tribe. I was born and raised in Fairbanks, Alaska. My family, blood-related and extended, live in villages near Fairbanks and along the Yukon River in the Interior of Alaska. Only a few relatives live in the lower United States, or "outside," as we Alaskans call the the other forty-nine states.

I have a very large family, including family from my mother's biological parents and her adopted parents. Then I have more on my father's side, numerous cousins, aunts, uncles, and grandparents. I even have family extending from my blood-related family, but I still call them my relatives. We all take care of each other whether we're related or not.

Most of my family in Alaska live a subsistence lifestyle. Our lifestyle is based on the

traditions and cultural values of living off the land by existing side-by-side with nature. We live mostly off the land by fishing, hunting, and trapping along the Yukon River.

During the summer, fish are caught by using fish-nets or fish-wheels. The fish-wheels, set in deep parts of the river, are constructed with two to four large baskets designed to catch fish. The fish-wheels put the the fish in a holding bin on the side, holding the fish until we get them. The fish-nets, set in shallow or deep water, are usually set with one end of the fish-net tied to a tree or post on land and the other end tied to an anchor in the river.

In the spring and fall, we hunt big game such as moose and bear. We eat or make use of every part of the animals we hunt or trap. Nothing goes to waste. For example, we eat everything of a fish—the head, the eggs—except the bones. We eat even the moose tongue. When dried, the moose skin is like a big fabric; it is used for slippers, gloves, purses, and bead work. Some people make carvings with the antlers. Both fishing and moose hunting make up our main diet and are most valuable in our way of life.

*In Alaska we all take care of each other whether we are related or not. I (right) am with my mother, Anna.*

My mother, sister, and I moved temporarily to Fredericksburg, Virginia, in 1994. Since then I have had many memorable experiences such as seeing the Atlantic Ocean and actually swimming in it. I've seen the Pacific before but never got the chance to swim at an oceanfront beach. One time, as my friends and I were walking to the Rappahannock River to go swimming, a king snake crawled across our path. I thanked God that it ate other snakes and did

not normally bite people. A little further down the path, I saw a lizard sitting on a tree. Just sitting there! And later, we saw three copperheads in all. Two of them were on land and one was in the water while we were swimming. There are no snakes or lizards in the Alaska where I am from, so this is why these experiences were very exciting and scary for me.

I did not appreciate my years in Alaska until I moved to Virginia. Most areas in the lower U.S., mainly in the inner cities and even small towns, are so commercialized—businesses, housing developments, automobiles, and just about anything that can be bought or sold. Seems to me that people can't get enough materialism and more of the world for themselves. It is like this in Alaska also, but Alaska has more nature than anything else. I miss

*Our fish camp with the smokehouse was set up right on the Yukon River.*

seeing more of what God put on this earth than what man has. Virginia has its place in my heart forever, but it is not my home. Alaska is where my heart belongs and that is where I will settle.

◻ In Alaska whenever there is a marriage, death, or any event that brings people together, we have a *potlatch,* or potluck. It is usually done inside a hall or large room, and everyone sits in a circle or around the edge of the area. The food is brought from the center, where it is set up, and served to everyone by the family of the occasion. The elders are served first, then the food is served to the others in the direct rotation of the sun or clockwise.

Peggy's meat loaf calls for moose meat, but I doubt you can find it in local supermarkets; beef is a good substitute. Moose meat has very little fat, so buy the leanest ground beef. Peggy is my paternal aunt.

### PEGGY'S MEAT LOAF

| | |
|---|---|
| 4 | lbs. ground moose or beef |
| 1 | onion, chopped |
| 4 | eggs |
| 1 | 10.75 oz. can tomato soup |
| 1 | cup oatmeal, cracker crumbs, or corn flakes |
| 1/2 | 12 oz. can evaporated milk |
| 1/2 | tsp. garlic powder |
| 1/2 | tsp. salt |
| 1/2 | tsp. pepper |
| 1/4 | tsp. Italian seasoning |

Combine all ingredients; mix well. Place in loaf pans. Bake at 400° for 45 minutes.
*10 to 12 servings*

◻ After catching many salmon, we cut the fish into strips. The fish is dipped into brine and hung over wooden poles outside under a canopy. The mixture of the brine, fish oil, and air creates a glaze around the strips. Then the strips are placed in the smokehouse. We make enough to last all year. By April the salmon is very precious!

This fish salad recipe is from my grandma, Angela Huntington.

### FISH SALAD

| | |
|---|---|
| 3 | medium potatoes, diced |
| 1 | pint salmon |
| 1 | small onion, chopped |
| 1 | 14.5 oz. can green beans, drained |
| 5 | small sweet pickles, chopped |
| 1-2 | Tbsp. catsup |
| | salt and pepper to taste |
| | mayonnaise |

Boil potatoes until tender; drain. Set aside to cool. Add remaining ingredients; mix well. Do not use too much catsup. Use mayonnaise to your preference, such as in potato salad.
*5 to 7 servings*

We have been in the Spotsylvania area of Virginia for over twenty years. We came down from Akwesasne, my Mohawk reservation in upstate New York. My dad was looking for a job. He was an iron worker and during the winter, men of this occupation didn't work because it was too cold. Most of them drew unemployment, or the wives went out to work.

I remember when we first came to Spotsylvania. It was strange when I came here in the '70's. I was fourteen and I had never been off the reservation. The students in my old school were all Native Americans and whites. I had never gone to school with black people. I felt left out.

Nobody had any idea who I was or where I was from. The kids asked me, "Are you Chinese? Are you Japanese? Are you Mexican?" When I finally said, "I'm Indian," suddenly everyone was saying,"Oh, you're *Indian*." Some would say they had ancestors who were Cherokee, Sioux, or whatever. It seemed like no one had ever seen a *real* Indian before. The kids in my new high school had this conception of the Indian reservation: teepees, riding horses, people still running around in buckskins and feathers.

I had to go back north for a funeral later that year. While I was there, I did a pictorial of Akwesasne for an English paper. Underneath the pictures I wrote, "This is my house. This is my car. The only pony I ever rode was a mustang and it was a 1966, V-8!" My English teacher gave me an "A" for the pictorial. It served a purpose for me and the kids at the school. They knew nothing about Indians; they still had the pictures from back in the old age of Indians.

Since then, exposure to Indian culture has improved, especially with more and more pow-wows. Some people think that a pow-wow is only for Indians, but it's for everybody. One of the reasons for the pow-

Donna (front right) with her
brothers and sisters.

*My parents had five kids.
There was no way Mom would
go out and work when Dad
couldn't work during the
winter. Dad found a job in
Maryland where he could
work all winter. Mom came
down with him one week,
looked around...and we've
been here ever since.*

wow is to let people know what Indian heritage is all about. Different tribes from all over the country come to celebrate, dance, dress up in their native costumes, and cook their native food. It's like what they did a long time ago: trade, see what's new in bead work, and exchange different ideas.

I have good memories of Akwesasne. Both my grandmothers made sweetgrass baskets on the reservation to sell when their husbands, who were also iron workers, weren't working. Sometimes Mom and I are driving along around here, and we'll just look over at each other and say, "Sweetgrass!" There's this one area where we can smell sweetgrass all over, especially after a rain. It has a soothing smell that reminds us of where we came from.

Now there is a nursing home on the reservation. We never had a nursing homes there before; we took care of our own. It's funny; the name of it is "Sweetgrass Manor."

❏ Now at pow-wows, there are people selling Indian tacos. I thought, "Indian tacos? I didn't know we made tacos." Some Indians just updated fried bread. In hard times, Indian food was cheap and made with the bare essentials, like our fried bread. Fried bread is flour, baking soda, lard, and a little water—all mixed together and fried. Now they put refried beans, lettuce, and cheese on the bread and call them "tacos."

It's not like it used to be a long time ago, but we still hang on to the old traditions as far as dancing, food, crafts, and baskets. Making Indian hash is a tradition that my family still carries on. It's made for special occasions, like weddings, for good luck. On the reservation, we'd say that a couple is "getting ready to throw the hash," meaning they're going to get married.

### INDIAN HASH

| | |
|---|---|
| 5 | lbs. potatoes, peeled |
| 1 | lb. lean ground beef |
| 1/2 | lb. pan or fresh sausage |
| 1 | large onion, chopped |
| 2 | tsp. sage |
| | salt and pepper to taste |

Boil potatoes until done. Drain and reserve water.

Boil beef, sausage, and onion in enough water to cover meat. Crumble meat while cooking; drain. Add potatoes to meat. Sprinkle sage, salt and pepper. Mash all ingredients, adding water from potatoes if needed.

*6 to 8 servings*

❏ This is a recipe that has been handed down many times. Mom and I make it together on New Year's. It's like the pork and black-eye peas tradition down south. Everyone has at least one bowl of soup with fried bread. If someone in the family doesn't make it over, we'll send over a jar.

We've gotten everyone eating it. We give some to the neighbors, friends, whoever is around that day. It's good luck, so they come in and have a bowl of corn soup—even if they think they won't like it. Usually, they do like it!

### INDIAN CORN SOUP

| | |
|---|---|
| 4 | thick country style pork ribs or any cut for seasoning |
| 2 | 28 oz. cans white hominy corn |
| 3 | 14 oz. cans red kidney beans |
| 1 | lb. carrots, diced |
| 1 | medium yellow turnip, diced |
| | salt and pepper to taste |
| 1/2 | large cabbage, shredded |

Boil meat until tender. Cool in refrigerator, preferably overnight. Skim fat and remove bones.

Bring meat and broth to a boil over high heat; reduce heat to medium. Add corn, kidney beans, carrots, turnips, salt and pepper. When turnips are done, add cabbage. Cook until cabbage is done.

*12 to 14 servings*

**I have been working** at the Morton's farm since I was six years old. I would plow the fields, work the corn and milk the cows, cut the wood—so many things. I also got water from the spring. The Mortons had a well, but they liked the spring water. Every day, I would bring a bucket of water from the spring just for them to drink. I've always worked there on the farm.

At first, I didn't fool with pigs. Then I began smoking hams for my boss, Mr. Morton. We started by raising the pigs, three to begin with. We raised them from piglets. We'd feed them every day until they got about 300 pounds. It took about six months for them to grow to that size. Someone else would come and pick them up to slaughter them. The pigs came back cleaned, but I had to cut them up for smoking.

After cutting, I laid the meat on the table and rubbed it down with salt, brown sugar, and black pepper. The meat stayed like this for six weeks in the smokehouse. My smokehouse was small, maybe only eight feet by eight feet, and made of cinder block. I always did this during the winter when the weather was cold.

Lewis, Josephine, his sister, and Mrs. Morton.

*I cut up and seasoned the meat for smoking. The women helped by grinding some of the meat for sausage.*

Afterwards, the ham was smoked for ten days. I hung the hams, shoulders, and midland—what we call fatback—on clothes hangers from the ceiling of the smokehouse. Then I built a fire on the floor, using hickory wood and all the corn cobs that we had been saving. For ten days I had to keep putting wood on the fire, twice a day and through the night. I had to get down on my knees—really low—or smoke would get in my eyes. During the smoking, the meat turns brown. You're supposed to wait another six months to eat the ham so the smoke soaks in. It's okay if you don't, but the ham is just not as good.

You can taste a difference between mine and the store-bought hams because the store-bought ones aren't smoked as long. My wife, Josephine, used to slice up and carry two hams to her church's homecoming and revival every year. They were the first thing gone. Of all the food on the tables, the people came to get the ham. They just loved my country ham. One year she didn't bring ham and everyone was upset.

Smoking the meat not only makes the ham taste better, it helps to preserve the meat. The meat will keep for three to four years if it is hung from the ceiling and the bugs don't get in it. Sometimes it becomes moldy, but that's even better for preserving it. Just scrape or wash the mold off before cooking. One time a woman said that she threw her ham away when she saw the mold because she thought the ham had gone bad. It's a lot of work smoking hams, so I don't smoke them anymore. But I haven't been able to find any store-bought ones as good as mine!

# Lewis Alsop

When I brought Lewis' ham to the homecoming and revival at church, the pastor's wife, sister, and sister-in-law would fight over the ham bone and skin. As soon as they saw me, they would ask, "Josephine, where's the ham bone? Where's the skin?"

If I said, "The pastor's wife gets it this year," they would say, "Oh okay. I get it next year, and you can have it the following year." Here is a recipe when I get the ham bone.

—Josephine Alsop

### SEASONED CABBAGE

|   |   |
|---|---|
|   | ham bone and drippings |
| 2 | large cabbages, quartered and sliced |
| 4 | cups water |
|   | salt and pepper to taste |

After cooking ham, skim grease and reserve drippings.

In a large pot, cook ham bone, drippings, cabbage, and water over medium heat for $1/2$ hour or until cabbage is cooked to preference. Add salt and pepper.

*10 to 14 servings*

When I was a little girl coming up, my father and I planted sweet potatoes. He would walk down the rows with a stick and poke holes for each slip. I had to drop the slips into the holes. He'd say, "Make sure you put one in each one of these holes and cover them up. Don't pack the dirt too tight." He'd tell me that every year. I also had to make sure the rows were straight and none of the plants were leaning. Sometimes, we'd plant 3,000 to 4,000 sweet potato slips.

Today my son, Dominic, helps his Pop Pop plant the sweet potatoes, and my mom still makes sweet potato pie. My mom loves to cook and is used to cooking for a lot of people. She gives the pies to neighbors and people who don't bake like this. This recipe makes six to eight pies; adjust the recipe to how many pies you want to make.

—Pam Alsop

### SWEET POTATO PIE

|   |   |
|---|---|
| 10 | large sweet potatoes |
| 12 | eggs |
| 4 | cups sugar |
| $1^1/2$ | cups milk |
| 2 | Tbsp. vanilla extract |
| 2 | Tbsp. lemon extract |
| $1/2$ | tsp. allspice |
| $1/2$ | tsp. cinnamon |
| $1/2$ | tsp. nutmeg |
| $1/2$ | tsp. ground clove |
| $1/2$ | tsp. mace |
| $1/2$ | cup butter, softened |

Boil sweet potatoes for 1 hour; drain. Rinse potatoes under running cool water. Peel with fork; mash well in a large bowl. Add remaining ingredients. Blend with mixer until smooth. Pour into 6 to 8 deep-dish pie shells. Bake at 350° for about $1^1/2$ hours or until brown.

*6 to 8 pies*

**I organized** Women of the World (WOW), an informal dinner and discussion group in the Fredericksburg area in 1989. We meet and share food and friendship.

The idea for WOW started in 1980 when I attended the United Nations Mid-Decade Conference for women in Denmark. I met women from around the world who share common problems and concerns. The women shared not only their problems and concerns, but also their solutions and ideas. We learned from each other.

When I returned to the USA, I was a graduate student at Florida State University. I knew that there were women who came from other countries either as students at the university or as wives of students. I decided to start a group of these women who could provide a unique opportunity for women of the American community to exchange their perspectives and knowledge with each other. Since then, I have organized other groups, and I believe that WOW benefits all of us who desire a deeper understanding of all people and a higher hope for peace.

The Fredericksburg group helped me to learn about other cultures and provided many delightful evenings of friendship and camaraderie. The group evolved to include men, as well as women. While the Fredericksburg group does not have the advantage of having access to many individuals from other cultures, as the one at Florida State, I discovered that there is an interest and desire among many individuals in the community to learn about the world beyond their front door. If we look, the world is there.

*I discovered that there is an interest and desire among many individuals in the community to learn about the world beyond their door. If we look, the world is there.*

In our seven years of monthly meetings, I have not had to look far for speakers. We have covered areas such as the Marshall Islands, Israel, Russia, Costa Rica, Argentina, Germany, Nigeria, and Saudi Arabia. Topics have ranged from folklore, cross-cultural marriages, migrant education, and language to the psychology of men, herbs, and women in military.

Not only has this group provided me with special friends and knowledge; it has provided me, and the community that attends, with the best ethnic food around. The variety of dishes brought to the pot luck gatherings has been exquisite!

❑ One of my favorite recipes is one my mother brought to the WOW meetings for the six years she attended. She created this dish from her memories of visiting me during the three years I lived in Beirut, Lebanon.

### MOM'S HUMMUS

2    15.5 oz. cans chick peas, drained and
      rinsed
      juice of 1 lemon
$^1/_4$   cup tahini
1    Tbsp. minced garlic

Combine all ingredients in a blender. Gradually add water until hummus is smooth but thick. Adjust amounts of lemon, tahini, and garlic to taste. Serve as a dip with warm pita bread or crackers.
*about 2$^1/_2$ cups*

❑ I fix salmon patties with peas often. They are nutritious and quite easy to prepare.

### SALMON PATTIES WITH PEAS

6$^1/_2$  oz. salmon in spring water, drained
$^1/_2$   cup rolled oats
$^1/_4$   cup egg beaters or 1 egg
1    16 oz. can sweet peas, no salt added
      olive oil

Combine salmon, oats, and egg; mix well. Let stand for 3 minutes. Form into patties, adding a small amount of water if needed. Cook in a small amount of oil until brown on each side.

In a separate pan, heat peas. Serve peas over salmon patties.
*2 to 4 servings*

❑ My mother and I created this recipe. The baking temperatures and times came by experimentation; Mom liked the muffins crunchy on the outside and soft on the inside.

These heavy muffins freeze and hold up well and may be taken as a snack when travelling. They are not very sweet. I like to have them with cream cheese or any nut butter.

### RAISIN BRAN BRAN MUFFINS

6    cups oat bran
2    cups wheat bran
2    cups rolled oats
1    cup powdered skim milk
$^2/_3$   cup flax seeds *
$^2/_3$   cup whole oats
$^1/_3$   cup molasses
$^1/_3$   cup brewer's yeast *
1    Tbsp. baking powder
2    eggs
4    cups water
$^1/_2$   cup yellow raisins
1$^1/_2$  cups black raisins

Combine all ingredients; mix well. Spoon into muffin pan. Bake on preheat at 400° for 20 minutes. After 20 minutes, turn to regular bake at 400° for 25 minutes. Reduce heat to 350°; bake for 30 minutes.
*24 muffins*

New Mexican food is a mixture of three main heritages: Spanish, Mexican, and Native American. Each group has added something different to New Mexican food; this is what gives New Mexican food its unique flavor. But New Mexico, the "Land of Enchantment," is known as the world's leading chili producer. The chilies are exported all over the place. August and September are the harvest months for the chilies. Chili farms are everywhere, but chilies from the town of Hatch are very famous.

If you go to the farms, they will roast the chilies for you by the bushel in a matter of minutes. You stand in line, then ask for hot, medium, or mild; green or red. Everyone buys at least a bushel. When the chilies come out of the field, they are dumped by the bushels into big round barrels made of wire; it's like a gas grill that turns. While the chilies are turning and roasting over the fire, they are sprayed with water to prevent burning.

New Mexican natives are known to eat chilies with just about everything, including pizza, steak, and spaghetti. They even make green chili jelly. My brother eats chilies straight, just chopped in the blender and warmed up. He'd sit there, eating warmed chilies, and sweat would be pouring down his face.

*It took a while for my husband, who is from Ecuador, to become accustomed to the New Mexican flavor, but now it's always a treat whenever I prepare the food that I grew up on.*

I've had green chilies here since I moved to Virginia, but after growing up with the ones in Albuquerque, they taste like bell peppers to me. I called Mom: "Mom, I need chili," so she shipped me a thirty-seven pound bushel of chili—first class. Dad went to the farm to get the bushel. He said he had to wait for an hour while they picked the chilies from the fields. They sell out quickly because people put them away for the winter.

I was all excited, waiting for the mailman to come. I went out and bought my baggies and got up the next day at eight o'clock in the morning to start roasting. I have fifty-two bags of frozen chili, but I need to make them last all year long. You just can't beat the flavor of New Mexico's chilies.

❑ Albuquerque is the home of the International Balloon Fiesta which runs for two weeks every October. My family would leave at four o'clock in the morning and wait for the sun to come up so we could watch the balloons inflate. We ate lots of food, then watched the mass ascension of hot air balloons with all the special shapes and colors, adding to the beautiful sky.

Green chili stew can be found at all the Mexican food stands at the balloon fiesta. It is also quick and easy to make it at home. Make it hotter and spicier by adding green chili powder. It's quite different from the common chili stew; for example, it doesn't have beans.

### GREEN CHILI STEW

| | |
|---|---|
| 5-6 | fresh green chili peppers, chopped |
| 1 | lb. ground beef |
| 5-6 | potatoes, peeled and diced |
| 1 | large onion, diced |
| | chopped carrots (optional) |
| 1 | 15.25 can whole sweet corn, drained (optional) |
| 1 | tsp. garlic powder |
| | salt and pepper to taste |

Broil raw chilies on both sides until blistered. Remove from oven; wrap in towel to sweat for 5 to 10 minutes. Peel skin and remove stem and seeds; set aside.

Cook beef over medium heat; drain excess oil. In a large pot, combine beef, potatoes, onion, carrots (optional), corn (optional), garlic, salt and pepper; cover with water. Chop chilies in blender; add to pot. Cook over medium heat for 30 to 40 minutes. Serve with flour tortillas.
*8 to 10 servings*

❑ Lilly is my mom. She makes the best chili beans. I probably was still in my high chair when I started banging, "I want beans! I want beans!" Mom had six kids and beans were really inexpensive. When there are eight people in a family, a pot of beans feeds everyone.

### LILLY'S CHILI BEANS

| | |
|---|---|
| 1 | lb. pinto beans, sorted and washed |
| 1 | tsp. garlic powder |
| | salt to taste |
| 1 | lb. ground beef |
| 2 | fresh basil leaves or 1 tsp. dry |
| 1-2 | Tbsp. red chili powder |
| 5-6 | fresh green chilies, chopped |
| 1 | 28 oz. can diced tomatoes |

Cook beans in water with garlic and salt until tender; do not drain.

In a separate pan, cook beef over medium heat. Add beef, basil, chili powder, chilies, and tomatoes to beans. Cook until slightly thick. Serve with Mexican corn bread.
*8 to 10 servings*

### MEXICAN CORN BREAD

| | |
|---|---|
| 1 | box self-rising yellow cornmeal |
| 1 | 15.25 oz. can whole sweet corn, drained |
| 2 | green chilies or 6 jalapenos, chopped |

Prepare corn bread recipe according to package instructions. Fold in corn and chilies or jalapenos. Bake according to package instructions. Serve with butter.

**Never a dull moment.** Travelling around the globe from northern New England to several southern states, Indonesia, Philippines, Germany, Israel, Paris, and London has enriched this "boiled dinner" chef into an international connoisseur of many tastes.

While living in Indonesia, my best friend and next door neighbor, Ibu Anna, taught me many new ways to enjoy foods of her culture. The very first time I invited her, Pak Marwan, and the three boys over for dinner was for Thanksgiving. I told them that there would be no rice and prawns, only American food; they still wanted to come. My husband and I explained the meaning of Thanksgiving and that we ate turkey for our meat dish.

"What is a turkey?" they asked.

"A big chicken," we replied.

After grace, I heard Anna mutter something. I asked her what she said.

"I prayed we would not be poisoned from eating this food," she said. From then on, we became good friends.

My love of cooking stems back to where I grew up in friendly Fort Fairfield, Maine, a progressive town in the great northeastern woods, one mile from the Canadian border. It all began with the woman who brought me into the world—mother.

She was a 5'4" peach with carrot-colored hair, freckles, and a sunny disposition. Cooking from morning until night over a wood burning stove, she filled the air with an aroma of fresh baked yeast bread,

*My husband, Sam, and I keep our American traditions alive even when we are outside of the United States. When we lived in Indonesia, we shared our Thanksgiving with our neighbor.*

pungent old-fashioned baked beans, and New England chuck roast with vegetables. We consumed potatoes every day but made it a special ritual on Saturday nights in the form of "Ma Ma's delectable potato salad." Dad was home at that time; usually he worked nights for the Bangor and Aroostook Railroad. All fourteen of us sat before a feast of fresh baked bread with a light golden crust, warm creamy butter, dark brown navy beans swimming in a molasses, brown sugar and mustard sauce, and Ma Ma's potato salad.

As we sprouted, we learned to depend on the Maine potato, one basic food that was essential to our culture. Fort Fairfield was the largest producer of potatoes, and all the farmers depended heavily on them for their livelihood. During the fall season, school would close for three weeks so all the kids could help bring in the harvest. A tractor pulling a "digger" would chug up and down rows of buried potatoes, laying those "spuds" on top for hands to scoop them into woven baskets that would then be emptied into wooden barrels.

We picked regardless of the weather. I can remember picking potatoes at five o'clock in the morning as falling snow threatened the crop. I felt the responsibility to help the farmer get his potatoes into the potato house before they froze and all would be lost. After all, he hired me knowing that I would aid him in supporting his family. These special hard times had their rewards. We were able to take some potatoes home. Some farmers gave a ten dollar bonus to the best picker, and I, happily, worked twice as hard when they did!

□ Here is "Ma Ma's delectable potato salad." I still make this salad for Sam and myself and for special outings, especially during the summer.

## POTATO SALAD

| | |
|---|---|
| 8-10 | new or boiling potatoes, preferably Maine, peeled and diced |
| $1/2$ | cup chopped sweet pickles or relish |
| 2 | Tbsp. juice from pickles |
| $1/2$ | cup chopped vidalia onion |
| 1 | cup diced celery |
| 4 | hard-boiled eggs, diced |
| $1/2$ | cup finely chopped fresh parsley |
| 2 | tsp. finely chopped dill weed spice or fresh dill |
| | salt and pepper to taste |
| 1 | Tbsp. mustard |
| $1/2$ | cup Hellmann's® light mayonnaise |
| 1 | hard-boiled egg, sliced for garnish paprika |

Cook potatoes until barely tender; drain. Set aside to cool.

Add remaining ingredients except mustard, mayonnaise, egg, and paprika to potatoes; toss lightly. Add mustard and mayonnaise; mix until evenly coated. Garnish with egg slices and sprinkle with paprika. Chill before serving.
*6 to 8 servings*

□ Growing up with five sisters and six brothers in New England was never dull. We had a birthday party every month. Devil's Food Cake with Seven-Minute Icing was Mother's most popular melt-in-your-mouth treat.

## DEVIL'S FOOD CAKE

| | |
|---|---|
| 2 | cups cake flour |
| 1 | tsp. baking soda |
| $1/4$ | tsp. salt |
| $1/2$ | cup cocoa |
| $1/2$ | cup buttermilk |
| $1/2$ | cup boiling water |
| $2/3$ | cup butter or shortening, softened |
| $1^1/2$ | cups sugar |
| 2 | eggs, beaten |
| 1 | tsp. vanilla extract |

In a small bowl, combine flour, soda, salt, and cocoa. Set aside.

In a separate bowl, combine buttermilk and water. Set aside.

In another large bowl, cream butter until smooth. Add sugar; mix well. Add eggs and beat until fluffy. Stir in vanilla.

Add flour mixture and buttermilk mixture alternately to butter mixture, beating until smooth after each addition. Grease and flour two 8-inch cake pans; shake excess flour. Pour batter into pans; bake in a 350° preheated oven for 27 to 30 minutes or until cake springs back when lightly pressed with fingertips. Remove from pan and cool thoroughly on cake racks before frosting.
*1 cake*

### SEVEN-MINUTE ICING

| | |
|---|---|
| 1 | egg white |
| $1/8$ | tsp. cream of tartar |
| | pinch of salt |
| 3 | Tbsp. cold water |
| $3/4$ | cup sugar |
| 1 | tsp. white corn syrup |
| $1/2$ | tsp. vanilla extract |

Cook all ingredients except vanilla in a double boiler over boiling water. Beat with hand mixer for 4 to 7 minutes until stiff peaks form. Remove from heat; add vanilla. Food coloring may be added for color. Spread immediately.

To a pre-teen, my pastor's home was a lively place: the doorbell, the telephone, someone at the back door, lots of teasing and humor. Compared to my quiet home, Bob and Ruthie's house was active.

On New Year's Eve after service had ended, Ruthie would put on a party for a congregation of about one hundred. She made a lot of food including sandwiches, fruit salad, and cookies. Ruthie made a six-dozen batch of sugar cookie dough and my mom made a three-dozen batch. I joined other teenaged girls to paint the cookies for the party. I had to take some home to finish as well.

Painting with a combination of egg yolk or white and food coloring, the girls and I turned out gingham dogs, polka-dotted saddled horses, pink and red poinsettias, and pale blue country churches with yellow lights streaming from the windows. What a festive table we set with the

Rootin'-tootin' "Becky Annie"
at nine years old.

painted cookies! Of course, when the boys came around to eat, they teased us and we would end up jabbing paint at them. I have fond, warm memories of painting the cookies...and the boys.

The last step before baking is sprinkling the cookies with sugar. One time, Ruthie picked up an identical salt shaker. When we tasted those salty little beauties, we promptly hung them on the Christmas tree! Ruthie never burned the cookies, but I had several catastrophes while I was in charge of the oven. I was always distracted by lively conversation, joking, and laughing.

My mom and I still give painted cookies for Christmas gifts. We present them in decorated bags covered with colorful tissue. They are especially appreciated by folks who work long hours and don't have time to bake.

# Rebecca Johnson

◻ Mom served dessert, traditionally a couple of cookies, even with lunch. She always kept a foot-high tin can filled with homemade sugar cookies with raisins in the middle.

My father was steeped in southern traditions. Why, if he did not have an entrée with salad, hot bread, and dessert for supper, he had not properly eaten. Mom would apologize if she had only store bought desserts.

For all of our hard work, we use butter instead of shortening for the sugar cookies.

## RUTHIE'S PAINTED SUGAR COOKIES

| | |
|---|---|
| $3/4$ | cup butter or shortening |
| 1 | cup sugar |
| 2 | eggs |
| 1 | tsp. lemon or vanilla extract or $1/2$ tsp. nutmeg |
| $2^1/2$ | cups flour, sifted |
| 1 | tsp. baking powder |
| $1/4$ | tsp. salt |

Cream butter and sugar. Add eggs and extract or nutmeg; mix well. Add flour, baking powder, and salt. Mix until smooth.

Roll out and cut with cookie cutters. Paint with egg paint. Sprinkle with sugar. Bake at 400° for 6 to 8 minutes. Bake lightly until edges are brown but not tops; colors will look better.
*3 dozen*

## EGG PAINT

| | |
|---|---|
| 4 | eggs |
| | water |
| | food coloring |

In eight small bowls, separate each yolk and egg white. Add 1 teaspoon water to each yolk. Add a lot of food coloring to the yolks for red, green, blue, and yellow food coloring. Use less in the whites to make light blue, pink, lavender, and light green.

Using children's dime store watercolor brushes, paint the cookies without letting colors make puddles.

◻ Mom and I make jelly cookies often, especially during the Christmas season to give as gifts.

## JELLY COOKIES

| | |
|---|---|
| $1^1/4$ | cups dates |
| $1/4$ | cup black walnuts |
| $1/2$ | cup sugar |
| $1/2$ | cup water |
| 1 | Tbsp. lemon juice |
| 1 | cup shortening or part butter and part shortening |
| $1^1/2$ | tsp. grated orange rind |
| $1/4$ | tsp. lemon rind |
| $1^1/2$ | tsp. salt |
| 2 | cups packed brown sugar |
| 2 | eggs |
| $3^1/3$ | cups flour |
| $1^1/2$ | tsp. baking soda |
| 2 | Tbsp. milk |

Grind dates, walnuts, sugar, water, and lemon juice. Cook over low heat, keeping warm until used.

Cream shortening, orange rind, lemon rind, salt, brown sugar, and eggs. Mix with flour, baking soda, and milk until dough is smooth.

Roll out dough. Spread date mixture over dough; form a roll on wax paper. Freeze overnight. Thinly slice; bake at 375° for 6 minutes.
*5 dozen*

I grew up on a tobacco farm in the Elk Creek section of Louisa County, Virginia. It was a time when children were allowed to be children and childhood was innocent. Let me share a few of my fonder memories.

I was a tomboy. I was the only girl of seven children and the only girl in the neighborhood. Whatever my brothers did, I did, too. Most of what we did was a matter of survival because my mother just didn't cook. My father worked from sun-up to sun-down, so he wasn't really there. When he was there, he did cook for us—beans most of the time. They were his specialty.

My uncle called me a "she-devil." I guess it was because my brothers and I plugged his watermelons in his watermelon patch. We'd cut a square in the watermelon and pull out the plug to see if it was ripe. If it wasn't ripe, we'd just put the plug back and, of course, the watermelon rotted. We did a lot of them like that to see if they were ripe. And when we found a ripe one, we'd eat it right there in the patch! We even stole corn from my uncle's corn patch.

We also trapped birds. We'd take an old door and prop it up with a stick. We'd tie a

*My husband and I are true country folks. Country folks have a peaceful, quiet nature that when awakened is full of humor and spirit.*

string to the stick and run it all the way from the trap to the house and through the window, then we'd just sit there and watch. When we saw a bird pecking at the corn under the door, we'd pull the string and the door would fall on him. We'd smush him! We did this all the time; it was the thing to do. They tasted like fried chicken. They were small, but when we were hungry, they were a lot of meat!

Once we had a pet pig named Pee Wee. We had hogs and we rescued Pee Wee from her mother who had eaten the rest of the litter. We adopted her as a pet and kept her in a shoe box in the house. Pee Wee was a true pet.

When we went to the mailbox, she would follow us, and if we left her, she'd start trotting after us. She stayed in the house until she was "shoat" size. She got so large until obviously we couldn't keep her in the house any longer. She had gotten so accustomed to being in the house that one afternoon when we came home from school, Pee Wee was in my mother's bed! Bed springs were all over the floor and Pee Wee, a big white sow, was in the bed. We just lost interest in Pee Wee as a pet because she got ugly. Later on, we slaughtered Pee Wee. I guess we ate her.

In Elk Creek, poor people ate biscuits; others ate light bread, or loaf bread as we call it today. If I brought biscuits to school for lunch, I would put my arm over my lunch pail to hide that I had a biscuit. I didn't want anyone to see that I was eating a biscuit. It even became an insult: "Look at all those *biscuit-eaters!*"

That's the way it was in Elk Creek during the late 1940's to the early 1950's. I lived in this time. Not everybody lived this way, with the outhouses for bathrooms and smokehouses for meat. It's kind of regional. I wouldn't say that my life was hard because I didn't realize it was hard then. I wouldn't say my life was mischievous because I didn't think I was mischievous then. I would just say that I have a lot of special memories of my childhood in Elk Creek in Louisa, Virginia.

❑ Chickens were a source of entertainment for me and my brothers in Elk Creek. I can recall watching a chicken lay an egg. The shell is really soft when it first comes out but hardens quickly. Many times—and I really feel bad when I think about this—we harassed hens while they were trying to lay their eggs. Some would run, dropping their eggs outside of the nest on the ground.

My cousin had a lot of chickens and we raided his chicken house all the time, almost on a daily basis. On several occasions, we got some eggs from under the setting hens, so when we cracked the eggs, there were baby chickens in them. Isn't that awful? Of course, we threw them away!

We chased the hens constantly until they grew tired. We didn't bother with the roosters; they were much faster than the hens. Besides, I was afraid of the roosters because, if provoked enough, they would not only turn and chase me, but also attack. Have you ever been spurred by a rooster? Ouch!

## BONNIE'S ELK CREEK-STYLE FRIED CHICKEN

| | |
|---|---|
| 1 | whole chicken, cut into pieces and remove skin |
| 1 | cup milk |
| | seasoning salt |
| | black pepper |
| 2-3 | cups flour |
| | paprika |
| 1/4 | cup parsley, finely chopped |
| 1 1/2 | cup olive oil |

Dip chicken in milk; shake off excess milk. Sprinkle with salt and pepper; roll in flour. Place on paper towels. Dip in milk; sprinkle with salt and pepper again. Sprinkle with paprika and parsley. Cook in oil over medium heat for about 35 minutes, turning every 10 minutes.

For crustier chicken, roll three times in milk, salt, pepper, and flour.

*5 to 7 servings*

❑ Hot fatback grease poured over thick caramel-colored molasses—not the runny stuff you see today—and hoecakes were a breakfast staple of black people living in Elk Creek. A cold glass of freshly churned buttermilk, with butter still swimming in it, topped off a delicious breakfast.

### HOECAKES

| | |
|---|---|
| 2 | cups flour |
| 1 | Tbsp. baking powder |
| 1/4 | tsp. salt |
| 1 | cup warm water |
| 4-6 | Tbsp. fatback grease |

Combine flour, baking powder, and salt. Gradually add water until batter is a pancake consistency. Stir in 2 tablespoons of fatback grease.

Heat remaining fatback grease in a large cast iron pan. Pour in batter. After hoecake has risen and browned, turn over and brown other side. Serve with fried fatback and warm molasses.

*4 servings*

❑ I remember many cold winter nights when my father awakened me to come and sit by the fireplace. Every winter, my father made ashcakes in the fireplace; he said his mother had made them for him. Watching my father make the bread was more enjoyable than eating it. The taste of ashcakes is not very different from hoecakes, but the gritty texture takes some getting used to!

Use the same ingredients as hoecakes. The only difference is the mode of cooking. My father would build a roaring fire in the fireplace and rake just enough hot coals onto the fire hearth to cover the bottom of a cast iron pan. He placed the pan containing batter on the coals and covered the batter with more hot coals. There was no turning. Once the ashcake was done, he would remove the bread and carefully wash it with water without making it soggy. My father and I enjoyed our ashcake by dunking chunks of it in a bowl of cold tomatoes that were retrieved from the cellar.

**People who liked** to go mountain climbing came from different places to the mountain near my family's house in Hawaii. A lot of them got stuck on the top. They got all the way to the top, then they couldn't get down. We always saw helicopters flying over our hut trying to rescue these people on the mountain.

My family lived on a one-acre piece of farmland near the Koolau Mountain range in a Quonset hut in Hawaii. We called our house a hut because Hawaiian houses were round with a thatch top. We didn't really have these type of huts in our days, but our house looked similar so we called it that. Our home was made from ridged metal sheets bent into a semi-circle. There were ten children in my family, and we were really poor. We paid one hundred dollars a month for three bedrooms. We had bunk beds everywhere.

When we moved to the hut, everybody hated it. It was on a farm and the cow pasture was next to us. It stunk so bad! In the back, there was a chicken farm, and further up, there was a pig farm—all these smells. And when the trade winds blew in our direction...oh, my god!

Our land was beautifully green. We grew every sort of vegetable and fruit. We had bananas, papayas, and mountain apples out there. We had ducks, a cow, chickens, and rabbits. But we never ate the rabbits. My brother caught crawfish from the river. There were cows next door, so we had fresh milk straight from the cow. We had whatever we needed in our backyard.

Food was a big part of getting together in my family. When we had luaus, the whole family would make the food. There was no gender thing in Hawaii; males and females cooked. Also luaus are not only tourist attractions. We called them luaus; others called them parties. We had luaus for many occasions such as weddings, anniversaries, and when a child turns one year old, especially if the child were a boy. They are just parties.

Sharleen with her husband.

*Food means more than just eating. It's like gaining family tradition and a feeling of warmth. It's not only about a food item that we prepare; it's about everyone working in the kitchen, preparing the food, and sitting down together to enjoy the meal.*

Luaus were mostly held outdoors under a canopy. Tables were set up and the food was buffet-style. Roasted pig and seafood were part of the occasion. Some foods were made ahead of time like *pasteles,* ground green bananas wrapped in tea leaves or banana leaves, and *lau lau,* meat or chicken mixed with butter fish and wrapped in *taro* leaves, then wrapped again in tea leaves. *Taro* leaves look like elephant ears.

On Saturdays, even if we were busy, we always prepared a big breakfast. It was a pretty big meal: bacon, sausages, waffles, fried rice, the whole nine yards. During the summertime, forget it. My family, aunts, uncles, cousins—everyone would take two weeks off and go camping on the beach. There were probably twenty-five people. We'd bring everything with us and set up tents. We ate fish fresh from the ocean and crabs. We'd bring steaks and hibachi grills to steam or grill our food. We're not gourmet cooks, we just have down-home cooking.

I think islanders find it hard to move away because of the fellowship around the table and the closeness in the families. Sometimes my family would come to my house and stay the whole weekend. I didn't have enough room, but everyone was still there!

❑ Hawaiians roast *Kahlua pig* in the ground. They put a certain kind of smooth lava rock which holds the heat for many hours on the bottom of a pit. Burlap bags and tea leaves are laid out, and the whole pig, head and all, is left to cook in this "oven" for about 24 hours. The inside of the pig is also stuffed with the lava rocks. There is no fire, just the hot rocks. The burlap bags and leaves hold the heat in.

The men cook the pig. They sit around all night, talking while the pig is cooking. I've never actually seen them put the pig in the ground because all the women stay inside to make the side dishes for the meal.

### OVEN-BAKED KAHLUA PIG
### Hawaiian Style Pork

| | |
|---|---|
| 1 | 5 lb. pork butt |
| | salt to taste |
| | liquid hickory smoke to taste |
| 1/2 | cup water |

Sprinkle pork with salt and liquid hickory smoke. Wrap in foil. Place in a shallow pan with water. Bake at 350° for 2 hours or until pork is fully cooked and meat easily falls off bone. Shred meat, adding a small amount of hot water. Serve with rice and a vegetable dish.
*6 to 8 servings*

❑ Cornmeal cake is a very light and fluffy dessert, not a bread.

### CORNMEAL CAKE

| | |
|---|---|
| 2 | cups Bisquick® |
| 1 | cup sugar |
| 3 | Tbsp. cornmeal |
| 1 | tsp. baking soda |
| 1/2 | tsp. salt |
| 2 | eggs, beaten |
| 1 | cup milk |
| 1 | cup butter or margarine, melted |

Combine Bisquick®, sugar, cornmeal, baking soda, and salt; set aside.

Combine eggs and milk; add to dry ingredients and mix well. Add butter; mix well. Pour into a floured 9 x 11 pan. Bake at 350° for 1 hour or until center is firm.
*1 cake*

❑ With ten children in my family, we were not able to have many toys but food was always available. If we didn't have anything to eat in the house, all we had to do was walk outside, pick fruits and vegetables from our yard, and make a salad or meat dish. They were delicious, or *ono,* as we say in Hawaii.

### CODFISH SALAD

| | |
|---|---|
| 4 | dried or salted codfish |
| 2 | tomatoes, diced |
| 1/2 | head of lettuce, torn |
| 1 | onion, sliced (optional) |
| 2 | avocados, sliced (optional) |
| | vinaigrette dressing to taste |

Cover codfish with water; boil for 25 minutes. Drain and add fresh water; boil again until codfish is soft and flaky. Drain; remove bones. Shred fish and mix with tomatoes, lettuce, onion (optional), and avocados (optional). Add vinaigrette; toss to mix.
*4 servings*

**Food was nothing** when I was a child living in Fredericksburg, Virginia. Sure, my family ate food every day: hot dogs, hamburgers, fried bologna—whatever was cheap and easy. Whenever I sat down at the table, there was rarely anything I liked. My mother liked pork brains and scrambled eggs. For some reason, she thought I also liked them. They were the worst things in my life, except for cooked carrots.

When I was older I found out that we ate such food because my parents didn't have money. Mom and Dad got married—bless their hearts—when they were seventeen. It was like the day after school let out on Mom's senior year.

One Christmas we even had hot dogs. They just couldn't afford to make the big Christmas dinner or give expensive gifts. We kids thought it was cool because everyone else had yucky turkey. Who wanted that? Mom gave me homemade Barbie clothes on that Christmas. She had scrap material from the pants factory where she worked. She stayed up all night sewing Barbie clothes as my present. My Barbie was the best dressed; she even had a fur coat. I didn't know any better. We had hot dogs for Christmas, and I got Barbie clothes for gifts. Mom and Dad felt bad, but I thought it was great.

*I got all these freckles from crabbing on a pier on the Eastern Shore!*

When I was about ten years old, we moved to the Eastern Shore because it was a chance for my parents to buy their own place. That's where my grandmother's family on my father's side is from. Moving to the Eastern Shore was real culture shock. Everything changed.

We were able to have more over there. We had so much seafood: baked or fried fish, clam chowder, steamed crabs. We either caught it, it was given to us, or we swapped for it. It was all free because water was all around us. I didn't like seafood because I never had it before. Fish sticks were the only fish I knew.

I returned to Fredericksburg at twenty-two years old. Only then did I realize that we had a gold mine on the Eastern Shore. Seafood prices in Fredericksburg were outrageous. I remember on the Eastern Shore we used to take a chicken back, tie it to a string, and throw it over the pier. We'd pull it up really slow, and the next thing we knew, we had a bushel of crabs. Now they're $100 a bushel, and that's not even cooked!

There were always people at our house on the Eastern Shore. Thanksgiving became a big thing and Christmas was even bigger. I don't know if I just started paying attention or I was getting older, but I have so many memories of the holidays, like smelling the turkey in the middle of the night. After we moved to the Eastern Shore, we always had a turkey on the holidays—except for once.

For some reason, Dad and my uncle went out hunting one year and brought back a goose. I remember that they had been "celebrating" the holidays with a good drink that day. When Dad came in, he stepped on the dog, then dropped kicked him out the door. I guess the goose would have been good except that we were supposed to watch it while it cooked. But we were just kids, and we let all the water boil out. The goose also wasn't very good because we had to keep pulling out little balls of metal! Since then, Mom only has turkey or venison on Christmas.

I still look forward to spending the holidays with my family on the Eastern Shore. It's the climax of the season. I have to go back or the holidays would not be the same.

◻ Mom started getting into Thanksgiving on the Eastern Shore. Now, it's a big production. The thing I remember most was not the turkey, not the sweet potatoes, but the dressing. Some call it stuffing. We never stuffed the turkey because it was a waste of time.

I have never had anything like it. She learned it from Dad's mom. We used to sneak up behind her and scoop some out of the bowl before it was cooked. That was half the fun!

## CORN BREAD DRESSING

| 2 | lbs. self-rising cornmeal |
| | milk |
| | oil |
| | salt and pepper to taste |
| 2 | Tbsp. sage |
| 1 | large onion, chopped |
| 2-3 | celery stalks, chopped |
| | turkey giblets, chopped |
| | turkey drippings |
| | butter |

Mix cornmeal with milk until batter is a pancake consistency. Fry into thin pancakes. Crumble pancakes into a large bowl.

Add salt, pepper, sage, onion, celery, and giblets to cornmeal; mix well. Add drippings to moisten. Spread in a baking dish and dot with butter. Bake at 350° for 1 hour or until brown on top.

*13 to 15 servings*

◻ I never saw or knew what a clam was until Dad came in with these "things," then steamed and ate them. Sometimes when he steamed clams, there were tiny crabs inside—maybe half an inch long—that looked like spiders. Mom and Dad would fight over those tiny crabs.

Dad learned how to cook clam chowder from the locals on the Eastern Shore. When he adds the bacon, he includes all the grease. He saves every amount of clam juice, or "liquor." Liquor is what everyone on the Eastern Shore calls all that slimy stuff that you can't believe you want to eat.

## EASTERN SHORE CLAM CHOWDER

| 1 | pint clams, chopped |
| 1 | cup diced potatoes |
| $^1/_3$ | cup chopped onion |
| $^1/_2$ | cup diced and fried bacon |
| | dash of bitters |
| | salt and pepper to taste |

Boil clams and liquor, potatoes, and onion in enough water to cover potatoes until potatoes are done. Add bacon, bitters, salt and pepper; cook for 10 minutes.

*4 servings*

**When the world** seems topsy-turvy and I'm stressed out from the hustle and bustle of raising three children and baby-sitting, I try to remember my great-great-aunts, Mable and Myrtle.

Mable and Myrtle, who lived and died old maids, not only raised me, but also three generations of my family. They bought a homestead in Fredericksburg, Virginia, with my mother. The homestead was a gathering place for the entire family; it was a safe haven for the wounded and the hungry. No one was ever turned away. Mable and Myrtle took care of everyone.

Mable and Myrtle were completely different, like night and day. One was long and linky; the other was short and stinky. That's what we called them. Mable, the oldest of the two, was a teeny, tiny, scrawny, little thing. Her glasses were as big as her face and her false teeth used to fall out when she was talking. We thought this was why she didn't do most of the yelling. We played with Mable's false teeth all the time. She would leave them by the sink, and we would put them in our mouths. She'd yell, "Get those out of your mouth. I have to wear those!"

Myrtle was short and stocky. She had the most beautiful white hair, as white as snow. She kept it short because she hated messing with her hair, but she liked her perms. Poor Myrtle, her glasses were always broken. She taped them, glued them, and mended them. She hated to spend money on her glasses, but not a week went by that she didn't spend money on sweepstakes. She pasted, peeled, ripped and wrote out her little checks to send away for free things. She got all kinds of nifty gadgets. She had a magnifying glass with lights, but when we put it to a book, the glass would fall out! Myrtle just knew she was going to hit the jackpot one day. She never did.

*A song, "Every Light In The House Is On," reminds me of the homestead where I grew up because no matter the time of day, my great-great-aunts, Mable and Myrtle, were always there for whoever need them. If anyone was ever having problems Mable and Myrtle would smooth over ruffled feathers and get things back to normal.*

Mable was the overall guardian and protector. She also did the manual labor, like cutting the grass or cleaning, and the heavy-duty work. Let's put it this way: she was the "man" of the pair. Mable was the ring leader, the controller; she made all the rules.

Myrtle was more relaxed. Most of the time we followed Myrtle's ways and Mable would get mad. At night when we were in trouble, Myrtle would come up and rub our backs because she knew we were upset. She taught us right from wrong. I remember Myrtle telling me not to play with birds' nests that fell out of this big oak tree in our backyard. One day I found a nest on the ground and baby birds calling out. So I picked up the nest. The next thing I knew, I was running through the yard with a big mother bird pecking my head! It was awful. This was one of the "Do as you're told" lessons that I will never forget.

Myrtle also cooked and made sure that my sister and I were always in the kitchen. She'd say, "You've got to learn how to cook. No man wants a woman who doesn't know how to cook." I was always in the kitchen with Myrtle because I loved to eat. She often called me her human garbage disposal because, to me, food was always better tasting the next day.

I see a little bit of Mable in me, but I'm more like Myrtle. I do all the cooking when we have family gatherings. I take care of the children; I take care of everybody. I'm the one who is always pointing the finger. My whole family—mother, brothers, sister, aunts—even tell me, "You're so much like Myrtle!"

Fortunately, Myrtle was always in the kitchen, especially the day that my youngest brother, Steve, woke up on the wrong side of the bed.

Myrtle fixed fried hash and grits one day for breakfast. We were all at the table except Steve, who came last. He came in, looked at the table and said, "What's this slop for breakfast?" We tried to tell him it was really good because Myrtle made it.

Steve sat down and tasted it. He didn't like it so he threw his fork across the table. I jumped up and yelled at him, and he punched me in the eye. I picked up a butter knife and started chasing him, not knowing what I would have done had I caught him. Myrtle was chasing me.

At one point, Steve turned around and punched me again—in the same eye! Myrtle ran to the refrigerator and grabbed a steak; this was her cure-all remedy. She put that steak over my eye and walked me to school so she could take the steak back home. I'm not sure if we cooked that steak or not. And it didn't work. My eye still blackened.

Everything Myrtle made was good. We just never questioned it—except for when Steve woke up on the wrong side of the bed. Myrtle made a corn pudding which a lot of people weren't sure if it was a dish to be served with dinner or if it was dessert.

### CORN PUDDING

| | |
|---|---|
| 2 | 15.25 oz. cans corn, drained, or 8 to 10 ears, kernels removed |
| 2 | Tbsp. flour or cornstarch |
| 2 | eggs |
| 1 | stick butter, cut into squares |
| 1 | tsp. vanilla extract |
| 1 | cup sugar |
| 1/2 | cup milk |
| | cinnamon |

Combine all ingredients except cinnamon; mix well. Bake in a 375° preheated oven for 15 minutes. Stir in cinnamon; bake for 30 minutes or until middle is done.
*4 to 6 servings*

I married into a family named Dickinson. When you think "clan," that's them. They are spread out all over Spotsylvania County in Virginia. What a wonderful bunch of people. They are always willing to give and help others in need. The whole family together is like a "jack-of-all-trades." Everyone has a different profession: electrician, builder, roofer, mechanic. When we needed a garage, we bought the materials, and they all came over. A couple of weeks later, the garage was done. And all I had to do was keep them fed.

All of the Dickinson bunch, including my husband, hunt every year. There is always enough meat to go around to the families, no matter who kills that day. Once we had a big get-together and everyone brought different meats. The menu was filled with deer, turkey, ham, snake, bear, turtle, rabbit, and more.

If you hunt or like venison, you simply must know about this recipe. My sons, W.C. and Tyler, say it's better than pizza. Now that's saying something! There are no measurements necessary.

### DICKINSON PARMESAN DEER

*deer hindquarters, cut into cubes*
*flour*
*Parmesan cheese*
*oil for frying*

Coat meat with flour and deep-fry until brown. Pour cheese into a container with a lid. While the meat is still hot, shake meat in the container with cheese until well-coated. Place meat on a baking sheet; bake at 375° for 10 to 15 minutes or until brown.

**It's nice to have a choice.** Fingers, forks, or chopsticks—which will I choose tonight? To be in America and to be American is to be in a culture of choice. America is a place where one can cherish the past or ignore it, revel in tradition or invent one's own. In America, I can ask "Why?" "Why must the table be set this way?" I can also expect a logical answer. When none is given, I can choose to accept or reject the premise.

Once while eating spaghetti with a friend's family, I was startled to see that all eyes were on me. I wondered what was wrong. I looked at my plate, then theirs. They started laughing. Feeling uneasy, I began eating again. I picked up my butter knife and fork and resumed cutting my spaghetti into fine pieces. It's good that way.

America is a land of tolerance. I cut up my spaghetti. Those who roll it in a spoon, well, they're okay, too. Tolerance is much greater than table manners. Tolerance encompasses religion, politics, styles of clothing, pretty much anything and everything. I can go to church, then eat lunch with someone who just came from a mosque. I can debate a socialist and invite him to my home afterwards. Tolerance is a virtue. America is a tolerant country. Anyone who doubts this needs only to look and see the diversity that surrounds each of us.

*Two hundred years ago, my dog and I would have died in a blizzard of this magnitude. But today we can both smile and know there is warmth waiting inside!*

To many, the nation's capital defines America. The Smithsonian museums, the Washington Monument, and the Lincoln Memorial are splendid attractions, but there are also experiences of diversity on every corner. Food and music that most would consider foreign are as American as the ice cream parlor and Elvis. An Ethiopian restaurant can be on one side of the street, an Indian restaurant on the other—Chinese, Thai, Italian, even an authentic English pub. These meeting places, along with the historical sights, are an important part of Washington D.C. because they are where people of the world come together, socialize, and communicate. They are examples of what makes this country America.

To me, small towns also define America. Even here in Fredericksburg, the diversity is obvious. Look at the faces, the dress, the food; diversity is everywhere. There is more to Fredericksburg than monuments of the old south; there are living monuments to the present-day. Restaurants, antique shops, pubs, clothing boutiques, and homes—each has a variety representing different cultures.

There is no single American culture. American culture allows individuals to decide. This is America: choice, tolerance, and diversity. Conforming to American culture is a decision. As an American, I always have a choice.

□ Now I don't care what anyone says. I've been to Italy, I've eaten their pizza, and "true pizza" is not Italian. It's American. Besides hamburgers and hot dogs, pizza is one of the most American foods anyone can eat. Trust me.

Please, please, whatever you do, use the highest quality ingredients for these recipes.

### AMERICAN PIZZA PIE

**crust:**

| | |
|---|---|
| 4 | cups flour, sifted |
| 1 | cake yeast |
| 1$^1$/$_3$ | cups 85° water |
| 2 | Tbsp. olive oil |
| $^1$/$_2$ | tsp. salt |

**sauce:**

| | |
|---|---|
| 2 | 15 oz. cans tomato sauce |
| 1 | Tbsp. oregano |
| 1 | tsp. garlic powder |
| 1 | tsp. crushed red pepper |
| $^1$/$_4$ | tsp. salt |
| $^1$/$_8$ | tsp. black pepper |

Combine all ingredients for crust; mix well into a dough. Knead for 10 minutes. Cover with damp cloth; let rise for 2 hours. Pat and stretch dough onto two greased 14-inch pizza pans. Pinch up a collar around edge.

Prepare sauce. Combine all ingredients for sauce; mix well. Adjust seasonings to taste. Spread over crust. Top with cheese and favorite toppings. Bake in a 400° preheated oven for 10 to 15 minutes.
*two 14-inch pizzas*

□ It's hard to believe, but this recipe has helped me see thirty countries including my own. Fifty cents a cookie adds up fast.

### COUSIN CLINT'S CHOCOLATE CHIP COOKIES

| | |
|---|---|
| 2$^1$/$_4$ | cups flour |
| 1 | tsp. baking soda |
| 1 | tsp. salt |
| 1 | cup butter |
| $^1$/$_2$ | cup packed brown sugar |
| $^1$/$_2$ | cup sugar |
| 1$^1$/$_2$ | tsp. vanilla extract |
| 2 | eggs |
| 2 | cups real chocolate chips |

In a small bowl, combine flour, baking soda, and salt; set aside.

In a large bowl, cream butter and both sugars until light and fluffy. Add vanilla and eggs; mix well. Add dry ingredients; mix well. Stir in chocolate chips. Roll a heaping tablespoon into a ball. Place each ball 2 inches apart onto an ungreased cookie sheet. Bake in a 300° preheated oven for 10 to 15 minutes. Cool before removing from pan.
*2$^1$/$_2$ dozen*

**My mother dropped me off** at Mother Flo and Papa Floyd's house every summer when I was a little boy. My grandparents lived in Suffolk, Virginia, a very rural community where peanuts, corn, and soybeans were the primary source of income for the people, who were pretty much all farmers at that time. My grandparents lived in a gigantic house which always reminded me of the Munsters' house on television. The house was so big that there were rooms upstairs that hadn't been used for years, and sometimes I sneaked up there to play.

Fridays were the days that groceries were purchased. I always looked forward to Fridays because Papa Floyd always had a special treat for me. Fridays were also the days when Mother Flo made pig's feet and black-eyed peas. Those pig's feet—those pink-looking things!—were put in a big tub and boiled so that the whole house had this certain smell to it. Pig's feet on Fridays! I tolerated the pig's feet, but really I wasn't too crazy about them. They felt sticky. Back then, it was just something that was part of the routine.

Every Friday night, we'd sit down and eat black-eyed peas, pig's feet, and home-cooked fries. The fries were the best. I never knew about buying French fries in the store. I think from a cultural point, this type of food was eaten for good luck. Pig's feet, black-eyed peas, lima beans, and cabbage—they were real soul food.

On special occasions, we had something I would not touch: chitterlings. When Mother Flo and Papa Floyd started cooking chitterlings, I kept my distance. I went to the other side of the house and disappeared. As a youngster, I thought the smell was so

Forest with Papa Floyd.

*My brother, Dwight, was Mother Flo's favorite. I knew this because I would find the cookies she always hid for him. But I was Papa Floyd's favorite. Besides the treat he brought me on Fridays, I usually got what I wanted from him.*

horrible that I just did not want to be around. I never acquired an appreciation for them because I couldn't stand the smell. Today, I have a neighbor across the street who is very good at cooking chitterlings. For some reason, hers don't stink.

When chitterlings were served, I ate chicken. It was nothing for Papa Floyd to go out and kill a chicken. That was strange to me. After the chicken's head is cut off, the chicken's body still runs around without the head. It's true! The chicken can run around for maybe a minute or so—not very long—without its head. It always scared the heck out of me!

Mother Flo could cook. I loved it when she'd cook fried potatoes and fried bread. She'd put some flour and lard together and fry them up into small pancakes. I could eat a hundred of them. She also made the best cakes and cookies—talk about stealing out of the cookie jar!

Papa Floyd passed away in 1988, and Mother Flo lived by herself at the homestead until 1994. Today, Mother Flo is ninety-one years old. The older, big house burned down back in 1968, but I still went to the new house during the summers. I recently bought their homestead. I don't plan on ever selling it; I plan to pass it on. It's so peaceful and quiet there with only the sounds of the birds and crickets.

When I go back now, I reminisce about being at the old house of Papa Floyd and Mother Flo. I have good memories of growing up there. I can still smell the odor of chitterlings, but I can also smell the pleasant odors of Mother Flo's home-cooked fries, cookies, and biscuits.

❑ Chitterlings and pig's feet are such a visible part of African-American cuisine. I don't know the truths of it, but I had been told that during slavery times the main parts of the animals were for the big house, and the leftover parts were given to the slaves and workers. The slaves and workers had to be creative in preparing dishes with intestines, feet, or whatever was readily available.

### CHITTERLINGS

| | |
|---|---|
| 10 | lbs. chitterlings, cleaned well |
| 1 | cup cold water |
| 1 | tsp. cayenne pepper |
| 1 | tsp. black pepper |
| 2 | Tbsp. salt |
| | vinegar (optional) |

Chitterlings come frozen and must be thawed completely; soak in cold water while thawing. Wash each strand separately under running cold water. Remove all dirt, foreign matter, and most but not all excess fat.

In a large pot with a tight-fitting lid, combine all ingredients. Cover and bring to a boil over medium heat. After boiling, drain. Add 1 cup of water and repeat seasoning. Cook over low heat for 3 to 4 hours. Stir occasionally; add water as needed. Add salt, pepper, and vinegar (optional) to taste.

For best results, use a pressure cooker. It cuts time to about 1 1/2 hours, and the chitterlings are more tender.
*10 to 12 servings*

❑ Mother Flo was one of the strongest women I have ever known. She had polio when she was about twenty-eight years old. I have never seen her not in a wheelchair. She had powerful arms from turning those wheels, and there were times that she'd tear my butt up!

I used to try to take advantage of her. If I did something bad, she'd say, "Boy, you better stop."

I'd say something like, "You can't stop me." Then I would forget. But she had a good memory. She'd lure me close enough and once she got a hold of me, she'd pull me toward her and body slam me with one arm!

Mother Flo could do anything. She was a very strong woman in the sense of pulling her own. She kept the house clean and always had dinner ready when Papa Floyd came home. Papa Floyd really loved Mother Flo's rice pudding. It was one of his favorite desserts.

### RICE PUDDING

| | |
|---|---|
| 1 | cup rice |
| 4 | cups cold water |
| 1/2 | cup butter |
| 1 | cup sugar |
| 2 | cups whole milk |
| 1 | 12 oz. can evaporated milk |
| 1 | Tbsp. lemon extract |
| 1 | tsp. nutmeg |
| 1/2 | cup raisins (optional) |
| 1 | egg, beaten |
| | dash of salt |

Cook rice in water over medium heat until water evaporates. Add butter, stirring until butter melts. Add remaining ingredients; mix well. Pour into a 2-quart casserole dish. Bake at 325° for 1 hour.
*8 to 10 servings*

**When I was a child**, our door was always open to the service boys. My father was an outgoing, loving person, and he always invited people in the military to our home. My father never asked if they were rich or poor or in-between. They were guys in the service protecting America; they were away from home, so our home was their home.

It was nothing for us to wake up after Daddy and Momma had gone out and see marines or sailors sitting at our table having breakfast. On Thanksgiving, if there were servicemen who couldn't make it home, they came to our house to share Thanksgiving dinner. It wasn't anything extraordinary. It was just a way of life.

I inherited my parents' heart for the military. My husband and I moved into a farmhouse where many of the guys stopped by as they came though the woods. The farmhouse was nicknamed the "Halfway house" because it was surrounded by Quantico Marine Base in Virginia. They could come any time to get away and still have a homelike atmosphere. We had a swing on the front porch, and if they wanted to pitch a tent in the backyard, they could. They'd come on Friday evening and if Monday was a holiday, they'd stay until Monday.

Claudia (bottom right).

*My mother would leave our Christmas tree up until all her boys in the military came home on leave to see it. It didn't matter if they didn't come for months; she would not let us take it down. This picture was not taken during Christmas. We were waiting for my brother, Bert, to come home.*

There were many times I came down the stairs and had to step over the servicemen who had spent the night. In the morning they would pass a hat around to pay for eggs and bacon, and I would cook breakfast for them all. I'd fix them up with scrambled eggs, bacon, and a couple gallons of milk and orange juice. They would come in the front door, go around the table just like they would in the mess hall, and walk right out the door.

The guys just learned how to be a part of the family. They would bring in a new group of fellows to replace them when they left. Each time they left, my heart would just break because I felt like I was losing my own kids.

We were a part of something that took place in their lives, just as they were a part of our lives. This is the part of me that bleeds from my parents.

When my children were in the service and away from home, I hoped—just like my parents—that someone was opening the door for them. If my grandsons go into the service, I hope that some form of hospitality is given to them while they are away from home. My husband and I moved away from the base, so we don't come in contact with many service personnel. However, our door still is and will always be open to the military.

❏ I was the tenth out of fourteen children, nine boys and five girls. Having big brothers in the service was the biggest cause for excitement when they came home on furlough for Thanksgiving and other holidays.

Thanksgiving at my home is as special to me now as when I was young, except now I have my own children and grandchildren. These recipes are a few of my children's favorite Thanksgiving dishes.

### ROASTED TURKEY AND STUFFING

| | |
|---|---|
| 1 | turkey |
| | turkey giblets |
| 1 | Tbsp. poultry seasoning |
| 1 | tsp. salt |

**stuffing:**

| | |
|---|---|
| 2 | loaves stale bread, chopped |
| 1 | cup chopped celery |
| 1 | cup chopped onions |
| 1 | Tbsp. poultry seasoning |
| 1 | tsp. sage |
| 1 | tsp. parsley |
| $^1/_2$ | cup butter, melted |

Cook turkey according to package instructions. Boil giblets in water with poultry seasoning and salt until neck meat is tender. Remove giblets from pan; reserve water.

Combine all ingredients for stuffing. Add 1 cup of reserved water; mix well. Stuff into turkey or bake alone. Use giblets and remaining water for gravy.
*10 to 12 servings*

### CANDIED SWEET POTATOES OR YAMS

| | |
|---|---|
| 6 | large sweet potatoes, peeled |
| 1 | cup brown sugar |
| 1 | cup chopped marshmallows |
| 1 | tsp. cinnamon |
| | butter |
| | whole marshmallows |

Boil sweet potatoes until tender. Remove sweet potatoes; reserve water. Set aside to cool.

In a separate pan, cook 2 cups of reserved water, brown sugar, chopped marshmallows, and cinnamon over medium heat until marshmallows are melted.

Grease bottom and sides of 2-quart dish with butter. Slice sweet potatoes. Layer potatoes, cooked mixture, and whole marshmallows until dish is almost full, leaving room for a last layer of marshmallows. Cook half an hour before serving dinner. Bake in a 375° preheated oven for 10 minutes, then broil until marshmallows are golden brown.
*10 to 12 servings*

### SCALLOPED POTATOES

| | |
|---|---|
| 6-8 | large potatoes, peeled and sliced $^1/_3$ inch thick |
| $^1/_4$ | cup butter |
| 3 | cups milk |
| 6-8 | slices American or Cheddar cheese |
| $^1/_2$ | cup flour |

Boil sliced potatoes until just tender; drain and set aside.

Cook butter, milk, and cheese over low-medium heat. Combine flour and enough milk to make a thin paste. Stir paste into cheese mixture gradually to prevent lumps. Add potatoes; cover well with sauce. Place in a buttered baking dish; top with a layer of extra cheese. Bake at 350° for 1 hour.
*12 to 14 servings*

**People adhered strictly** to their own kind, back in the days of my parents. My parents are American. My father, John Barrett's, side was Irish-Catholic, and my mother, Florence Courtney Jones', side was Anglo-Episcopal. Dad was a pharmacist from Pennsylvania; Mom was from a first family in Virginia. So there was much ado about an Irish-Catholic Yankee marrying a Protestant southern girl.

Mom and Dad revered their parents and were considerate of their differences. However, Mom and Dad were determined to teach us nine children not to be prejudiced or bigoted on all fronts. They both were deeply religious and loved politics, and they raised us to be devout and politically active.

My husband, Harry, was raised similarly. We believe that love and service with honor and integrity to each other, our families, and our community equate to the best of our American Dream. Being frugal and sharing the extra from our abundance—what we grow in our garden of life and the food we prepare—are part of that philosophy. Feed the body and the soul will be enriched with the love that is served therewith.

*Harry and I have such similar backgrounds in faith, politics, and roots that our marriage of thirty-two years has been fruitful and loving. Here we are doing the twist on St. Patrick's Day.*

Part of being an American is caring for my community and involving myself in local politics and civic groups. Through the Ancient Order of Hibernians, an Irish-Catholic group, I have found a way to express my political and religious concerns. Cherishing my Irish and English backgrounds, I try to understand the likes and differences between the Irish and English and between the Protestants and Catholics. I give my love to both groups and offer a prayer for a peaceful solution. There's no use taking sides when trying to make peace.

I treasure my roots. I love the democratic view of life and the great Catholic faith that my Anglican-Catholic parents practiced. My parents raised nine children and my husband's parents raised ten, and neither family could have succeeded without the appreciation of our American democracy and faith. With hard work, faith in God, and love of family, we have succeeded in finding the American Dream. It does work!

◻ This trifle, an Irish-American dessert, is for those frugal souls who never make waste and use leftovers in the most creative and delightful ways. It never tastes the same twice, but it is always a delicious surprise. Have fun and serve it in a festive glass bowl, punch bowl, or just a salad bowl.

## CRISP'S TIPSY TRIFLE DELIGHT

| | |
|---|---|
| 1 | package instant vanilla pudding |
| 2 | Tbsp. Irish Mist, sherry, or any liqueur |
| 1 | 14 oz. can fruit cocktail or |
| | cherry or blueberry pie filling |
| $^1/_3$ | cup Irish Mist, sherry, or any liqueur |
| 1 | vanilla, lemon, or any flavor layered |
| | cake, cut into wedges |
| | jelly or jam to spread on cake (optional) |
| | leftover vanilla wafers, graham |
| | crackers, or any cookies, crumbled |
| 3 | oz. slivered almonds |
| | whipped cream |

garnish:
cherry halves
almonds
dash of nutmeg
dash of cinnamon

Prepare pudding according to package instructions, stirring in 2 tablespoons liqueur.

Drain fruit cocktail, reserving juice. Mix $^1/_3$ cup liqueur with juice to make "tipsy sauce"; set aside.

In a large serving bowl, layer cake and half of fruit cocktail; sprinkle with crumbled cookies, almonds, and "tipsy sauce." Spread $^1/_2$ of pudding.

Repeat layering, ending with cake. Spread whipped cream over cake. Garnish with cherries, almonds, nutmeg, and cinnamon. Chill for 2 to 3 hours before serving.

◻ We've always believed that you've got to nourish the body before you can feed the soul, so all the men in the family like to cook, too. This recipe was passed on when Uncle Harry Mash married Dad's sister. The coleslaw is perfect to bring for any family gathering.

## PAPAP'S COLESLAW

| | |
|---|---|
| 1 | small cabbage |
| 1 | small purple cabbage |
| 4 | celery stalks |
| 4 | carrots |
| 1 | medium onion |
| $^1/_2$ | cup sugar |
| $^1/_4$ | cup apple vinegar |
| $^1/_2$-1 | cup low-fat mayonnaise |

Shred all vegetables in food processor or chop finely; toss to mix. Mix sugar and vinegar; stir in mayonnaise. Combine with vegetables; mix well.
15 to 20 servings

**We lived in an area** of Vietnam where we didn't travel by mechanical transportation. The north of Vietnam has most of the cities, so the transportation is different; they use cars, bicycles, buses. The south of Vietnam has more farms and bigger bodies of water. If we wanted to go places or travel around, we would use canoes called *ghe*.

When I married I moved from the city to An Lac Tay, an island with the mainlands on both sides of it. Being from the city, I wasn't used to travelling by boat, but the only way for all the people living on the island to go to the mainland was by boat.

Every morning we went by boat to the mainland to go shopping. The food we bought, we bought day by day; we didn't store it up. Now here in America, we do store food, but not then in Vietnam. We went shopping every day, especially for meat because we didn't have a refrigerator.

We had to leave very early because the market opened at seven o'clock in the morning and was over by nine o'clock. If we were late, there would be no food left; it would all be sold. Mainly we just bought meat and oil. Sometimes we just made our own oil out of animal fat by frying the skin until the oil came out. It was very rare that we bought vegetables in the market. We grew our own. Most of the people where we lived owned a certain amount of land to plant many kinds of fruits and vegetables for their families.

*When I think of Vietnam, I always remember the green countryside with all the rice fields, coconut tree, and banana trees.*

This is just the way we lived because we were on an island in the south. There is so much water in the south that even if we wanted to go from the top of the mainland to the bottom of the mainland, we would still need a boat.

It's really the same here. When I need something here, I get into my car and drive to buy it. When I needed something in Vietnam, I got into the boat and paddled to buy it. But it took a lot longer by boat to go shopping, maybe a half an hour to one hour. If we went far, maybe it took two to four hours. The boats are not fast like a car; they're very slow.

We didn't have problems, like here, with parking or someone stealing our boat. There was always room on the piers, and no one would ever think about stealing another person's boat. And it's not like here with teenagers either. American teenagers want their own cars, but in Vietnam, teenagers would never ask for their own boat!

I actually loved travelling by boat. I remember standing up—everyone stands up while rowing—and rotating the two long oars with my arms crossing in front of me. I paddled by myself, but I didn't know how to swim. I think that had I tipped the boat over, I would have died!

I moved here to America, and I don't have to paddle anymore. When I'm about to drive my car—holding the steering wheel like the oars with both hands—I always remember Vietnam. But now I don't have to move my arms for rowing.

◻ We grew our own pineapples in Vietnam, so we always used fresh pineapples, not canned.

## GA XAO KHOM
### Stir-Fried Chicken with Pineapple

| | |
|---|---|
| 1 | fresh pineapple, sliced $1/2$ inch thick, or 2 cans |
| 2-3 | Tbsp. oil |
| 3 | garlic cloves, chopped |
| 2 | boneless chicken breasts, sliced |
| | salt to taste |
| | msg (monosodium glutamate) to taste |
| $1/2$ | bunch green onions, cut into 2-inch pieces |

If using fresh pineapple, marinate with 2 tablespoons sugar before using; if using canned, reserve juice from one can.

Heat oil over medium-high heat. Add garlic; cook until fragrant. Add chicken; cook until done outside. Add salt and msg. Add pineapple with juice. Reduce heat to medium; cook, covered, for 15 minutes. Stir in green onions. Serve with rice and soy sauce or fish sauce on the side.

*4 servings*

◻ The first thing Vietnamese people do before going out is put on a *non la*, a palm leaf hat. It's very hot in Vietnam, so the hat protects the face from the sun. It's also waterproof.

The hat is especially worn by people in the country. Everyone working in the rice fields is wearing one. In the city, not many people wear one; they think the *non la* is old-fashioned. Tourists buy the hats as souvenirs. I wore my *non la* whenever I went shopping on the mainland for meat and other groceries.

If I buy ribs, I may prepare *suon ram*. I make the dish whenever my family feels like having stir-fried pork ribs.

## SUON RAM
### Vietnamese Pork Ribs

| | |
|---|---|
| 2 | lbs. small pork ribs, cut short |
| 1 | Tbsp. green onion stalk, chopped |
| 1 | cup water |
| 4 | Tbsp. soy sauce |
| 2 | tsp. sugar |
| 1 | tsp. salt |
| $1/4$ | tsp. msg (monosodium glutamate) |
| $1/4$ | tsp. black pepper |
| 1 | medium onion, sliced |

Cook ribs and green onion over medium-high heat for 10 minutes. Add water. Reduce heat to medium; cook, covered, until water is reduced to half. Add soy sauce, sugar, salt, and msg; cook for 5 minutes. Remove any liquid fat. Add pepper and onion; cook until liquid is almost gone and meat is tender. Serve with rice.

*4 to 6 servings*

**Vietnamese families** stick together. They love each other, and they will do everything for each other. I love going back home because the Vietnamese always have respect. I love the culture and the way people sit and talk with me and treat me so nicely. We can sit and talk for hours about life a long time ago.

It is poor in Vietnam—so poor that the people have to cook outside in a pot on top of three rocks, over a fire made with wood or straw. But anything I wanted to eat, they would cook it for me. I went back to Vietnam during the summer of 1996. My family, everybody, wanted to cook all the food I like such as *bun man*, noodles with duck and bamboo shoots; *lau luong*, eel with sweet and sour soup; and *banh uoc*, steamed rice flour dumplings eaten with cucumber and fish sauce. This is why I went to Vietnam: I miss my country's food!

I am from Hue, a big town between Saigon and Hanoi. There is a beautiful big river called *Song Huong,* meaning Perfume River, that flows through Hue. It is so clear, the sand can be seen.

Coi with her husband.

*The last time I went to Vietnam I visited my house where my husband, daughter, and I used to live. Now it belongs to someone else. We visited our old neighbors and relatives and shared lots of good memories of when we lived in Vietnam.*

My husband comes from Gio Dau, a small village outside of Saigon. There are no rice fields, banana or coconut trees where I am from, but in Gio Dau, there are many rice and sugar cane fields, bamboo, and banana trees. I remember riding on the train and seeing that everything was green, and outside the window, there were many Vietnamese fruits and jackfruits and oranges. Oh, so many! Sometimes the people plant bananas up in the mountains. I don't know how in the world they climbed up there.

The last time I went to Vietnam was for my mom's *Dam Do*. *Dam Do* is a remembrance of family members who had passed away. The family gathers on the day before the anniversary of the person's death, this time being my mom's *Dam Do*. We invited family and neighbors to eat and drink tea. We wanted to call her to eat with us, so we prayed that she would come back.

Every year on *Dam Do*, we cook a lot of food. No one cares if the family doesn't have money. It doesn't matter if they have to borrow the money just for that day. Traditionally, when the parents are gone the house goes to the oldest son, so he is usually the one who hosts the remembrance. He must cook everything. No one brings a dish—maybe just fruit—but not cooked food.

A big table is set and everyone sits down to eat. It is like a wedding feast but without the cake. We fix stir-fry, shrimp, noodles, pork with egg, fish, crabs, whatever the person who died liked to eat—which is everything, because when a person lives, he or she likes to eat everything.

Even though the last time I went to Vietnam was for my mom's *Dam Do*, the trip was still a happy occasion. I feel good every time I go, and I am very happy. If I had the money, I would like to go home every year.

# Coi Mai Truong

❑ Squid is common in Vietnam. They come in all kinds of sizes. This is an excellent dish and can be easily prepared at home.

## MUC NHOI THIT
### Meat-Stuffed Squid

| | |
|---|---|
| 12 | small squid |
| 3/4 | lb. ground pork |
| 1 | garlic clove, chopped |
| 2 | shallots, chopped |
| 1/4 | tsp. black pepper |
| 1 1/2 | tsp. fish sauce |
| 1/4 | tsp. sugar |
| 1/4 | tsp. salt |
| | oil for frying |

Clean squid under cold running water; remove purplish skin by rubbing. Cut off tentacles. Finely chop 5 tentacles; set aside. Discard heads and thin cartilage from inside body. Drain in a colander; pat inside and outside with paper towel. Set aside.

Combine pork, garlic, and shallots. Sprinkle with pepper, fish sauce, sugar, and salt. Add chopped tentacles; mix well. Firmly stuff squid 2/3 full.

Heat 1/2 inch oil over medium-high heat. Carefully place squid into oil. Reduce heat to medium. Cook for 20 minutes without turning. Increase heat to medium-high; cook until squid is brown. Turn and cook other side for 10 minutes.

*4 servings*

❑ I often prepare *thit bo xao ot xanh,* or beef with green peppers and broccoli. Sometimes I fix a big pot earlier in the week then eat it almost every day.

## THIT BO XAO OT XANH
### Stir-Fried Beef with Green Peppers and Broccoli

| | |
|---|---|
| 1/2 | lb. beef, thinly sliced |
| | freshly ground black pepper |
| 1 1/2 | tsp. fish sauce |
| 2 | garlic cloves, chopped |
| 1 | tsp. oyster sauce |
| 1/2 | tsp. soy sauce |
| 1/2 | cup water |
| 1 | Tbsp. cornstarch |
| 2 | shallots, chopped |
| 1 1/2 | Tbsp. oil |
| 1 | cup broccoli florets |
| 1 | large tomato, cut into wedges |
| 1/2 | large onion, cut into wedges |
| 1 | green pepper, cubed |
| 1 | celery stalk, thinly sliced |

Sprinkle beef with pepper, 1/2 teaspoon fish sauce, and 1/2 of chopped garlic; set aside.

In a separate bowl, combine remaining fish sauce, oyster sauce, soy sauce, water, and cornstarch; set aside.

Cook remaining garlic and shallots in oil over high heat. Add meat, stirring constantly. Add broccoli and 1 tablespoon water. Cook, covered, for 3 minutes. Add tomato, onion, green pepper, and celery; stir constantly. Stir in oyster sauce mixture. Cook for 5 minutes.

*6 servings*

Good cooking runs in my family. My uncle and my mom were chefs in Vietnam, and my family owned a bakery. At our bakery we also made French food like *paté choux,* a meat pie in puff pastry, and eclairs, and we made them well.

There is a big French influence in Vietnamese cooking, especially in pastries because the French were in our country for about seventy years. We have adopted some of their culture: All of our sandwiches are in baguettes, not sliced bread. Instead of having stew with rice or noodles, we may just dip a baguette. A Vietnamese submarine has French sausage, paté, coriander, Vietnamese pickled vegetables, and spring onions.

I want my daughter and son to have the same talent I have. I tell them to come to the kitchen to watch me cook and not to be afraid. If it is not good, throw it away and keep trying. I want them to experiment, and I leave them alone to do so. I show them how to cook, but they can create their own ways. My daughter, Hanh, and son still call me all the time to ask me how to cook certain dishes.

My children always say that my food has more flavor and tastes better than other Vietnamese cooking. I used to help my friends cook for big parties, some having 300 people. That was a few years ago; now I'm getting old and too slow!

Although men don't usually cook in Vietnam, my husband cooks a lot, too. He was in the States on his own in 1968 and 1969 while we were dating. He wanted to learn how to cook so he wrote to me in Vietnam asking how to cook this and that. Now he cooks very well.

When we came to America in 1975 together, we were poor but I still loved to feed the family well. We didn't have an Asian store around then, but I always found substitutes in American food. For example, I used spaghetti noodles for Vietnamese rice noodles. Vietnamese eat a lot of fresh herbs like cilantro, mint, purple mint, purple basil, and Vietnamese celery, which we now grow in our yard. But back then we lived in an apartment so we couldn't grow fresh herbs; we just lived without them.

*We not only prepare Vietnamese food, we love food from every country, and we respect everyone else's food as much as we respect ours.*

Now it is easy to find ingredients. Our food even tastes better than when we lived in Vietnam because America has fresh, rich food and more of a variety. Sometimes we make Vietnamese dishes more luxurious, like adding shrimp to a dish because they are easy and inexpensive to buy here. We believe that no matter how much money you have or what culture you live in, creativity helps you make the best of what you have.

◻ If you go to a Vietnamese party, there will always be food. If you don't bring food to the party, that is pretty rude. Even if the hostess says don't bring anything, you better bring something.

Typical foods at parties are *cha gio*, spring rolls; *thit nuong*, barbecued pork; and *che*, a general term for a drink dessert which can be made of corn, bananas, coconut, or dried fruit.

◻ We all love to cook, but we are all dominating in the kitchen. When my mother cooks, she wants me to watch and learn from her, but not necessarily cook. She'll have me chop carrots or something. When she cooks, she likes it done her way. I find myself acting the same with my friends. Just like my mother, I like to cook my own way.

—Hanh Le

### GOY CUON
### Fresh Spring Rolls

| | |
|---|---|
| 20 | sheets rice paper* |
| 2 | lbs. pork loin, boiled and thinly sliced |
| 1 | lb. shrimp, deveined and boiled |
| 1/2 | 17.5 oz. package rice vermicelli, cooked and drained* |
| 1 | leaf lettuce |
| 1 | bunch cilantro |
| 1 | bunch watercress |
| | mint or purple basil (optional) |

Prepare rice paper by running warm water over *one* side only. Place wet side down onto plate; repeat with remaining sheets, always placing wet side against dry side of previous sheet. Cover with damp cloth.

Layer a small amount of each ingredient on each sheet and roll like an egg roll. Serve with tuong or nuoc mam.
*4 servings*

### TUONG
### Peanut Butter and Hoisin Sauce

| | |
|---|---|
| 3 | garlic cloves, chopped |
| 1 | Tbsp. oil |
| 1 | cup hoisin sauce* |
| 1/2 | cup water |
| 2 | Tbsp. peanut butter |

Cook garlic in oil over medium-high heat until brown. Add remaining ingredients; cook over medium heat until boiling, stirring constantly. Garnish with finely chopped peanuts or garlic chili pepper sauce.
*1³/4 cups*

### THIT NUONG
### Vietnamese Grilled Pork or Chicken

| | |
|---|---|
| 5 | lbs. pork or chicken |
| 1/2 | cup soy sauce |
| 1/2 | cup oyster sauce |
| 1/3 | cup sugar |
| 1 | tsp. black pepper |
| 4 | garlic cloves, crushed |
| 1 | Tbsp. white wine |
| 2 | green onions or lemon grass, chopped |

Combine all ingredients; marinate overnight. Grill to desired doneness. Serve with nuoc mam.
*8 to 10 servings*

### NUOC MAM
### Fish Sauce Dip

| | |
|---|---|
| 1/4 | cup fish sauce |
| 1/4 | cup sugar |
| 1/2 | cup water |
| 1/8 | cup white vinegar |
| | garlic chili pepper sauce (optional) |

Combine all ingredients; mix until sugar dissolves.
*1¹/8 cups*

**It was a really long walk** going up Blue Beard Castle Hill. I can see it now. I used to run up that hill from school whenever I knew Grandma was fixing red pea soup. But that was a long time ago when I was just a little girl. I was born there—on Blue Beard Castle Hill—in the Virgin Islands. It was so beautiful on top of the hill; we had a wonderful view of St. Thomas. On Sunday morning, the church bells would toll to remind people to go to church. I loved the simple life on the Virgin Islands, even going to marketplace.

Grandma used to take me to the big marketplace on Saturday mornings. It was really exciting with all the hustling and bustling. People came to sell everything: their fish, their conches, their whelks. They sold green bananas, plantains, and *tania*. *Tania* is a starchy black vegetable with no taste, but I still love it. Grandma would buy a big stalk of sugar cane, peel it for us, and we'd eat it—just like that.

We saw shoppers going very early to the marketplace to get fresh parsley, thyme, and chervil. These are the kinds of seasonings we grew accustomed to. Back home, everyone knew each other. If we didn't see what we wanted while we were shopping, the merchant would happily tell us, "Go over there to Sandy," or to whoever had what we needed.

Other merchants sold prepared foods like roti, fried fish, fried Johnny cakes. They had sugar cakes and coconut cakes. The prepared food section was not very big, but it had a lot of variety. After all the shopping, we'd carry everything home in bags or baskets made of straw. Some carried the baskets in their arms, but Grandma could balance it on her head without even holding it.

I remember the donkeys that came from the countryside where most of the French people lived. They brought their farm goods by donkeys over the mountains to sell at the marketplace. The donkey had a seat in the middle and boxes, filled with fruits and vegetables, on the sides. In those days, there wasn't much traffic like today. Nowadays when you take the bus, it's better if you just get off and walk.

*My grandchildren will grow up with many conveniences that I didn't have, but I wouldn't change how I grew up in the Virgin Islands for anything in the world. No way!*

Back home, we didn't have electricity, indoor plumbing, or refrigeration. We carried our own water. We had to come down the hill to the faucet, which was turned on only during certain times of the day. Grandma used to go up and down the hill carrying water in a square five-gallon lard tin. I carried a little one because I was just a kid. Sometimes there were long lines, and people would fight if they thought that they may not get their water in time or if a person jumped the line. Yeah, they used to fight—over water.

We cooked "dumb bread" in a homemade oven. The oven was an iron pot with coals underneath and on top; I guess that's why it was called dumb bread. Our clothes iron had an opening in the front where we would put hot coals inside. There was no indoor plumbing. The bathroom was an outhouse, and we took baths using buckets of water. If we wanted ice, Grandma would go to the ice plant to buy a block of ice. When it was gone, that was it!

We got electricity afterwards, but when I was growing up, we still had oil lamps and used kerosene for cooking. When I stop and think about it, living as we did really was a lot of fun. Everybody was like us, so I never felt like I was missing out on anything.

□ We always bought goat. Besides the fruit and vegetables, the marketplace in St. Thomas also sold fresh meat, like goat, which we call mutton. I've noticed that mutton is trying to be introduced here, but we had been eating mutton from the time I knew myself. Beef is a good substitute for the goat in this recipe.

## MUTTON (GOAT) STEW

| | |
|---|---|
| 1 | Tbsp. rock salt |
| 1 | tsp. black peppercorns |
| 3 | garlic cloves, chopped |
| 3 | cardamom pods, seeds only |
| 2 | parsley sprigs, chopped |
| 2 | thyme springs, chopped |
| 2 | celery stalks, chopped |
| 1 | large onion, chopped |
| 5 | lbs. goat, cut into pieces |
| 1 | cup oil |
| 1 | Tbsp. curry or turmeric |
| 1 | tsp. grated ginger |
| | salt and pepper to taste |

In a mortar, pound salt, peppercorns, garlic, and cardamom seeds. Combine this mixture, parsley, thyme, celery, onion, and meat; mix well. Add oil; mix well. Marinate for several hours or overnight.

Skim oil and set aside. Drain meat, reserving marinade. Cook meat in oil over medium-high heat until brown. Add marinade, curry, ginger, salt, pepper, and enough water to cover. Cook, covered, over medium heat until meat is tender.
*14 to 16 servings*

□ My favorite of all Grandma's cooking was red pea soup with dumplings. Oh, Lord! It didn't matter what kind of soup, as long as it was red pea soup, I was happy.

If I can't find the tails when I make the soup, I use smoked ham hocks or smoked neck bones.

## RED PEA SOUP

| | |
|---|---|
| 1 | pig tail, pig nose, or smoked ham hocks |
| 1 | lb. dried red peas or kidney beans |
| 3 | garlic cloves, crushed |
| 1 | 1- inch piece of ginger, crushed |
| 1 | large onion, chopped |
| 1 | plantain, sliced |
| 1 | bunch seasoning (chervil, thyme, and parsley) |
| | dumplings (see below) |
| 1 | Tbsp. butter |
| | black pepper to taste |

Soak meat and peas in water for several hours or overnight in refrigerator; drain.

In a large pot, combine meat, peas, garlic, and ginger; cover with cold water. Cook over medium-high heat for 2 hours or until peas break. Add onion, plantain, seasoning, dumplings, butter, and black pepper. Cook for 20 minutes.
*8 to 10 servings*

## DUMPLINGS

| | |
|---|---|
| 1 | Tbsp. rock salt |
| 2 | cups water |
| 2 | tsp. butter |
| 4 | cups flour |

Dissolve salt in water. Set aside.

In a separate bowl, cut butter into flour. Gradually add salted water to flour mixture until dough is stiff. Cut off pieces with spoon for dumplings.

The spark that lit my earliest interests in the world and its people came from a slide presentation shown to me by the father of my Big Sister, Winnie O'Driscoll, née Bergen.

I don't believe that Mr. Bergen and Winnie could have ever imagined the profound impact that sharing their memories with me had—then or now. I was only about nine years old and their sharing of travels has remained and will forever remain with me. For this, I thank them for a moment that none of us knew would last a lifetime.

The bloodline for *Coming Home* was the word-of-mouth recommendations from a handful of core contacts. From there, the list just naturally grew. I extend my most gracious appreciation to the countless people who made recommendations, whilst giving me an overview of our diverse community.

I thank the Stafford County Sun and The Free-Lance Star newspapers for running articles during my search for the different peoples in the area. I also thank Steve Manster at the Rappahannock Area Development Commission, the Department of Modern Languages and the Multicultural Center at Mary Washington College, the Ancient Order of Hibernians, Women of the World, the Fredericksburg Area Community Relations Organization (FACRO), the Rappahannock Regional Library, the Virginia Cooperative Extension, and the many organizations that allowed me the opportunity to speak about the book or distribute information.

I particularly thank Sharleen Sanchez, Tony Gilbert, and Juan Chaves of the National Organization Association of Hispanics (NOAH) for their referrals, which were not restricted to only people of Hispanic background. NOAH is a splendid example of working with different people outside of the confines of its organizational boundaries.

A very special thanks goes to my editor. I truly appreciate her patience, advice, and great enthusiasm.

Indubitably, the people in this book deserve the greatest applause. They welcomed me, a stranger, without hesitation into their homes. They spoke freely of their lives in their home countries with a deep release of sentimentality. They treated me like family. Some fed me; some even gave me unexpected gifts. To all of them, who cared enough to spend the time so others could learn about their culture, I am sincerely touched by their trust in me and their eagerness to share a piece of their lives. Without them, there would be no book. This book is a priceless gem; each person's story is a facet that adds to the beauty and value of the insatiable learning experience.

a c k n o w l e g e m e n t s

## notes

One of the beauties of America is the absorption of different foods from around the world. Food such as paté, tahini, feta cheese, and plantains are almost standard in community grocery stores. Depending on where you live, you may have to search for certain ingredients mentioned in this book. However, it should not be difficult to find ingredients in communities where there may be even just a small number of international people; it is rare for people to give up the food they were brought up on. Only a fraction of the recipes call for a "special" ingredient. Most have been selected for their ease of preparation in the American marketplace.

Ingredients with an **asterisk** (*) indicate that the item can be found in a respective international store, but check your grocery store first. Besides the larger grocery store chains, look for international ingredients in locally-owned grocers. For example, in downtown Fredericksburg, Nader's Grocery, owned by Palestinians, has been carrying an assortment of Middle Eastern and Mediterranean foods since 1989.

# *Index*